ENEMY OF THE STEAK

VEGETARIAN RECIPES TO WIN FRIENDS AND INFLUENCE MEAT-EATERS

NIKKI & DAVID GOLDBECK

SQUAREONE PUBLISHERS

COVER DESIGNER: Jeannie Tudor
COVER PHOTO: Getty Images, Inc.
INTERIOR ART: Jeannie Tudor
EDITOR: Joanne Abrams
TYPESETTER: Gary A. Rosenberg

Square One Publishers
115 Herricks Road
Garden City Park, NY 11040
(516) 5335-2010 • (877) 900-BOOK
www.squareonepublishers.com

Library of Congress Cataloging-in-Publication Data

Goldbeck, Nikki.
Enemy of the steak : vegetarian recipes to win friends and influence meat-eaters / Nikki and David Goldbeck.
p. cm.
Includes index.
ISBN-13: 978-0-7570-0273-1 (pbk.)
1. Vegetarian cookery. I. Goldbeck, David. II. Title.

TX837.G624 2007
641.5'636—dc22

2006031046

Printed in the United States of America

10 9 8 7 6 5 4 3 2 1

CONTENTS

1. INTRODUCTION

It's funny that we vegetarians find ourselves in this position—enemies of the steak. We are not really looking for a fight. As it happens, our aim is simply to show the pleasures of plant-based eating because we have learned that meatless cuisine has much to offer in terms of both health and sheer enjoyment. That's what *Enemy of the Steak* is all about—making vegetarian dishes that are tempting and nourishing, and that fit easily into today's busy lifestyles.

Never before has it been so easy to create food that is both good-tasting and good for you. Over the past few decades, North America has become one of the world's great culinary incubators. Our markets are filled with an abundance of fresh and varied foods. Moreover, a new health-oriented approach to cooking has emerged that has gained respect from both nutrition experts and gourmet food enthusiasts. The two of us have personally spent more than thirty years working in the areas of cooking, nutrition, and health. During that time, we have enjoyed making a contribution by developing a more accessible, attractive, and healthful vegetarian cuisine. Now, in *Enemy of the Steak,* we apply both our creativity and our kitchen expertise to preparing this bounty of food in more than two hundred convenient, interesting, and satisfying ways.

As you are about to discover, *Enemy of the Steak* is not like other vegetarian cookbooks. It is not filled with the stock vegetarian dishes already found in so many books. This is because *Enemy of the Steak* is more than a collection of tasty, meatless recipes. It takes healthy dining to new heights by formulating dishes that are a marriage between the science of nutrition and the art of cooking. How have we made our dishes not only delicious but also healthful? First, our recipes rely on wholefoods—that is, unprocessed ingredients. This is not necessarily the case with other vegetarian cookbooks, but has always been our practice. Second, our recipes are based on a set of nutritional principles that have evolved over three decades of study and nutrition practice. (To learn more, see "About the Recipes" on page 2.) The result is a truly enjoyable collection of dishes that assure the variety and balance a healthy diet requires.

Why don't our recipes contain meat? The answers can be found in the inset on page 4. Despite the many reasons to be a vegetarian, you don't have to ban meat from your table. But for everyone who is a vegetarian, for people interested in exploring meatless dining, and for those who simply want more good food on their daily menu, we know that *Enemy of the Steak* offers nutritionally sound and great-tasting options.

Although this is not a "diet" book or nutrition manual, the recipes were spurred by Nikki's work as a nutritionist and her decades of research into healthy diets. Her experience working with people who are at risk or have already faced a variety of conditions and illnesses—including weight problems, heart disease, diabetes, cancer, and eating disorders—has given her a rare perspective on the health-diet-cooking-lifestyle relationship. She has met with many people eager to embrace a healthy diet, and has learned what they are looking for and what concerns they have in common. Likewise, she has grown in her work as clients revealed the secrets of their successes, as well as the pitfalls, frustrations, and confusion they've encountered along the way. Since, in addition to providing nourishment, food plays a strong cultural and social role in most people's lives, these experiences have all helped us develop recipes that fit comfortably into modern life.

To achieve optimal nutrition, we believe that people must relax and fully enjoy what they eat. We can think of no better way to do this than to sit down to a meal knowing that the food is of the highest caliber, the recipes were professionally tested, and the results have won widespread praise from those who have shared them.

The philosophy behind these dishes is one that has guided us in all our previous cookbooks, and is tied to the way our bodies are designed. You see, the human digestive system is essentially the same one our ancestors had 50,000 years ago. It best digests and utilizes the foods provided by our habitat. For the most part, these basic foodstuffs were discovered by our Stone Age ancestors in a hit-or-miss fashion. Those who ate best tended to live longest, and consequently their heirs and friends followed their example. The accepted diet became the one that maintained the species, and thus you might say it is a Darwinian diet. Additionally, as certain foods have become more constant in the diet, our bodies have accommodated these choices.

Processed and fragmented foods, as well as those that include unnatural amounts of sugar, salt, and fat, or any amount of modern food chemicals, are still very new to our system. We have seen many problems created by the fragmentation of wholefoods.

The challenge has always been to find the best way to enjoy vegetarian wholefoods dining in a modern context. That is the essence of *Enemy of the Steak*.

ABOUT THE RECIPES

As mentioned earlier, the recipes found in *Enemy of the Steak* will help you create dishes that are far more than just enticing and easy to prepare. They represent a new level of cooking that evolved from decades of study and nutrition practice. As such, when creating the dishes found in this book, we followed these simple but important guidelines.

- The recipes are based on wholefoods—that is, foods that are processed as little as possible and contain no chemical additives. In keeping with this, no refined ingredients are used. This means that the recipes include only whole grains, whole-grain products, and unrefined sweeteners.

- All ingredients are free of hydrogenated (trans) fats.

- Organic ingredients are favored.

- The recipes balance carbohydrates and protein to improve health and assist in weight management.

- Either few or no fats are used. Instead, recipes are designed to take advantage of the fats found within foods. This technique accomplishes three things. First, it lowers the overall amount of fat. Second, it helps create a more favorable balance of fats in the diet. Third, it decreases the use of concentrated fats in the form of oils, which are not really wholefoods and thus are missing some of their native constituents.

- The use of vegetables and fruits is maximized. This strategy—which naturally increases the amount of vitamins, minerals, fiber, and other important nutrients found in each dish—is agreed on by all health authorities.
- Soy foods, legumes, and yogurt are used often to encourage consumption of these valuable foods.
- Dishes and suggested menus incorporate a broad variety of ingredients to support a healthful intake of all nutrients.

To follow the guidelines presented above, we occasionally revamped traditional dishes to make them healthier without sacrificing enjoyment. You will see this in our Black Bean Hummus, Superior Spinach Dip, Mashed Potatoes with Garlic, Creamy Italian Dressing, Chickpea Pesto, and Gold Chip Cookies, among others. You will also notice that *Enemy of the Steak* employs a few cooking techniques that are not widely found in other cookbooks, including stir-steaming and the stewing of foods in their own juices.

Enemy of the Steak provides a solid core of recipes that will allow you to substantially improve your diet and feel comfortable in the kitchen. Before you turn to the first recipe chapter, though, you should take a look at Chapters 2 and 3. Chapter 2, "Stocking the Pantry," will guide you in filling your kitchen with the foods you'll want to have on hand so that you can easily put together the dishes presented in this book. Chapter 3, "Basic Training," offers some key recipes, flavoring tips, and comprehensive guidelines for preparing the beans, grains, and vegetables that hold a prominent place in the vegetarian repertoire.

The hardest part of planning healthy vegetarian meals is knowing where to start. *Enemy of the Steak* will take you beyond pasta and pizza. Remember, you do not have to be a full-time vegetarian to enjoy and benefit from meatless meals.

Twenty-One Reasons to Eat Like a Vegetarian

Not so long ago, the word *vegetarian* was sure to elicit laughter on late night talk shows. But not anymore. Many people now recognize that vegetarian meals are not only familiar—think peanut butter sandwiches and bean burritos—but that these meat-free meals have a lot going for them. Even if you do not want to become a vegetarian, you may wish to consider adding more meat-free days to your week.

People often say to us, "I could be a vegetarian. I love vegetables." Loving vegetables is a very good thing, since collectively they are probably the most health-protective of all foods. However, they are certainly not just for vegetarians, and despite the name, vegetarianism is not about eating vegetables.

The vegetarian diet is defined by its protein source. Meat-eaters get their protein from animal flesh. The typical vegetarian obtains protein from beans, nuts, seeds, eggs, yogurt, cheese, and milk. Another group of vegetarians known as *vegans* refines this to exclude any food of animal origin, including dairy products, eggs, and even honey.

While at one time people were concerned about the adequacy of vegetarian diets, today even the American Dietetic Association confirms that they are healthy. Here are our twenty-one reasons to go meatless:

1. Less fat and calories. One noteworthy feature of a vegetarian diet is the potential for less artery-clogging saturated fat. For example, beans, which are a focal point of healthy vegetarian meals, contain very little fat. Soybeans and products made with them are somewhat higher in fat than other beans, but the fat they contain does not promote heart disease. In fact, the protein in soy is believed to have just the opposite effect by reducing cholesterol levels.

Nuts and seeds are indeed high in fat, but again, not the kind that is bad for your heart. In small quantities, these foods help satisfy your appetite and can thereby actually curtail overeating.

Low-fat and nonfat dairy products are another example of protein in a lean package. As you will soon see, in *Enemy of the Steak,* we sometimes make use of a little-known food called yogurt cheese, which is easily made from yogurt. We also use eggs in moderation because, contrary to what many people believe, eggs are low in fat and calories relative to their nutritional return.

Finally, because many vegetarian staples are high in fiber, and because the vegetarian meals we promote emphasize more vegetables and whole grains than meat-based meals, a sound vegetarian menu is likely to fill you up with fewer calories.

2. Better nutrition. Getting adequate amounts of most vitamins and minerals is often easier with a vegetarian diet than it is with a meat-based diet. By its very nature, vegetarian eating includes abundant amounts of vegetables on a daily basis. While there is no reason meat-eaters can't eat similar amounts of vegetables, in general, they give these foods a lower priority. The same is true of whole grains. Due to these choices, as well as the fact that beans and nuts are high in fiber while animal foods contain little, vegetarians also get far more health-promoting fiber in their diets.

This is not to say that all vegetarians enjoy better nutrition. Poorly chosen diets are unhealthy irrespective of the diet's protein source. And vegans do need to put more effort into getting adequate calcium. Moreover, it is possible to become deficient in vitamin B_{12} after years of vegan eating, which is why nutritionists recommend a B_{12} supplement for vegans.

3. Mad cow. Concerns about animal husbandry have motivated vegetarians for years. Practices such as the overuse of antibiotics, hormones, and pesticides in animal feed were what prompted our own turn to a meat-free diet in the 1970s. Now there is another compelling reason for people to consider vegetarian eating—the disturbing news about the health of cows, and the possibility that the meat they yield may be deadly. Mad cow disease was first seen in British cattle. Initially, most scientists insisted that it could not be transmitted to people. It seems they were wrong. Suspected cases have been traced to Canada, and several deaths have occurred in the United States.

4. Mad Dow. The fact that meat-free meals are generally less expensive than their meat-based counterparts is another selling point for most people.

5. Easy, interesting, and convenient dishes. One of the best reasons to try meatless dining is that with the increased selection of inviting ingredients and appealing recipes, vegetarian dining is easier and more exciting than ever. And despite rumors to the contrary, preparing meals without meat is no more difficult or time-consuming than preparing food in general.

6. Concern for animals. Practically all animals destined for the table are raised in inhumane conditions. They are crowded together in unclean quarters, with some rarely breathing fresh air or seeing the light of day. Lack of exercise makes their lives miserable, but it is also what makes their meat tender and juicy.

7. Concern for people. The feeding of plant protein to animals has been called a "food factory in reverse," in that it takes almost six pounds of plant protein—soy, grain, and forage—to produce just one pound of animal protein. While not all of this plant material is suitable for people, the growing of feedstuffs has reduced the amount of land devoted to edible food production, and is a contributing factor to world hunger.

8. Concern for the environment. One of the most alarming consequences of commercial meat production is the resulting air and water pollution. In areas surrounding large-scale feedlots and factory-like poultry facilities, the stench of urine and feces is far more noxious and pervasive than the odors found on a small-scale farm. Moreover, the methane gas emitted by livestock adds to the buildup of greenhouse gasses associated with global warming, while the massive accumulation of manure in feedlots leaches toxins into the ground and, ultimately, the waterways.

On the waterfront, the fishing industry is heading toward self-destruction by compromising the oceans' ecosystems. The demand for reef-fish has contributed to the loss of coral reefs, some said to be over a million years old. Fish farming is no less damaging, since shoreline aquaculture has led to the decimation of mangroves—the trees and shrubs that protect the landmass. In fact, mangroves are considered natural shields against tsunami waves.

9. Concern for the future. According to United Nations Food and Agriculture Organization estimates, 70 percent of the world's commercial fish stocks are in danger due to unsound fishing practices and overfishing. Industrial-scale commercial fishing has been blamed for the severe depletion of many fish species over the past fifty years. In addition, the escape of farmed fish can spread disease and threaten the genetic purity and survival of wild species. On land, the loss of arable soil to animal raising and animal feed production threatens the future of farming.

10. Concern for your health. Numerous studies point to the connection between meat-eating and many types of cancer and heart disease. Every leading health agency, from the American Cancer Society to the American Heart Association, promotes a diet emphasizing vegetables, fruit, grains, and legumes (beans).

11. Resistant bacteria. Antibiotics are routinely administered to animals for enhanced growth as well as disease prevention—a constant threat due to overcrowded, unsanitary living conditions. This practice has led to a surge of antibiotic-resistant bacteria, and is adding to the increasing world crisis of drug-resistant diseases.

12. Food-borne pathogens. While meat is not the only source of food-borne disease, the majority of deadly *E. coli* cases have been traced to meat products. Moreover, factory-raised poultry is notorious for the presence of Salmonella and Campylobacter. While these bacteria are not likely to kill you if you are in good health, they can make you mighty sick. Moreover, for the very young, the elderly, and anyone with a compromised immune system, the outcome can be much worse.

13. Kitchen contamination. Poor food-handling practices in home kitchens are far more serious when meat, poultry, and fish are on the menu. Failure to properly sanitize cutting boards, knives, utensils, and other items that come in contact with food can result in the spread of harmful bacteria to the rest of the meal.

14. Persistent pesticides. Pesticides, heavy metals, and other environmental toxins found in all industrial societies accumulate in the fat tissues of both animals and humans. When people consume fat-containing meat, poultry, and fish, they simultaneously take in these accumulated chemicals. These concerns are so serious that the US government advises pregnant women and young children to avoid eating certain fish altogether, and suggests limits on the consumption of others.

15. Protein loading. Even if no other protein-providing foods were eaten in the course of a day, it would take only about 6 ounces of meat to satisfy the 45-gram protein needs of the average woman, and just 3 ounces more to take care of a man's 65-gram protein need. For people with higher protein needs, including athletes, heavy laborers, and pregnant women, only 100 grams (what you would find in about 14 ounces of meat) are required. Consuming protein above these levels serves no useful purpose. Furthermore, animal-focused high-protein diets like those touted by some weight-loss programs can disturb liver and kidney function, as well as increase the loss of bone calcium. While these are long-term consequences, more immediate effects such as dizziness, nausea, and bad breath can reduce the general quality of daily life.

16. Feisty phytochemicals. A newly identified class of food components called *phytochemicals*—nutrients derived from a plant source—is believed to be among the most health-protective elements in food. Some phytochemicals are potent antioxidants. Others can alter human enzyme production in order to subdue inflammatory ailments. Some regulate hormones in a manner that may enhance bone strength. Phytochemicals have been shown to help cells resist cancer-causing agents and fight retroviral infections, including AIDS. In addition, they have been credited with having a positive effect on circulation, vision, blood clotting, cholesterol production, and more, thereby preventing or curbing a wide range of ailments.

17. Fortifying fiber. Only plant-based foods contain the fiber that aids digestion, contributes to satiety and thereby curbs overeating, slows down the release of carbohydrates into the blood stream to help maintain proper blood sugar levels, and reduces the body's production of artery-damaging cholesterol. The majority of meat-centered diets are deficient in fiber.

18. Happy hearts. The fat in animal foods is mainly saturated fat, which has been directly implicated in heart disease. Conversely, the predominant fats in nuts and seeds—the plant foods most likely to contain fat—are believed to raise levels of the so-called "good" HDL-cholesterol, which appears to reduce the risk of heart disease.

19. Living longer. Longevity studies from around the world—including studies of Seventh-day Adventists in North America, wartime Europeans, and populations in China and Okinawa—indicate that the healthiest and longest-living people eat relatively few foods of animal origin. While genetics may play a part, peers and progeny who eat a more meat-centered westernized diet do not enjoy similar longevity.

20. Weight control. British researchers studying the eating habits of 22,000 people over five years, including meat-eaters and vegetarians, found that while all put on a few kilos, meat-eaters who changed to a vegetarian or vegan diet gained the least.

21. Adventures in eating. Because vegetarian meals are not routinely available everywhere, vegetarians become more resourceful and adventurous away from home. They seek out different international cuisines, venture off the beaten path, and look beyond the meat entrées on the menu. As a result, they are apt to engage in more conversation when they travel, be open to trying new places, and be on the lookout for options that others might never notice.

2. Stocking the Pantry

To follow the recipes in *Enemy of the Steak* with ease, we recommend stocking your pantry with some basic ingredients. In this chapter, you'll find comprehensive lists of items you'll want to keep in your cupboard, refrigerator, and freezer. With these foods on hand, you will have no trouble following our recipes and devising other delicious, nourishing meals and snacks.

Note that many pantry staples can be found in the supermarket. However, for a larger selection, the natural foods store is your best bet. And whenever possible, choose organic products.

THE GRAIN PANTRY

Grains are milled into flour, and are the predominant ingredient in hot and ready-to-eat cereals, pasta, breads, crackers, cookies, and cakes. Those grains that are left intact—which means that most of the bran and all of the germ remain—have the most to offer, nutritionally speaking. The bran is the source of fiber and the germ is the nutrient-rich core of the grain kernel, so to reap the real benefits of grains, the word "whole" should precede "wheat"; brown rice should take priority over white rice; and whole-grain cornmeal—sometimes called "stoneground" or "unbolted"—should be chosen over the more typical "degermed" cornmeal.

Although a variety of grains has long been available on supermarket shelves, in the last few years, the roster of grains has been expanded by varieties that have long been used in other parts of the world. This makes it easier and more interesting than ever to cook with grains. Spelt and kamut flour, for instance, can be used in recipes calling for whole wheat flour.

Grain and Flour Storage

Grains should be stored in airtight containers in a cool, dark, dry place. Heat and light lessen the quality of grains, and moisture encourages the growth of mold. Properly stored, whole grains can last for years, although it is best to use them within six to nine months. Whole grains that have been ground into flour or meal have a briefer shelf life, and should be refrigerated and used within two to three months.

Recommended Grains

The following grains are commonly used in our recipes, either as is or ground into flour. As explained above, all grains should ideally be purchased and used with both bran and germ intact.

- Barley
- Brown rice
- Cornmeal (whole grain, unbolted)
- Cracked wheat (bulgur)
- Kamut
- Kasha (buckwheat groats)
- Millet
- Oats
- Quinoa
- Rye
- Spelt
- Wheat germ
- Whole wheat
- Wild rice

THE BEAN PANTRY

Beans add flavor, fiber, protein, and other important nutrients to a wide variety of dishes, from soups to stews to side dishes and salads. In general, cooked dried beans have a better texture and flavor than canned beans, but the convenience of a can is a big attraction. Canned beans suffer from two culinary limitations—they tend to be mushy, and they tend to be salty. Because of their soft consistency, canned beans work best in recipes that call for puréeing or mashing. If using them in a cooked dish that does not involve mashing, be sure to keep cooking time to a minimum to avoid softening them any further. If you want to avoid a high-salt product, look for brands geared to the health food market, as they tend to be unsalted or relatively low in salt, or seek out low-sodium versions of major brands. To reduce the salt content of regular—in other words, highly salted—canned beans, rinse them for a few minutes under cold water, a process that washes away a substantial amount of salt. Avoid brands that are sweetened.

Bean varieties can be interchanged in recipes if you want to experiment or if you have run out of the specified type. However, if you are starting with uncooked dried beans, you may have to make adjustments for variations in cooking time. (See page 23 for information on cooking dried beans.)

Bean Storage

Dried beans can be stored almost indefinitely if maintained in a dry, airtight container, preferably away from heat and light. However, the sooner they are eaten, the better they taste. Beans toughen with storage and as they age, they take longer to cook. Try to use them within a year of purchase. Canned beans, of course, can be stored indefinitely.

Once dried beans are cooked, you can store them in the refrigerator for about a week. If longer storage is needed, place them in the freezer for up to six months.

Recommended Beans

The following beans are readily available in most supermarkets and natural foods stores, and are used frequently in the recipes in this book. You probably won't want to stock all of them, but it is a good idea to have a few favorites on hand and to add some new ones to your pantry now and then—just to keep things interesting.

- Adzuki beans (aduki beans)
- Black beans
- Black-eyed peas
- Cannellini beans
- Chickpeas (garbanzo beans)
- Great Northern beans

- Kidney beans
- Lentils (red, green, and French)
- Lima beans
- Navy beans
- Pea beans
- Pink beans
- Pinto beans
- Red beans
- Soybeans
- Split peas (yellow and green)
- White beans

THE NUT AND SEED PANTRY

Packed with fiber, protein, and B vitamins, as well as other vitamins and minerals, nuts and seeds are also among the most calorie-dense foods available. Moreover, they add flavor and crunch to many dishes, from salads to pastas to desserts. Just keep in mind that they are also relatively high in fat—albeit, heart-healthy fat—and should therefore be eaten in moderation.

For the most wholesome product possible, choose unsalted nuts and seeds that are either raw or dry roasted. When buying nut butters—peanut butter, almond butter, tahini (sesame seed paste), etc.—choose brands that contain nothing but the nuts and seeds. Never buy nut butter made with hydrogenated oils or sweeteners.

Nut and Seed Storage

Because nuts and seeds have a high fat content, they must be stored properly to keep them from becoming stale or rancid. Unshelled nuts store well for several weeks at room temperature. If you're going to keep shelled nuts for only a few days before using them, simply place them in airtight containers and keep them at room temperature. To preserve them for more than a few days, the refrigerator is a far better option. There, they will stay fresh for up to a year. If longer storage is desired, seal the nuts well and place them in the freezer for up to two years. Keep in mind, too, that nuts in the shell keep longer than shelled nuts; and whole nuts keep better than nuts that have been chopped or ground.

All nut butters should be stored in the refrigerator to prevent them from spoiling. Tightly covered, these nutritious products should remain fresh for up to three months.

Recommended Nuts and Seeds

You will find many of the following nuts and seeds included in the recipes in this book. Moreover, as long as they are eaten in moderation, nuts and seeds are a good snack choice.

- Almonds
- Brazil nuts
- Butternuts
- Cashews
- Flaxseeds (for more about flaxseeds, see page 17)
- Hazelnuts (filberts)
- Peanuts
- Pecans
- Pine nuts (pignoli)
- Pistachio nuts
- Pumpkin seeds
- Sesame seeds
- Soy nuts (technically not nuts, but roasted soybeans)
- Sunflower seeds
- Walnuts

THE OIL PANTRY

Because the recipes in *Enemy of the Steak* rely mostly on the fats naturally found within foods like nuts, seeds, and whole grains, rather than on concentrated extracts such as oils and butter, you will need only a limited supply of items in this category. But when used in moderation, oils are invaluable ingredients. Olive oil is the preferred all-around choice for cooking and salads. Canola oil, which is essentially flavorless, is perfect for baking. Flaxseed and hemp oils, both of which add healthy omega-3 fats to the diet and act as flavoring agents, are always used uncooked. And sesame oil—especially toasted sesame oil—adds wonderful taste and aroma when used in small amounts.

Oil Storage

Cooking oils can become rancid over time, especially when exposed to their chief enemies: oxygen, light, and heat. Rancidity not only destroys the taste of oils, but also makes them unfit for consumption. Most unopened oils have a shelf life of about a year, but some—sesame oil and flaxseed oil—have even shorter shelf lives.

Whenever possible, buy your oil in small amounts so that you will use it up before it can spoil, and look for opaque containers that limit exposure to light. Store olive oil at room temperature, preferably in a dark, cool cupboard. Store canola oil, flaxseed oil, hemp oil, and sesame oil in the refrigerator. This will keep canola oil fresh for up to a year; sesame oil, for up to four months; and flaxseed and hemp oil, for up to two months.

Recommended Oils

We've already mentioned the handful of oils that we use in our recipes, but the following list may be helpful when it's time to stock your pantry.

- Canola oil (cold-pressed)
- Flaxseed oil
- Hemp oil
- Olive oil (virgin or extra virgin)
- Sesame oil (regular or toasted)

THE HERB, SPICE, AND CONDIMENTS PANTRY

Dried herbs and spices are an easy means of adding flavor and color to your dishes without adding a lot of calories. Your supermarket, natural foods store, or specialty store should offer a wide range, including both single spices and herbs, and blends designed for all occasions. And now that fresh herbs are available in nearly every produce section, you'll find it easy to enhance your food's nutritional value as you boost its flavor.

A wide variety of condiments are also available. In our recipes, we use mostly mustard, hot pepper sauce, and vinegar. We have limited our recipes to balsamic, wine, white rice, and cider vinegar, but if you enjoy experimentation, you'll be pleased to find an ever-increasing number of flavored and unflavored vinegars on the shelves of your local stores. Use them in your cooking and, of course, on fresh salads.

Herb, Spice, and Condiment Storage

Store dried herbs and spices in airtight containers away from heat and light. Although just about every spice is available ground, you'll get better flavor and longer shelf life if you buy your nutmeg and black pepper in whole form, and grate or grind the spice as needed. Be aware that these products will lose their pungency over time, though, so buy them in the smallest quantities you can find and use them quickly.

As mentioned earlier, you'll also want to use fresh herbs—garlic, ginger, parsley, cilantro, basil, dill, and mint, for instance. Although garlic and ginger will keep for weeks, leafy herbs are much more fragile, and should be used up within a few days. You'll increase their "shelf life" if you refrigerate them in tightly closed plastic bags in which you've placed a sheet or two of paper toweling to absorb any excess moisture. Be sure to change the paper every day or so.

Bottled condiments keep for a long time. Stored in a dark cabinet, vinegars stay fresh indefinitely, as does hot pepper sauce. Mustards, of course, should be kept in the refrigerator, where they will last for many months.

Recommended Herbs, Spices, and Condiments

The following list contains the herbs, spices, and condiments we use most often in our recipes. Feel free to experiment, though, with all of the many seasonings and flavorings that are now so easy to find.

- Balsamic vinegar
- Basil (fresh and dried)
- Bay leaf
- Black pepper
- Cayenne pepper
- Chili powder
- Cider vinegar
- Cilantro (fresh)
- Cinnamon (stick and ground)
- Crushed red pepper
- Cumin
- Curry powder (preferably imported from India)
- Garlic (fresh)
- Ginger (fresh)
- Hot pepper sauce (any type you like)
- Mint (fresh and dried)
- Mustard (dry and prepared, any type you like)
- Nutmeg
- Oregano (dried)
- Paprika
- Parsley (fresh)
- Rice vinegar
- Salt
- Turmeric
- White vinegar
- Wine vinegar (red and white)

THE SOY FOOD PANTRY

Made from soybeans, soy foods like soy milk, tofu, and tempeh are good sources of protein and other nutrients. Moreover, unlike the meat and dairy products they are often used to replace, they are believed to reduce artery-clogging cholesterol and thereby lessen the risk of heart disease.

A number of soy foods are used in the recipes in *Enemy of the Steak*. These nutritious foods are each briefly discussed below, along with storage recommendations.

Soybeans

One of the many healthful beans listed on pages 10 and 11, soybeans should be stored like all other beans—in a dry, airtight container. Canned soybeans, available in natural food stores, can be stored indefinitely.

Soy Flour

Made from roasted soybeans that have been ground into a powder, soy flour is a great means of adding a protein boost to a range of recipes, including baked goods. Both full-fat and defatted version are available, but we prefer full-fat soy flour because it imparts better taste and texture.

Because full-fat soy flour has all the natural oil found in soybeans, it can easily turn rancid, and should be stored in the refrigerator or freezer.

Tofu

Also known as *soybean curd,* tofu is a soft cheese-like food made by combining soy milk with a coagulating agent. It comes in silken, soft, regular, firm, and extra firm varieties, and can be found preseasoned as well. If the recipe does not specify the form, firm is always a safe choice, although in most cases, regular and extra firm tofus will also work. Soft and silken varieties are usually used to make sauces and desserts.

Unless aseptically packaged in shelf-stable boxes, tofu should be kept cold. Sealed containers are usually dated. Once opened, the tofu should be submerged in fresh water that is changed daily. Stored this way, tofu will keep for about a week. Tofu that's sold loose from bulk containers should be handled in the same way.

Tofu can be wrapped tightly and frozen for up to six months. Just be aware that the freezing process dramatically changes the texture of tofu, making it the preferred form for some recipes, but unsuitable for use in recipes that call for fresh tofu.

Tempeh

Made from cracked, cooked, fermented soybeans, tempeh is molded into cakes that have a yeasty, nutty taste. Tempeh is sometimes made with soybeans alone, and sometimes also contains grains, vegetables, or flaxseed. For the most protein and soy benefits, all-soy tempeh is suggested. However, some people prefer the milder flavor of tempeh that is prepared with grains.

Tempeh is usually found in the refrigerated case of natural food stores, and can be stored in the refrigerator until the recommended pull date, or kept frozen for three to six months. White or gray patches on the surface are normal, but avoid tempeh that's covered with black patches or that shows mold of any other color. When spoiled, tempeh has an ammonia-like odor.

Soy Milk

The liquid that remains after soybeans have been cooked, crushed, and strained, soy milk can be consumed as a beverage or used in recipes, just as you would use cow's milk. Select full-fat soy milk because it has greater nutritional value, choosing a brand that has been fortified with calcium and vitamins if you prefer.

Fresh soy milk, open containers of aseptically packaged soy milk, and reconstituted powders require refrigeration, just like regular milk.

Soy Sauce

A salty seasoning liquid, soy sauce is available in several forms. Genuine (traditional) soy sauce, sometimes known as *shoyu,* is prepared by aging soy beans along with cracked roasted wheat, salt, and water, and squeezing the resulting cake to produce the characteristic brown liquid. The soy sauce known as *tamari* is also made naturally, but does not contain wheat. Nontraditional soy sauce relies on a chemical process that uses defatted, hydrolyzed soy protein, corn syrup, and caramel coloring; no aging or fermentation take place. For the best flavor and nutrition, you'll want to look for shoyu or tamari, and to avoid chemically processed sauces. Just be aware that all soy sauces—including so-called low-sodium versions—are very high in salt.

Soy sauce keeps indefinitely at room temperature, but can be stored in the refrigerator if you prefer.

Miso

A thick paste made from fermented soybeans, salt, and sometimes grains, miso is a popular Japanese condiment often used in the preparation of soups and sauces. The darker the miso, the stronger the flavor. Lighter miso is a bit sweet. All miso is salty.

Stored in the refrigerator in an airtight container, miso will keep for several months. The white mold that sometimes forms on the surface is harmless, and can be scraped off and discarded or simply mixed into the miso paste.

THE VEGETABLE PANTRY

Variety and abundance is the goal when it comes to choosing vegetables, as vegetables provide a wealth of important nutrients, including a healthy dose of fiber. To maximize taste and nutrition, you'll want to use fresh vegetables whenever you can. And when possible, by all means choose organic produce, particularly when it comes to those varieties you eat most frequently.

Frozen vegetables can be a great convenience. For example, frozen corn and peas can be easily added to grains, soups, and mixed vegetable dishes to enhance color, flavor, and nutrition. Frozen spinach is particularly handy when chopped spinach is called for in a filling mixture. (See Eggplant Rollatini on page 128.)

The only canned vegetables used in this book are canned artichoke hearts and bottoms, and canned tomato products—including whole and crushed tomatoes, tomato purée, tomato paste, and tomato juice. If salt is a concern to you, you'll want to look for low-sodium versions of these products, as they are often quite salty.

In the dried vegetable category, mushrooms of all varieties are quite useful for intensifying the flavor of numerous dishes, as are sun-dried tomatoes. When sun-dried tomatoes are referred to in our recipes, we mean the leathery moisture-free product, not the kind swimming in oil. Dried seaweed is another vegetable that we use quite often. With one or more varieties of seaweed in the pantry, you will be able to make our Sea Vegetable Topping (see page 208) or our Orange Arame Salad (see page 92), and even do some experimenting on your own. Seaweed, also called sea vegetables, can be purchased in Asian markets and natural food stores.

THE FRUIT PANTRY

Like vegetables, fruits are loaded with vitamins, minerals, and fiber. Again, you'll want to choose fresh fruits whenever you can, and to opt for organic produce when possible. This is especially important when your recipe calls for the *zest*—the outer skin, minus the bitter white pith—of a citrus fruit.

Although fresh fruits are the most healthful, some good alternatives are available. Dried fruit, for instance, adds nutrients, sweetness, and flavor to a range of recipes, and also makes great snacks. Just be aware that cup for cup, dried fruit provides more calories than its fresh counterpart. Other handy fruit items include unsweetened applesauce for use in baking; canned unsweetened pineapple; unsweetened fruit juices—especially orange and apple juice; and frozen berries.

THE WINE PANTRY

A number of different wines can be used to enhance the flavor of dishes without adding fat. To begin, sherry makes an excellent cooking medium. Either purchase inexpensive dry sherry in your local liquor store—you can usually find a nice-size bottle for about $5—or opt for cooking sherry, which can be found in most supermarkets. Just be aware that cooking sherry has added salt (to make it undrinkable) and is generally of an inferior grade. Both regular and cooking sherry can be stored nearly indefinitely at room temperature.

Another product you may want to keep in your pantry is Chinese cooking wine. Like cooking sherry, this product is not suitable for drinking because it contains added salt. But used in small amounts, it can add wonderful flavor to your dishes, and it will keep forever if stored at room temperature.

Dry red and white drinking wines are also included in some of our recipes. If you enjoy a glass of wine, conserve the rest of the bottle in the refrigerator for cooking. Nondrinkers need not purchase a high-priced wine for cooking, but be sure to pick a dry (not sweet) variety. Once opened, wine should be refrigerated.

THE SWEETENERS PANTRY

The only concentrated sweeteners we use in our recipes are honey, molasses, and pure maple syrup. As they keep for a very long time—honey and molasses, in the food cabinet; maple syrup, in the refrigerator—we stock them all.

THE DAIRY

The principal dairy items you'll need to complete the recipes found in *Enemy of the Steak* are yogurt, homemade yogurt cheese (see page 21), and eggs. Both yogurt and eggs should, of course, be purchased fresh, refrigerated promptly, and used as quickly as possible.

A few of the recipes in this book use cheese, usually feta or Parmesan cheese. Even when added in small amounts, these products can greatly enhance the flavor of your dishes.

Now that your pantry is stocked, you're probably eager to turn to the recipe chapters and start cooking. Before you do, though, it's a good idea to take a brief look at the next chapter, "Basic Training." There, you will find simple step-by-step instructions for the techniques used throughout this book.

3. BASIC TRAINING

Before you move on to the recipes in *Enemy of the Steak,* we would like to acquaint you with some favorite preparation techniques that appear throughout the book so that you will feel comfortable when you begin cooking. Included here are basic approaches to cooking the beans, grains, and vegetables that form the backbone of many of our recipes, along with techniques for making some special ingredients, such as spiced sherry and ground mushroom seasoning. Some of these methods may already be part of your culinary repertoire, while others may be entirely new.

We suggest that you take a few minutes to skim this chapter, briefly familiarizing yourself with the information that's offered here. Then, when you choose a recipe that requires flaxseed meal, for instance, you'll know where to go to find the simple instructions that will allow you to prepare the dish with ease.

MAKING FLAXSEED MEAL

In order to get the benefits of flaxseed, the seeds must be ground before eating. This is done by processing the seeds in a blender or spice mill, which creates the reddish brown powder referred to as flaxseed meal. Having a delicate nutty flavor, the meal can be sprinkled on cereal; added to spreads, toppings, and casseroles; or used in baking to replace some of the flour. Because of the meal's natural oil content, incorporating it into a recipe for baked goods substantially reduces the need for added fats. In addition, the fiber in flaxseed slows down the rise in blood sugar that normally follows the consumption of carbohydrate-rich foods.

When ground, flaxseeds produce a little less than twice as much meal as the original measure of seeds. Thus, a half cup of flaxseeds will yield a scant cup of flaxseed meal. Grinding can be done as needed, or you can prepare a modest quantity in advance and store it the refrigerator for use over the coming week or two. Ground flaxseed can also be stored in the freezer.

Step-by-Step Flaxseed Meal

1. Place the flaxseeds in a blender or spice mill, and grind at high speed until reduced to a soft powdery consistency.

2. Use the flaxseed meal immediately, or store the meal in a tightly covered container in the refrigerator or freezer.

MAKING TOMATO PUREE

We prepare this handy purée when tomatoes are at their peak, and then are able to recapture the flavor of fresh tomatoes after the season is over. The purée can be stored in the refrigerator for several days or frozen for future use, and can be used in any recipe calling for tomato purée or juice. Just be sure to check for salt when using your homemade purée. Most commercial tomato products are highly salted, so your finished dish may taste "flat" to you if you switch to an unsalted purée without correcting the seasoning.

Step-by-Step Tomato Purée: Method 1

This method uses a food mill, which purées the tomatoes while straining out skin and seeds.

1. Cut the tomatoes into wedges, place them in a saucepan, and bring to a boil over medium heat. Simmer for about 10 minutes, or until the tomato pieces have softened.

2. Process the tomatoes through a food mill, place in containers, and store in the refrigerator or freezer.

Step-by-Step Tomato Purée: Method 2

This method uses a blender or food processor. Because these tools will not remove the peel from the tomatoes, you will have to do so manually.

1. Bring a large pot of water to a boil, and plunge the whole tomatoes into the boiling water for a minute or two—just until the skins break.

2. Transfer the tomatoes to a colander to drain and cool. When the tomatoes are cool enough to handle, peel.

3. Place the peeled tomatoes in a blender or food processor, and process to the desired consistency.

4. Transfer the purée to a pot and simmer for 5 minutes. Cool, transfer to containers, and store in the refrigerator or freezer.

Step-by-Step Tomato Purée: Method 3

This method is useful when you're making stuffed tomatoes, and therefore are using only the "shells" while discarding the pulp.

1. Slice the tops from the tomatoes, and use a curved

Tips for Storing Tomato Products

When using a prepared tomato product such as tomato paste, tomato juice, tomato purée, or canned crushed tomatoes, you often need only part of the contents for your recipe. Fortunately, these products are easy to store for future use.

Place the leftovers in airtight nonreactive containers—glass, plastic, or stainless steel. Then refrigerate for up to three days, or freeze for up to six months. If using the freezer, try to divide the product into suitable amounts so that you will be able to defrost only what you need. Thaw your frozen tomato product in the refrigerator or at room temperature, or add to hot dishes to defrost during cooking.

If you think you'll need only small amounts of the leftover product—if you're going to use it as a flavoring agent, for example—create portions in ice cube trays, placing about 2 tablespoons in each of the small compartments. When the product is frozen solid, remove the cubes from the tray and store in freezer-safe plastic bags until needed.

grapefruit knife and serrated grapefruit spoon to remove the pulp.

2. Place the pulp and all the liquid you can capture in a blender or food processor, and process to the desired consistency.

3. Transfer the purée to a pot and simmer for 5 minutes. Cool, transfer to containers, and store in the refrigerator or freezer.

MAKING SPICED SHERRY

To zip up the flavor of dishes that call for sherry, use spiced sherry in its place. Easy to make, this product will keep for several weeks in the refrigerator. Once the sherry has been prepared, you'll even be able to use the sherry-infused pepper in your dishes.

Step-by-Step Spiced Sherry

1. Roast one hot chili pepper—use any type you like—over an open flame or in a broiler, turning to char all sides. (See page 20 for more information on roasting peppers.)

2. Wrap the charred pepper in a clean cloth towel, and leave covered for 5 minutes. Then scrape off the skin with a small paring knife.

3. Place the pepper in a glass jar, and mash gently with a fork to break it up into pieces and release the seeds.

4. Pour in enough sherry to cover the pepper well. Cover the jar and refrigerate for at least several hours. Either remove the pepper before using, or keep the pepper in the jar and replenish by adding more sherry as needed.

TOASTING NUTS AND SEEDS

Toasted nuts and seeds can be used to garnish salads, vegetable dishes, and cooked grains. In our recipes, we mostly use toasted pumpkin seeds and pine nuts, but a variety of nuts and seeds can be enhanced by toasting. Plan on using one tablespoon for every two servings. For the crispest, tastiest results, toast all your nuts and seeds just before using.

Step-by-Step Nut and Seed Toasting

1. Arrange the nuts or seeds in a single layer in a dry skillet, and place over moderate heat.

2. Cook, shaking the pan frequently, for several minutes. You'll know that pine nuts are fully toasted when they are just golden. Pumpkin seeds are done when they are lightly colored and fragrant, and most of them have "popped." When toasting other varieties of nuts and seeds, take the ingredient off the heat when it smells nutty and is just beginning to color. Pay close attention throughout the process, as nuts and seeds can quickly turn from toasted to burned.

MAKING ROASTED GARLIC

Roasted garlic pulp is a great means of seasoning a wide range of dishes, or can simply be used as a delicious spread for your favorite bread. We have seen various methods for roasting whole garlic heads. Some recipes call for cutting off the top third of the head and rubbing it with oil, while others have you wrap the head in foil. The approach described below is the simplest method we've tried, and has always given us good results. For those times when you need only a small amount of roasted garlic, we've also included instructions for roasting a few garlic cloves rather than a whole head.

Step-by-Step Roasting of a Head of Garlic

1. Preheat the oven to 400°F.

2. Place the whole head of garlic on an ungreased

baking sheet intact (without cutting open). Bake for 40 minutes or until the head yields easily when gently pressed.

3. Remove the garlic from the oven. When cool enough to handle, remove the outer papery layers, and expose the pulp by slicing off the top with a knife or cutting it with scissors.

4. Remove the pulp either by using the tip of a knife to scoop it out of the paper, or by separating the individual cloves and squeezing to force out the creamy interior.

Step-by-Step Roasting of Garlic Cloves

1. Preheat the oven to 400°F.

2. Arrange the individual unpeeled cloves of garlic in a single layer on an ungreased baking sheet. Bake for 20 to 25 minutes, or until the cloves are soft when pressed and are very lightly colored. Remove each clove as it is done. Do not allow the garlic cloves to become too brown or they will be bitter.

3. When cool enough to handle, peel the cloves or simply cut off the ends and squeeze out the pulp.

ROASTING PEPPERS

Roasting makes the flesh of both bell and hot peppers tender rather than crisp and enables you to easily peel the pepper, leaving just the meat. It also adds another dimension to their flavor.

The roasting process is easy, and can be done a number of different ways. Use the method that suits the equipment you have on hand (you'll need a gas stove for the open-flame method), the number of peppers you're roasting, and your own personal preferences. And when cooking with hot peppers—jalapeño, Serrano, and the like—remember that it's usually a good idea to wear thin, disposable surgical gloves, and to remove the gloves before touching your skin. These gloves will protect you from the chili's hot juices.

Step-by-Step Roasting Over an Open Flame

This traditional method of roasting peppers—which requires a gas stove—is useful when you're preparing one pepper only.

1. Hold the pepper with tongs and place over a gas flame, rotating the pepper as necessary until the skin is charred and blistered all over.

2. Wrap the charred pepper in a clean cloth for about 5 minutes.

3. When the pepper is cool enough to handle, scrape off the skin using a small paring knife, cut the pepper open, and remove the seeds. Use the pepper as desired.

Step-by-Step Roasting Under a Broiler

This roasting method is fast, and allows you to prepare a number of peppers at a time.

1. Preheat the broiler.

2. Arrange the peppers in a single layer on a baking sheet, place 4 to 6 inches below the broiler, and broil for about 15 minutes, turning several times during cooking, until the skin is charred and blistered all over.

3. Wrap the charred peppers in a clean cloth for about 5 minutes.

4. When the peppers are cool enough to handle, scrape off the skin using a small paring knife, cut the peppers open, and remove the seeds. Use the peppers as desired.

Step-by-Step Roasting in the Oven

This approach takes longer than the other two, but

requires less monitoring. Like the broiler method, it allows you to easily prepare a number of peppers.

1. Preheat the oven to 450°F.

2. Arrange the peppers in a single layer on a baking sheet and bake for 30 minutes, until the pepper skins are a bit crisp and pull away from the flesh. Turn several times to promote even cooking.

3. Wrap the charred peppers in a clean cloth for about 5 minutes.

4. When the peppers are cool enough to handle, scrape off the skin using a small paring knife, cut the peppers open, and remove the seeds. Use the peppers as desired.

USING DRIED MUSHROOMS

Dried mushrooms are a terrific flavor enhancer and can be utilized in a number of different ways—either ground and used as a dried seasoning, or rehydrated and used hot or cold.

Step-by-Step Ground Mushroom Seasoning

1. Place the dried (unsoaked) mushrooms in a coffee grinder or mini food processor, and process until you have a powdery consistency.

2. Store in a clean airtight jar, and use a generous pinch to flavor broths, soups, salad dressings, and yogurt cheese.

Step-by-Step Dried Mushroom Rehydration

Once you learn how easy it is to rehydrate dried mushrooms, you'll find many ways to use them. After soaking, they can be drained and added as is to recipes that require further cooking, such as casseroles, soups, and sauces. Or you can cook them briefly in a saucepan and add them to salads and cooked grains and pasta.

1. Place a handful of dried mushrooms in a bowl, and pour on enough warm water to cover.

2. Allow to soak uncovered for about 10 minutes, or until the mushrooms are tender.

3. If using the mushrooms in a dish that requires further cooking, gently squeeze the moisture from the uncooked mushrooms and use in the recipe as directed. If using the mushrooms in a salad or a dish that's already been cooked, transfer the mushrooms and liquid to a small pot, add a pinch of salt, and simmer for 2 minutes before draining and using.

4. Pour the soaking or cooking liquid through a coffee filter or fine sieve to remove any sediment. Use in broths, sauces, stews, salad dressings, or recipes that call for a little simmering liquid.

MAKING YOGURT CHEESE AND YOGURT CREAM

Both yogurt cheese and yogurt cream are made by draining the liquid whey from yogurt to create a thick, mild-tasting product. Yogurt cream can be used like sour cream, while yogurt cheese can be used in dips, spreads, toppings, baking, sauces, soups, fillings, and more, as many of the recipes in this book demonstrate.

In countries where yogurt cheese originated, yogurt is commonly hung in a linen bag to drain. You can also line a strainer with cheesecloth or a coffee filter. Or you can make life easier for yourself by purchasing a reusable device designed specifically for this purpose. (You can order one online at www.HealthyHighways.com.)

Both yogurt cheese and yogurt cream can be made with any unflavored or flavored yogurt, so long as it does not contain gelatin or modified food starch, which will hold the liquid whey in suspension and prevent it from draining off. The time it takes to drain the liquid and the final yield will vary slightly from brand to brand. On average, it takes about 2 hours to reach sour cream consistency and 12 hours until a soft spreadable cheese is achieved. Maximum thickness is reached within 24 hours. Two cups of yogurt will yield about 1 cup of yogurt cheese or a larger amount of yogurt cream.

Step-by-Step Yogurt Cheese or Cream

1. Set your straining device of choice on a stable container large enough to hold the liquid that drains off. If you're using 2 cups of yogurt, you can expect about 1 cup of liquid to collect once it is fully drained.

2. Fill the selected strainer with yogurt and cover with a plastic lid, plate, or waxed paper to keep the yogurt from absorbing refrigerator smells.

3. Place the strainer in the refrigerator and allow to drain until the desired consistency is reached, or up to 24 hours. (After this time, the yogurt will not get any thicker.) A draining time of 2 hours will yield yogurt cream, while more time will be needed to yield yogurt cheese.

4. Discard the accumulated liquid, and transfer the yogurt cream or yogurt cheese to a covered container. Store in the refrigerator for 7 to 10 days.

COOKING DRIED BEANS

As discussed in Chapter 2, beans can be purchased dried or canned, with each form having its own distinct advantages and drawbacks. Even the casual cook has probably used canned beans, but many people have spent little or no time working with dried beans. Because beans have such an important place in vegetarian cooking, and because home-cooked dried beans will provide you with the very best flavor and texture, this section will tell you first how to soak beans, and then how to successfully cook them for use in your recipes. (For information on using canned beans and on storing all types of beans, see page 10.)

When using dried beans, keep in mind that most dried beans measure 2 to 2½ cups per pound. In general, a cup of dried beans will yield 2½ to 3 cups of cooked beans.

Soaking Dried Beans

Most dried beans require soaking prior to cooking to replace the water lost in drying, to quicken cooking time, and to increase digestibility. The exceptions to this rule are lentils—red, green, and French—and both green and yellow split peas. Baby lima beans don't have to be soaked prior to cooking, but will cook more quickly if they are first soaked. If you choose to cook the beans in a pressure cooker, you will be able to skip the soaking regardless of the type of bean used. (See page 30 for information on using a pressure cooker.)

Two soaking methods are offered below. Whether you choose the traditional or quick-soak method, be sure to select a pot that will accommodate both the beans and the large amount of water needed for soaking. Beans can actually triple in volume during this process.

Step-by-Step Traditional Soaking

1. Sort out any beans that are shriveled, damaged, or severely discolored, as well as any stones or other foreign objects. Place the remaining beans in a colander and rinse in cool water.

2. Transfer the beans to a large pot and cover with cool water, adding about 3 cups of water for each cup of dried beans. Soak for up to 8 hours at room temperature, or soak overnight in the refrigerator. Proceed with cooking the beans.

Step-by-Step Quick Soaking

1. Sort out any beans that are shriveled, damaged, or severely discolored, as well as any stones or other foreign objects. Place the remaining beans in a colander and rinse in cool water.

2. Transfer the beans to a large pot and cover with cool water, adding about 3 cups of water for each cup of dried beans. Bring the beans to a boil over high heat, and boil for 2 minutes. Then cover the pot, remove from the heat, and let stand for 1 to 2 hours. Proceed with cooking the beans.

Cooking Dried Beans

Whether you've used the traditional or quick method of soaking your beans—or even if you're using a type of bean that doesn't have to be soaked—the cooking method is the same. Be aware that some people prefer to discard the soaking water, rinse the beans, and cook them in fresh water to get rid of the hard-to-digest sugars that have been accused of causing gas. For the same reason, some people add herbs and spices such as caraway seed, dill, fennel, coriander, and ginger to the cooking water, and others cook the beans with the seaweed kombu. If this is of concern to you, try changing the cooking water and using different herbs until you get the desired results.

The cooking time for dried beans varies according to the type used. Table 3.1 offers the approximate cooking times for common beans. Remember that older beans take longer to cook, and that the more you place in the pot, the longer you will have to cook them before they are tender.

Step-by-Step Bean Cooking

1. If replacing the soaking water with fresh water, add about twice as much cool water as beans.

2. Place the uncovered pot over high heat, and boil vigorously for 5 to 10 minutes. This will help destroy the substances that can interfere with digestion.

3. After this brief boiling period, add spices, herbs, or kombu if desired. Then reduce the heat, cover the pot, and simmer gently, keeping the heat as low as possible. Low heat conserves the liquid and helps prevent the beans from splitting. It is a good idea to

TABLE 3.1. COOKING TIMES OF COMMON DRIED BEANS

Bean	Cooking Time*	Bean	Cooking Time*
Adzuki beans	1 hour	Lentils (unsoaked)	30 to 45 minutes
Black beans	1½ to 2 hours	Lima beans	45 minutes to 1½ hours
Black-eyed peas	1½ hours	Navy and pea beans	1 to 1½ hours
Chickpeas (garbanzo beans)	2 to 3 hours	Pinto beans and other brown or speckled beans	1½ to 2 hours
Great Northern, cannellini beans, and other large white beans	1½ to 2 hours	Soybeans	3 to 3½ hours
Kidney beans and other large red beans	1½ to 2 hours	Split peas (unsoaked)	30 to 45 minutes

*Note that except when otherwise noted, these cooking times apply to beans that have been soaked.

check the beans' progress occasionally, stirring and adding more liquid if needed.

4. Cook until the beans are completely tender and have an even creamy texture throughout the interior. If the center is still hard, you should continue cooking. Beans should not be eaten raw or undercooked, but if they are to be cooked again in a recipe, be sure to stop cooking as soon as they become tender.

5. If desired, salt the beans, adding about $\frac{1}{2}$ teaspoon per cup of dried beans. Do not salt until cooking is almost complete, as salt will toughen the skins of beans if added at the beginning of cooking time. Similarly, acidic ingredients such as tomatoes, wine, lemon juice, and vinegar should not be added until the last half hour of cooking time.

COOKING GRAINS

The preparation of whole grains is almost effortless. It merely involves combining the grain with a suitable amount of liquid, and simmering gently until the liquid has been absorbed and the grain is soft. The amount of liquid and length of time needed vary according to the grain used, and are listed in Table 3.2. The liquid can be plain water, diluted tomato juice, broth, or just about any other flavorful medium.

Two different methods can be used to cook grains—the boiling water method and the cold water method. Regardless of the technique chosen, during cooking the liquid should barely simmer. Furious boiling causes grains to burst, making them gummy rather than fluffy. Do not stir during cooking unless directed in the recipe, as this will loosen the starch on the outer surface and alter the texture. (In dishes like risotto and polenta, stirring is called for to create the characteristic creaminess.)

The need for salt varies according to the liquid used, as well as personal preferences. When using an unsalted liquid such as water, the general guideline is to add $\frac{1}{2}$ teaspoon of salt per cup of dry grain. This can be added during cooking or afterwards. For rice and millet, the addition of salt tends to harden the grain and add to the cooking time. Thus, it is best to wait at least 15 minutes into cooking before salting these foods.

When cooking time is almost over, you can determine doneness by moving the grains aside to see if all the liquid has been absorbed at the bottom of the pot. You can also chew a few of the top grains to check tenderness. If the grains are not done, continue to cook, adding a little more liquid if needed to prevent scorching. If the grains are tender but a little liquid still remains, partially uncover the pot and cook a little longer, until dry. When cooking is completed, remove from the heat and, if possible, let sit in the covered pot for 10 to 15 minutes before serving.

Finally, when planning meals, be aware that a cup of dry grain produces two to three times as much cooked grain, or about four side dish servings. For a main dish or when catering to large appetites, plan on 1 to $1\frac{1}{2}$ cups of cooked grain per serving. (For information on cooking grains in a pressure cooker, see page 35.)

Step-by-Step Grain Cooking—The Boiling Water Method

The boiling water method of cooking makes the grains swell rapidly, causing them to remain separate when done.

1. Place the specified amount of liquid in a pot, and bring to a boil over high heat.

2. Slowly sprinkle the grain into the liquid, cover, and reduce the heat so that the liquid barely simmers. Cook until the grain is tender and the liquid has been absorbed.

TABLE 3.2. COOKING GUIDE FOR COMMON GRAINS

Grain	Liquid for Each Cup of Dry Grain	Cooking Time
Barley, hulled (whole grain)	$2\frac{2}{3}$ cups	75 to 90 minutes
Brown rice	2 to $2\frac{1}{4}$ cups	45 to 50 minutes
Couscous (whole wheat)	$1\frac{1}{2}$ cups	10 minutes
Cracked wheat (bulgur)	2 cups	15 to 20 minutes
Kamut	$2\frac{1}{2}$ cups	75 minutes
Kasha (buckwheat groats)	2 cups	20 minutes
Millet	3 cups	30 minutes
Oat groats	2 cups	45 minutes
Quinoa*	2 cups	15 minutes
Rye berries	2 cups	50 minutes
Wheat berries	2 cups	50 minutes
Wild rice	$2\frac{1}{2}$ cups	50 minutes

*Rinse quinoa thoroughly in cold water before cooking to remove the bitter residue that coats the seeds.

Step-by-Step Grain Cooking–The Cold Water Method

Because this approach makes the grains swell slowly, it tends to yield a slightly stickier dish than the boiling water method.

1. Place the grain in a strainer, and rinse under cold running water to remove surface starch.

2. Place the grain and the specified amount of liquid in a pot, and bring to a boil over high heat.

3. Cover, and reduce the heat so that the liquid barely simmers. Cook until the grain is tender and the liquid has been absorbed.

STEAMING

Steaming is one of the simplest ways to prepare food without adding fat. It is most commonly used for vegetables, but tofu and tempeh can also be cubed and steamed. For even cooking, keep the size of the pieces uniform and spread them out over the bottom of the steamer, rather than piling them too deeply. If using a collapsible steaming basket, choose a broad pot that allows the bed to fully expand.

Keep in mind that while steaming conserves the natural flavors of foods, it does not *add* flavors as frying or grilling does. For this reason, you'll want to try one of the following ways to enhance the taste of your steamed dishes:

- While the food is still hot from the steamer, add a splash of soy sauce, freshly squeezed lemon juice, or a flavorful vinegar.

- Sprinkle the cooked food with chopped fresh herbs, grated lemon zest, and/or freshly ground black pepper.

- Drizzle the cooked food with a small amount of olive, flaxseed, or hemp oil, or toss with your favorite salad dressing.

Although it takes very little time to steam vegetables, be aware that you can speed the process even more by using a pressure cooker. For information on pressure-cooking vegetables, see page 32.

Step-by Step Steaming

1. Fill a large pot with one to two inches of water, and bring to boil over high heat.

2. Place the steamer in the pot, and arrange the food in the steamer. Cover the pot and reduce the heat just to maintain a boil.

3. Cook as directed in your recipe, or to taste. Keep in mind that the smaller the pieces, the faster they will cook. If a range of times is given in a recipe, test by piercing the food with a fork after the minimum suggested time. Continue cooking, if necessary, until the food reaches desired doneness.

STIR-STEAMING

Stir-steaming refers to a technique of quickly cooking vegetables in a wok or skillet without the addition of fat. As long as you use a heavy, well-seasoned wok; a nonstick wok or skillet; a well-seasoned cast-iron skillet; or a high-quality stainless steel skillet, the food will not stick.

Step-by-Step Stir-Steaming

1. Heat a wok or heavy skillet over medium-high heat.

2. Add the vegetables and stir almost constantly until they begin to wilt. If needed, add a bit of liquid such as wine, sherry, diluted soy sauce, vegetable broth, lemon juice, or even water to prevent sticking.

3. Cover the pot with a tight-fitting lid. Cook briefly, letting the food steam in its natural juices or a little added liquid, just until cooked through.

STEWING

Stewing is a slow method of cooking in which foods are cut into pieces and cooked under cover in their own juices, or in a minimal amount of added liquid. This technique is suitable for produce that is inherently moist, such as onions, mushrooms, and peppers.

Step-by-Step Stewing

1. Place the vegetables in a heavy, high-quality stainless steel or cast-iron pot. For additional flavor, or whenever a food's own juices are insufficient, add a few spoonfuls of broth, diluted soy sauce, wine, sherry, mild vinegar, or even water.

2. Cover the pot with a tight-fitting lid, turn the heat to medium, and cook, stirring occasionally, until done to taste.

OVEN ROASTING

Roasting is an excellent way to intensify the flavor of vegetables, and although most cooks do not realize it, no added fat is required. The fragrance of the vegetables permeates the kitchen as they cook, and they emerge from the oven tender and golden. If roasting several vegetables together, keep their individual cooking times in mind; the goal is to have them all done at about the same time. This can be done either by adding them at appropriate intervals according to the estimated times given in Table 3.3, or by cutting longer-cooking vegetables into smaller pieces so that they cook more quickly.

Do not crowd the pan when roasting, as this encourages vegetables to steam and inhibits browning. As the directions on page 27 demonstrate, it is not necessary to coat vegetables with oil for roasting. However, for increased browning and deeper flavor, you can toss them in a little olive oil infused with herbs or spices before placing them in the pan. A modest but adequate ratio is one tablespoon of oil per cup of vegetables. For added flavor, to each tablespoon of oil, add one to two teaspoons of dried oregano, rosemary, thyme, chili powder, curry powder, or another favorite seasoning. A good pinch of cayenne would also work well.

A generous serving of roasted vegetables makes a good accompaniment to beans, and is practically a meal in itself on top of pasta, polenta, or cooked grains. If you opt for grains, just be sure to include protein in your meal, either in a separate dish or by topping the vegetables with a generous amount of yogurt cheese, cooked beans, or a bean- or nut-based sauce. Leftovers can be transformed into a salad by tossing them with lemon juice, balsamic vinegar, or red wine vinegar and herbs.

The following steps will enable you to successfully roast a range of vegetables. Table 3.3 not only provides cooking times but also details how each vegetable should be cut up so that it turns a golden brown on the outside and is moist and tender inside.

Step-by-Step Oven Roasting

1. Preheat the oven to 500°F.

2. Generously oil one or more baking sheets or shal-

TABLE 3.3. OVEN ROASTING GUIDE FOR VEGETABLES

Vegetable	Preparation	Roasting Time
Asparagus	Whole, tough ends broken off	20 minutes
Beets	1/2-inch to 1-inch pieces, peeled or unpeeled	40 minutes
Brussels sprouts	Halved lengthwise (through stem)	20 to 25 minutes
Carrots	Quartered lengthwise, peeled	30 to 40 minutes
Eggplant	1/2-inch slices	15 minutes
	1-inch cubes	30 minutes
Fennel	1/2-inch-thick wedges	15 to 20 minutes
Mushrooms	Whole	20 minutes
Onions	1-inch-thick crescents	15 minutes
Potatoes, large white	1 1/2-inch cubes	30 to 40 minutes
	1/4-inch slices	30 minutes
Potatoes, small new or red	Quartered	30 minutes
Sweet potatoes	1-inch chunks, peeled	30 minutes
	French fry-size sticks, peeled	15 to 20 minutes
Zucchini	Quartered lengthwise	30 to 40 minutes

low roasting pans with olive oil, making sure you have enough space to arrange the vegetables without crowding.

3. Spread the vegetables in the pans in a single layer. If cooking several types of vegetables at once, you may want to organize them according to baking time so that you can easily remove or add them at appropriate intervals.

4. If desired, toss the vegetables with a little olive oil, and scatter them with your seasonings of choice, including slivered garlic, rosemary, oregano, and such.

5. Place the pans in the preheated oven and bake, checking on them occasionally and using a spatula to loosen and move the vegetables around to promote even roasting and prevent sticking. Cook as indicated in Table 3.3, or until the vegetables are done to taste.

6. Transfer the vegetables to a serving bowl, and season with freshly ground pepper. If desired, sprinkle with soy sauce or balsamic vinegar.

GRILLING

Many vegetables lend themselves to grilling, which adds both a distinctive flavor and an appealing look to foods.

The easiest approach to grilling is to simply place the prepared vegetables on the preheated grill and, if desired, season them afterwards. Of course, you may find they taste so good plain that no seasoning is necessary. Our favorite tactic is to sprinkle the vegetables while still hot with a little balsamic vinegar. This works particularly well with slices of grilled zucchini, eggplant, mushrooms, carrots, broccoli trees, and cauliflower. Sometimes we use soy sauce instead of the vinegar.

If desired, you can marinate the vegetables before grilling, or baste them while they're on the grill. For marinating, we recommend Spicy Marinade (see page 216) or the marinade in Asian Grill (see page 136). If you prefer basting, try Sweet Mustard Basting Sauce (see page 215).

Cooking time will vary with the intensity of the heat as well as the distance between the grate and the heat. A common mistake people make is to grill foods too close to the heat source. This causes the food to char on the outside before it has a chance to cook. Table 3.4 indicates cooking times.

Because vegetables can easily slip between the grill bars, a mesh grill rack is a worthwhile tool to have. You'll also want long tongs with heatproof handles so that you can keep a safe distance from the heat when turning the food.

It's tricky to gauge the amount of vegetables to cook. Since grilled vegetables are so tasty, people tend to eat a lot, especially if you serve them an assortment. We suggest choosing four to six items and planning the following amounts per serving: 3 to 4 mushrooms, half an onion, 5 to 6 ounces cauliflower or broccoli, half a large sweet potato, 8 ounces eggplant or acorn squash, 1 small zucchini or crookneck squash, 2 plum tomatoes, and half a red or green pepper.

If you love grilling as we do, don't limit yourself to vegetables, but also try fruit. We recommend peaches, nectarines, and pineapple.

The following steps will help insure grilling success. Refer to Table 3.4 for preparation and timing guidelines.

Step-by-Step Grilling

1. Marinate vegetables, if desired, for 30 minutes to 2 hours at room temperature, or longer in the refrigerator.

2. Oil the grill grates and preheat a charcoal grill until the coals are glowing. If using a gas grill, preheat the grill on high.

TABLE 3.4. GRILLING GUIDE FOR FRUITS AND VEGETABLES

Fruit or Vegetable	Preparation	Total Grilling Time	Suggestions
Broccoli	Thin trees with peeled stalks	6 to 10 minutes	Cook plain and sprinkle with soy sauce or balsamic vinegar; marinate before cooking for 1 hour or more; or baste during cooking.
Carrots	¼-inch-thick lengthwise slices, peeled	10 to 16 minutes	Cook plain and sprinkle with balsamic vinegar; marinate before cooking for 1 hour or more; or baste during cooking.
Cauliflower	Florets or ¼-inch-thick slices	14 to 20 minutes	Cook plain and sprinkle with balsamic vinegar; marinate before cooking for 1 hour or more; or baste during cooking.
Corn	Whole with husks intact	15 to 20 minutes	Cook until the husks are charred, turning frequently. Then remove husks and silk and return the corn to the grill until the kernels are slightly browned.
Eggplant	¼-inch-thick rounds	10 minutes	Cook plain and sprinkle with soy sauce or balsamic vinegar; marinate before cooking for 30 minutes or more; or baste during cooking.
Mushrooms	Whole, threaded on skewers or placed directly on mesh grate	6 to 10 minutes	Cook plain and sprinkle with soy sauce or balsamic vinegar; marinate before cooking for 30 minutes or more; or baste during cooking.
Nectarines	Halved and pitted	6 to 10 minutes	Cook plain and dust with cinnamon after cooking.
Onions	Halves, wedges, thick slices, or chunks	10 minutes	If using chunks, thread onto skewers. Cook plain or marinate before cooking for 30 minutes or more.
Peaches	Halved and pitted	6 to 10 minutes	Cook plain and dust with cinnamon after cooking.
Pineapple	½-inch-thick slices, peeled	10 minutes	Cook plain and dust with cinnamon after cooking.
Red or green peppers	Halved, cut in strips, or 1- to 2-inch wedges	6 to 10 minutes	If cutting into wedges, place on skewers or directly on mesh grate. Cook plain.
Summer squash (crookneck, pattypan, or zucchini)	¼-inch-thick lengthwise slices	6 to 10 minutes	Cook plain and sprinkle with soy sauce or balsamic vinegar; marinate for 30 minutes or baste during cooking.

Fruit or Vegetable	Preparation	Total Grilling Time	Suggestions
Sweet potatoes	1/4-inch-thick slices, peeled.	14 to 20 minutes	Cook plain; marinate before cooking for 30 minutes or more; or baste during cooking. For a softer interior, cover or make a foil tent over potatoes for the first few minutes of cooking.
Tomatoes, plum preferred	Halved lengthwise.	6 to 10 minutes	Cook plain.
Winter squash	1/4-inch-thick rounds, peeled and seeded.	14 to 20 minutes	Cook plain; marinate before cooking for 30 minutes or more; or baste during cooking. For a soft interior, cover or make a foil tent over the squash slices for the first few minutes of cooking.

3. If using a charcoal grill, if desired, you can impart flavor and aroma by adding a handful of fresh or dried herbs, tea leaves, or dried citrus peels to the fire.

4. Place food on grill grates about 3 to 6 inches above heat.

5. Cook as indicated in Table 3.4, turning several times, until the vegetables are nicely seared on all sides with grill marks, and done to taste. If basting, you can do so just before turning. It is important to stay at the grill during cooking so you can watch and turn the foods, or move them towards the hotter center or the cooler edges as necessary.

6. As they are done, transfer the food to a serving platter. If desired, sprinkle with soy sauce or balsamic vinegar while still hot.

7. Serve at once or at room temperature.

PRESSURE-COOKING

The pressure cooker is one of our most prized kitchen tools. An airtight metal pot, it cooks food quickly by using steam under pressure at high temperatures. If you want to enjoy wholefoods with fast-food convenience, nothing beats the pressure cooker. Most foods cook in about 30 percent of the usual time, and flavor and nutrients are well conserved.

Although a pressure cooker may be intimidating at first, it is really a very easy tool to use, especially if you get a model with a quick pressure-release valve. The inset on page 31 will tell you a little more about pressure cookers so that if you don't already own one, you can learn about this tool before making a purchase.

Basic Pressure-Cooking

When using a pressure cooker, be sure to follow the manufacturer's instructions for assembling and operating. The following basic principles, though, can be applied to all units. Later in this chapter, you'll find more specific guidelines for pressure-cooking vegetables (see page 31), beans (page 33), and grains (page 35).

Step-by Step Pressure-Cooking

1. Load the cooker with the prepared ingredients and

Selecting a Pressure Cooker

There are many different pressure cookers on the market. Older models feature a weight balanced loosely on top. The weight jiggles as it releases bursts of steam. When cooking is complete, you must wait for the pressure to reduce naturally or carry the loaded pot to the sink and run it under cold water. This type of pressure cooker is the most temperamental to use.

Newer pressure cookers utilize a spring valve that allows you to set specific pressure, or rely on a concealed weight that can be regulated somewhat by listening to the pot hiss. Both of these designs are easy to use, and although the latter model is not always as precise in timing, it usually sells for less. We have used this less expensive model with great success. Since just a little steam is released during cooking, these newer cookers are also relatively quiet. Moreover, most new pressure cookers have several built-in safety mechanisms, as well as a button for quickly releasing the steam, which is a very worthwhile convenience.

Whatever model you choose, make it stainless steel, not aluminum, which has potential health risks. A 6-quart pressure cooker is suitable for most households, but if you're cooking for more than six, an 8-quart cooker may be a better choice.

the required amount of liquid. Never fill the cooker more than two-thirds the height of the pot.

2. Close the cooker and place on high heat. Be sure the pressure-release valve is properly aligned to prevent steam from escaping.

3. Once full pressure is achieved as indicated in the operating manual, reduce the heat to just maintain the pressure. Begin timing at this point, following the timing tables found on pages 32, 34, and 35. For best results, use a kitchen timer to avoid miscalculation. If you are uncertain of the target time, it is best to underestimate. You will be able to bring the pressure up again if you find that the food is undercooked.

4. When the recommended cooking time is over, remove the cooker from the heat.

5. Reduce the pressure by carefully and slowly opening the pressure-release valve (if applicable), until the steam no longer escapes and the safety lock recedes. For models without a pressure-release valve, the cooker can be cooled down under cold water.

Pressure-Cooking Vegetables

Vegetables cook quite quickly under pressure. The preferred technique is to place the prepared vegetables in a steaming basket above boiling water. As a general guideline, add $\frac{1}{2}$ cup water for up to 5 minutes of pressure cooking, 1 cup water for 6 to 10 minutes, and another cup for each additional 10 minutes. Table 3.5 provides more precise cooking times, as well as preparation methods and water amounts, for a number of common vegetables.

Be aware that when the pressure-cooking time is given as "0," you should remove the cooker from the stove as soon as full pressure is achieved, and reduce the pressure quickly. When a range of times is given, variations are due to size and age. For example, larger, older vegetables require more cooking than smaller, younger produce.

TABLE 3.5. PRESSURE-COOKING GUIDE FOR VEGETABLES

Vegetable	Preparation	Amount of Water	Cooking Time
Artichokes	Whole	1½ cups	11 minutes
Asparagus	Whole, ends trimmed	½ cup	1 to 2 minutes
Beets	Small whole	1 cup	10 minutes
	Medium whole	1½ cups	12 to 16 minutes
Broccoli	Full stalks	½ cup	2 minutes
	Florets	½ cup	1 minute
Brussels sprouts	Whole	½ cup	3 minutes
Cabbage	Quartered	1 cup	5 to 6 minutes
	Strips	½ cup	2 minutes
Carrots	½-inch-thick coins	½ cup	1 minute
	Large chunks	½ cup	2 minutes
	Whole	1 cup	4 to 7 minutes
Cauliflower	Whole	1 cup	5 minutes
	Florets	½ cup	2 minutes
Green beans	Whole, ends trimmed	½ cup	1 to 2 minutes
	1-inch lengths	½ cup	0 to 1 minute
Leeks	3-inch lengths	½ cup	3 minutes

Step-by-Step Vegetable Pressure-Cooking

1. Bring the amount of water specified in Table 3.5 to boil in the pressure cooker.

2. Place the vegetables in the steaming basket and set over boiling water.

3. Close the cooker, and bring the pressure up over medium heat.

4. Reduce the heat to just maintain the pressure, and cook for the time indicated in the table. If the pressure-cooking time is given as "0," you should remove the cooker from the stove as soon as full pressure has been achieved.

5. At the end of the cooking time, reduce the pressure by removing the pot from the heat, waiting 5 minutes, and then slowly turning the steam-release valve to allow the gas to escape gradually (do not open all at once); by removing the pot from the heat, waiting 5 minutes, and running the pot under cold water; or by removing the pot from the heat and letting it cool down on its own.

Vegetable	Preparation	Amount of Water	Cooking Time
Onions	Wedges	$\frac{1}{2}$ cup	1 minute
Parsnips	Whole	1 cup	8 to 10 minutes
	1-inch chunks	$\frac{1}{2}$ cup	3 to 4 minutes
Peppers	Halved, stuffed with precooked filling	$\frac{1}{2}$ cup	3 minutes
Potatoes	Whole, new	$\frac{1}{2}$ cup	5 minutes
	Whole, small (3 ounces each)	1 cup	10 minutes
	Whole, medium (5 ounces each)	$1\frac{1}{2}$ cups	15 minutes
	Whole, large (8 ounces each)	$2\frac{1}{2}$ cups	25 minutes
	3-inch cubes	$1\frac{1}{2}$ cups	12 minutes
	$1\frac{1}{2}$-inch cubes	1 cup	6 minutes
	$\frac{1}{2}$-inch-thick slices	$\frac{1}{2}$ cup	2 minutes
Pumpkin	Large wedges	1 cup	8 to 10 minutes
Squash, acorn	Halved, seeds removed	1 cup	7 minutes
Squash, yellow	Halved, stuffed with precooked filling	$\frac{1}{2}$ cup	3 minutes
Sweet potato	Whole	1 cup	6 to 8 minutes
	Halved	$\frac{1}{2}$ cup	3 to 4 minutes
Turnips	1-inch cubes or $\frac{1}{2}$-inch-thick slices	$\frac{1}{2}$ cup	3 to 4 minutes
Zucchini	$\frac{1}{2}$-inch rounds	$\frac{1}{2}$ cup	1 minute

Pressure-Cooking Dried Beans

Beans may be soaked prior to pressure-cooking, or they may be pressure-cooked without soaking. Just be aware that unsoaked beans need a longer cooking time and more water, but also create less froth and hold their shape better. To reduce the froth and foam that develops when cooking beans, be sure to do the following:

- Never fill the cooker more than halfway.
- Never use less than $1\frac{1}{2}$ cups of water.
- Before cooking, wipe the inside of the pressure cooker lid with oil.

Whether you're cooking soaked or unsoaked beans, the technique is the same. In Table 3.6, you'll find both the amount of liquid and the amount of time needed to cook several different common varieties of beans, from adzuki to soybeans. Since the water amount and cooking time vary according to whether the beans have been presoaked, for each variety, you'll find information listed for both unsoaked and soaked beans. Once you have this basic information in hand, you'll be able to turn to the step-by-step instructions provided directly below.

Step-by-Step Bean Pressure-Cooking

1. Combine the beans and water in the amounts recommended in Table 3.6. You can alter the amounts proportionately, but be sure the pot is not more than half full.

2. Bring the water to a boil over high heat, and skim off any surface froth.

3. Close the cooker, and bring the pressure up over medium-high heat.

4. Reduce the heat to just maintain the pressure, and cook for the time indicated.

5. At the end of the cooking time, reduce the pressure by removing the pot from the heat, waiting 5 minutes, and then slowly turning the steam-release valve to allow the gas to escape gradually (do not open all at once); by removing the pot from the heat, waiting 5 minutes, and running the pot under cold water; or by removing the pot from the heat and letting it cool down on its own.

6. Test one of the beans. If the beans are not completely cooked, bring back up to pressure and cook

TABLE 3.6. PRESSURE-COOKING GUIDE FOR BEANS

		Amount of Water		**Cooking Time**	**Amount of**
Water	**Cooking Time**				
		for Presoaked	**for Presoaked**	**for Unsoaked**	**for Unsoaked**
Bean	**Amount**	**Beans**	**Beans**	**Beans**	**Beans**
Adzuki beans	2 cups	3 cups	10 minutes	4 cups	15 minutes
Black beans	2 cups	3 cups	6 minutes	5 cups	25 minutes
Black-eyed peas	2 cups	3 cups	5 minutes	4 cups	15 minutes
Chickpeas (garbanzo beans)	2 cups	2 cups	18 minutes	5 cups	48 minutes
Great Northern and cannellini beans	2 cups	4 cups	7 minutes	5 cups	35 minutes
Kidney beans	2 cups	4 cups	8 to 10 minutes	5 cups	35 to 40 minutes
Lentils*	2 cups	Not applicable	Not applicable	4½ cups	10 minutes
Lima beans	2 cups	3 cups	5 minutes	5 cups	15 to 18 minutes
Navy and pea beans	2 cups	3 cups	7 minutes	5 cups	30 minutes
Pinto beans	2 cups	3 cups	7 to 8 minutes	5 cups	35 minutes
Soybeans	2 cups	4 cups	16 to 18 minutes	5 cups	45 minutes

* Lentils should not be soaked.

for another 5 minutes. Repeat this as necessary until the beans are cooked to your liking.

7. Add salt and other seasonings as desired. (Never add salt until the beans are cooked.)

Pressure-Cooking Grains

Using a pressure cooker slashes the cooking time for grains approximately in half, making it easier to incorporate healthful grains into your diet. Table 3.7 provides the guidance you need regarding water amounts and cooking times. Just keep in mind that because the volume of grains more than doubles during cooking, the dried grains should not fill the pressure cooker more than halfway.

Note that while pressure-cooking is a great way to cook grains, not all grains are appropriate for this method of preparation. Millet, quinoa, kasha, and cracked wheat are all too small, and can clog the valve of the pressure cooker. For this reason, you'll want to stick to the grains listed in Table 3.7, and prepare all others using the traditional method discussed earlier in the chapter.

Step-by-Step Grain Pressure-Cooking

1. Wash and drain the grains well.

2. Combine the grain and water in the amounts recommended in Table 3.7. You can alter the amounts proportionately, but be sure the pot is not more than half full.

3. Close the cooker, and bring the pressure up over high heat.

4. Reduce the heat to just maintain the pressure, and cook for the time indicated.

5. At the end of the cooking time, reduce the pressure by removing the pot from the heat, waiting 5 minutes, and then slowly turning the steam-release valve to allow the gas to escape gradually (do not open all at once); by removing the pot from the heat, waiting 5 minutes, and running the pot under cold water; or by removing the pot from the heat and letting it cool down on its own.

6. Test the grains. If they are not tender, bring back up to pressure and cook for another 5 minutes. Re-

TABLE 3.7. PRESSURE-COOKING GUIDE FOR GRAINS

Grain	Liquid for Each Cup of Dry Grain	Cooking Time
Barley, hulled (whole grain)	2 cups	30 minutes
Barley, pearled	2 cups	20 minutes
Brown rice	1 cup	15 minutes
Kamut	2 cups	45 minutes
Rye berries	2 cups*	35 minutes
Wheat berries	2 cups*	35 minutes
Wild rice	2 cups	25 minutes

* For a drier texture, reduce liquid to $1\frac{1}{2}$ cups.

The Master Rule

Before you start preparing a dish, read through the recipe completely. Then gather all the ingredients and appropriate utensils in your workspace, prepare any pans, and preheat the oven, if necessary. Do as much measuring, peeling, chopping, and such as is practical before combining the ingredients. You are now ready to assemble, mix, cook, and concentrate on any unfamiliar techniques—mastering the recipe.

peat this as necessary until the grains are cooked to your liking. If a little liquid remains in the cooker, stir well and it will probably be absorbed in a few minutes. If more than a little liquid remains, drain it off before serving.

7. Add salt and other seasonings as desired. (Never add salt until the grains are cooked.)

Your basic training is now complete. As you experiment with the dishes in this book and with recipes from other sources as well, don't hesitate to turn back to this chapter and re-acquaint yourself with these techniques as necessary. A mastery of these basics are sure to help you in all your cooking adventures.

4. Breakfast

A healthy day starts with a good breakfast. It is important to eat something sustaining in the morning. If you get up too early to face a complete meal, consider dividing breakfast into two snack-type meals before lunch.

People have different opinions about what foods qualify as breakfast fare. In our view, most foods that are good for you are good for you at *any* time of day. Nonetheless, in this chapter we offer some breakfast tips, some menus, and a selection of recipes that we feel stand out in quality and breakfast appeal.

Here are some pointers you can use regardless of whether you eat your morning meal at home or on the go:

■ Carbohydrate-dominant foods such as bagels, rolls, and pastries are typical of many breakfasts. Be sure to balance your carbohydrates with protein, making soy- and yogurt-based dishes your breakfast choice as often as possible.

■ Choose cereals, breadstuffs, crackers, and pancakes made from whole grains. Top cereal with ground flaxseed and wheat germ—ingredients that should also be included when making your own baked goods.

■ Eat cereal with yogurt or soy milk, both of which have proven health benefits.

■ Give each person a bowl of yogurt; set out a selection of fresh and dried fruits, nuts and seeds, and honey and maple syrup; and let everyone make their own "breakfast sundae."

■ Top pancakes with yogurt or yogurt cheese and fruit, instead of drowning them in butter and sweet syrup.

■ Try to include vegetables at breakfast. Add a slice of tomato, cucumber, sprouts, and/or lettuce to the filling of a bagel or sandwich, or include mushrooms, peppers, onions, leftover vegetables, and the like in tofu scrambles or omelets. A baked potato—white or sweet, made in advance—topped with dairy or soy cheese is an easy breakfast addition.

■ Include fresh fruit on cereal, on pancakes, or in nut butter sandwiches.

■ Make soy part of your breakfast fare. Along with using soy milk on cereal and in shakes, add soy flour to muffins, biscuits, and pancakes. And try the Soybean Pancakes and tofu and tempeh breakfast recipes found in this chapter.

Finally, realize that just as breakfast need not be limited to traditional foods, the recipes in this section do not have to be reserved for the morning. For example, Vegetable Tofu Scramble and Mexican Scramble make excellent dinners. For a light evening meal, griddlecakes can fill the bill.

Sample Breakfast Menus

Scrambled Eggs with Cheese (page 42)
on whole grain toast

Mexican Scramble (page 43)
with corn tortillas and sliced avocado

Ultimate Oatmeal (page 39)
with fresh berries or sliced banana

Appleberry Corn Muffins (page 48)
with yogurt cheese (page 22)
or almond butter

Orange Griddlecakes (page 44)
with Tempeh Breakfast Links (page 41)

Yogurt with fresh fruit

All-in-One Breakfast Shake (page 39)

All-in-One Breakfast Shake

YIELD: 4 SERVINGS

2 1/2 cups soy milk

1 cup orange, apple, or pineapple juice

1/2 cup oats

2 medium bananas, cut into chunks

1/4 cup wheat germ

4 to 8 ice cubes, optional

Ground nutmeg, optional

This shake combines cereal, soy, and fruit in one easy-to-fix, easy-to-enjoy package. You can add variety by trying different juices and by altering the fruit according to the season, replacing the bananas with a very ripe pear, a large peach, or 3/4 cup of sweet berries.

1. Combine everything except the ice cubes and nutmeg in a blender, and process at high speed until smooth. For a frothier shake, add the ice cubes and process until completely melted.

2. Divide the shake among serving glasses and sprinkle with the nutmeg, if desired.

Ultimate Oatmeal

YIELD: 4 SERVINGS

1 1/3 cups oats

1/2 cup oat bran

5 cups water

Pinch salt, optional

1/4 cup flaxseed meal (page 17)

1/4 cup wheat germ

Ultimate Oatmeal shows how easy it is to nutritionally upgrade familiar dishes. Here, oats are enhanced with oat bran, wheat germ, and flaxseed. The recipe produces a thick porridge that can handle a generous amount of soy milk. If a thinner cereal is preferred, add some freshly boiled water at the end as needed.

1. Combine the oats, oat bran, water, and salt, if desired, in a medium-size pot.

2. Bring the oat mixture to a boil over medium heat, reduce the heat, and simmer gently for 5 minutes, stirring once or twice during cooking.

3. Remove the pot from the heat and stir in the flaxseed meal and wheat germ. Cover and let sit for a few minutes before serving. If desired, garnish with sunflower seeds, chopped walnuts, and cinnamon.

Orange Frosty

YIELD: 4 SERVINGS

3 cups plain nonfat or low-fat yogurt

1 cup orange juice

1 to 2 tablespoons honey

8 ice cubes

This tasty drink combines the familiar breakfast juice with dairy.

1. Combine everything in a blender, and process at high speed until smooth.

2. Divide the shake among serving glasses.

Light Granola

YIELD: ABOUT 5 CUPS

4 cups oats

1/2 cup wheat germ

1/2 cup chopped nuts and/or seeds of choice, such as pecans, walnuts, almonds, hazelnuts, peanuts, sunflower seeds, and pumpkin seeds

1/2 cup dried fruit of choice, such as raisins, chopped dates, apples, apricots, or pears

1/4 cup oat bran

1 teaspoon vanilla extract

1/2 teaspoon ground cinnamon

3/4 cup apple or apple-berry juice

This healthy granola is fruit-juice sweetened and contains no added fat.

1. Preheat the oven to 375°F.

2. Combine the oats, wheat germ, nuts and seeds, dried fruit, and oat bran in a large bowl.

3. Add the vanilla extract and cinnamon to the juice, and stir the mixture into the cereal until evenly moistened.

4. Spread the cereal over a large, shallow baking pan and bake, stirring occasionally, for about 20 minutes or until dry and lightly browned. Be sure to check frequently towards the end of the cooking time to avoid overbrowning.

5. Cool the cereal and store in an airtight container. Serve with soy milk or yogurt.

TEMPEH STRIPS

YIELD: 4 SERVINGS (6 STRIPS EACH)

2 tablespoons water

1 tablespoon soy sauce

Canola or olive oil

8 ounces tempeh, cut into 1/8-inch-thick strips

These tasty strips are good with pancakes, alongside eggs, or on a sandwich. They can also be served over a cooked grain—brown rice, millet, quinoa, or kasha, for example.

1. Combine the water and soy sauce in a small bowl, and set aside.
2. Place just enough oil in a 12-inch skillet to coat the bottom, and place over medium heat. Add the tempeh strips and brown lightly on both sides.
3. Sprinkle the soy sauce mixture over the browned tempeh. Cover and cook for 1 to 2 minutes, or until most of the liquid has been absorbed.
4. Remove the lid and cook to evaporate any remaining moisture.

TEMPEH BREAKFAST LINKS

YIELD: 4 SERVINGS (3 LINKS EACH)

1/4 cup water

1 tablespoon soy sauce

8 ounces tempeh, cut into 1/4-inch "fingers"

Fat, juicy tempeh links can be served in the same way as the crisper Tempeh Strips above. Enjoy these links alongside pancakes or eggs, or with a cooked grain.

1. Combine the water and soy sauce in a small bowl, and set aside.
2. Heat a heavy 12-inch skillet, preferably cast iron, over medium heat. Add the tempeh and about half of the diluted soy sauce to the skillet.
3. Cook until the tempeh starts to color on the bottom. Turn the tempeh over and add the remaining liquid. Cover and cook for 5 minutes.
4. Remove the cover and cook until the liquid has evaporated and the tempeh is nicely colored on both sides.

Vegetable Tofu Scramble

YIELD: 4 SERVINGS

2 cups mixed vegetables of choice, such as asparagus, broccoli, celery, carrots, cauliflower, corn, green beans, mushrooms, red cabbage, snow peas, and zucchini, cut into small pieces

1/2 cup chopped onion

1/2 cup diced green pepper

2 tablespoons water

2 teaspoons soy sauce

1 pound firm tofu

1/2 teaspoon ground turmeric

Salt

Freshly ground pepper

Many people find scrambled tofu a marvelous replacement for scrambled eggs. The addition of turmeric is more for color than taste, and truly gives tofu the appearance of the conventional egg dish. Serve on a plate with brown rice or potatoes, stuff into a whole wheat pita, fold inside a tortilla, or pile on toast.

1. Combine the vegetables, water, and soy sauce in a 12-inch skillet, and place over medium heat. When hot, turn the heat to low, cover, and cook, stirring occasionally, for 10 to 15 minutes, or until the firmest vegetables are fork tender.

2. Add the tofu to the skillet and mash into rough chunks with a potato masher. Sprinkle the entire dish with the turmeric.

3. Raise the heat a little and continue to cook and stir for a few minutes, until the tofu is hot.

4. Season to taste with salt and pepper.

Scrambled Eggs with Cheese

YIELD: 3 SERVINGS

3 eggs

3 tablespoons yogurt cheese (page 22)

Salt

Freshly ground pepper

A single egg goes farther when you combine it with yogurt cheese. This recipe's technique of beating the egg in the hot pan requires a bit more skill than the conventional approach, but involves less cleanup. Move quickly or the egg may set too rapidly and you will end up with unblended whites, rather than consistently yellow eggs.

1. Heat a 12-inch seasoned omelet pan over medium heat. If not well seasoned, wipe with oil.

2. When the pan is hot, break the eggs directly into the pan and quickly beat with a fork until the yolks and whites are integrated. Cook, stirring with a spoon or lifting the cooked portion with a spatula as it sets, and allowing the uncooked portion to flow underneath.

3. When the eggs are almost cooked to your liking, drop the yogurt cheese in several dollops on top. Fold the eggs over the yogurt cheese and cook briefly, until the yogurt cheese is creamy.

4. Season to taste with salt and pepper.

Mexican Scramble

YIELD: 4 SERVINGS

- 2 cups fresh or frozen corn kernels, optional
- 1/2 cup chopped onion
- 1/2 cup diced green pepper
- 2 tablespoons minced hot pepper, such as jalapeño or Serrano
- 2 tablespoons water
- 2 teaspoons soy sauce
- 1 teaspoon dried oregano
- 1/2 teaspoon ground cumin
- 2 teaspoons chili powder
- 1 pound firm tofu
- Salt
- Freshly ground pepper

If desired, top each serving with 2 tablespoons of warm salsa. Serve with corn tortillas, sliced avocado, and additional salsa for those who want a bit more seasoning.

1. Combine the corn, if using, with the onion, green pepper, hot pepper, water, and soy sauce in a 12-inch skillet, and place over medium heat. When hot, reduce the heat to low, cover, and cook, stirring occasionally, for 5 minutes.

2. Stir in the oregano, cumin, and chili powder, and cook briefly.

3. Add the tofu to the skillet and mash into rough chunks with a potato masher. Raise the heat a little and continue to cook and stir for a few minutes, until the tofu is hot.

4. Season to taste with salt and pepper.

Mixed Grain Griddlecakes

YIELD: 4 SERVINGS (3 PANCAKES EACH)

1 cup cornmeal
1/2 cup whole wheat flour
1/4 cup wheat germ
1/4 cup soy flour
1/4 cup flaxseed meal (see page 17)
5 teaspoons baking powder
1/2 teaspoon salt
2 1/2 cups soy milk
2 teaspoons maple syrup
2 teaspoons canola oil
2 bananas, sliced, optional

Try these hearty pancakes with one of the delicious toppings offered in the inset on page 45.

1. Combine the dry ingredients in a mixing bowl. Add the soy milk, maple syrup, and oil, and stir until the dry ingredients are completely moistened. Let stand a few minutes, until the batter absorbs the liquid and thickens.

2. If desired, stir the sliced bananas into the batter.

3. Preheat a nonstick or lightly oiled griddle or large skillet over medium-high heat. Pour generous 1/4-cup portions of the batter onto the skillet, and cook until bubbles form on the surface of the cakes and the bottoms are lightly browned. Turn and cook until the other side is set.

Orange Griddlecakes

YIELD: 4 SERVINGS (4 PANCAKES EACH)

1 1/2 cups whole wheat flour
1/4 cup wheat germ
1/4 cup soy flour
1/4 cup flaxseed meal (page 17)
2 teaspoons baking powder
1 teaspoon baking soda
1/2 teaspoon salt
2 1/2 cups orange juice
2 teaspoons canola oil

These sweet, cakelike pancakes are delicious topped with yogurt or yogurt cheese, and sliced bananas, peaches, or berries. A good choice for a brunch or even a light dinner.

1. Combine all of the dry ingredients in a mixing bowl. Add the juice and oil, and stir gently until the dry ingredients are completely moistened.

2. Preheat a nonstick or lightly oiled griddle or large skillet over medium-high heat. Pour 1/4-cup portions of the batter onto the skillet, and cook until bubbles form on the surface of the cakes and the bottoms are lightly browned. Turn and cook until the other side is set.

Soybean Pancakes

YIELD: 4 SERVINGS (5 PANCAKES EACH)

2 cups cooked soybeans

4 eggs

1/2 cup soy milk

High in protein, these flourless pancakes are surprisingly delicate.

1. Combine all the ingredients in a blender or food processor, and purée until smooth.

2. Preheat a nonstick or lightly oiled griddle or large skillet over medium-high heat. Pour 1/4-cup portions of the batter onto the skillet, and cook until bubbles form on the surface of the cakes and the bottoms are lightly browned. Turn and cook until the other side is set.

Pancake Toppings

What's a fast and easy way to turn pancakes into a more balanced meal? Add a topping that contains some protein. The following toppings will enhance your griddle cakes with both flavor and a healthy dose of protein.

Maple Cream

YIELD: 1 CUP

1/2 cup plain nonfat or low-fat yogurt

1/2 cup maple syrup

1. Place the yogurt and maple syrup in a bowl, and mix together until well blended.

2. Serve chilled or at room temperature.

Berries and Cream

YIELD: ABOUT 1 1/4 CUPS

1 cup fresh or frozen (thawed) unsweet-ened strawberries or raspberries

2 tablespoons honey

1/2 cup plain nonfat or low-fat yogurt

1. Place the berries in a bowl and crush with a fork.

2. Stir the honey into the berries. Add the yogurt and mix well.

3. Serve chilled or at room temperature.

GOLDEN BISCUITS

YIELD: 8 BISCUITS

1 3/4 cups whole wheat flour

1/4 cup soy flour

1/4 cup flaxseed meal (page 17)

1 teaspoon baking powder

1/2 teaspoon baking soda

1/2 teaspoon salt

3/4 cup plain nonfat yogurt

1/4 cup unsweetened applesauce

Homemade biscuits are surprisingly easy to make, and ours provide far better nutrition than you'll get from a mix or a package of refrigerated dough. In fact, Golden Biscuits offer fewer calories, almost twice the protein, about a third the fat, and just half the sodium of most commercial biscuits, along with a hefty serving of fiber.

1. Preheat the oven to 425°F.

2. Combine all of the dry ingredients in a mixing bowl.

3. Make a well in the center of the flour mixture, and add the yogurt and applesauce. First using a spoon and then your hands, mix until all the ingredients are moistened and you have a soft dough.

4. Transfer the dough to a cutting board and pat into a 1-inch-thick square. Cut into eight 2-inch squares.

5. Arrange the biscuits about 1 inch apart on an oiled baking sheet and bake for about 15 minutes, or until golden.

"Nothing will benefit human health and increase the chances for survival of life on Earth as much as the evolution to a vegetarian diet."

–Albert Einstein

Savory Oat Biscuits

YIELD: 10 BISCUITS

1 cup oats

1 cup whole wheat flour

$\frac{1}{4}$ cup sliced scallions

1 tablespoon baking powder

$\frac{1}{2}$ teaspoon dried dill or basil

$\frac{1}{4}$ teaspoon salt

$\frac{1}{8}$ teaspoon freshly ground pepper

$\frac{1}{4}$ cup canola oil

1 cup plain nonfat yogurt

A generous dose of oats enables these biscuits to provide the important cholesterol-lowering fiber that makes oats so popular. Each biscuit also includes as much calcium as you'll find in a half cup of milk. The final product is a rough-textured biscuit that gets dropped onto a baking sheet rather than being rolled and cut, and is best eaten warm.

1. Preheat the oven to 400°F.

2. Combine the oats, flour, scallions, baking powder, and dry seasonings in a mixing bowl.

3. Add the oil to the oat mixture, and stir until the mixture resembles coarse crumbs. Add the yogurt, and mix just until the dry ingredients are evenly moistened.

4. Mound the biscuits by $\frac{1}{4}$ cupfuls on an oiled baking sheet. Bake for 20 minutes or until nicely browned.

Variation

- For Savory Oat-Vegetable Biscuits, add $\frac{1}{4}$ cup chopped green pepper and/or $\frac{1}{2}$ cup fresh or frozen corn kernels to the dry ingredients before stirring in the oil.

Appleberry Corn Muffins

YIELD: 10 MUFFINS

1 cup whole wheat flour

1 cup cornmeal

1/4 cup flaxseed meal (page 17)

2 teaspoons baking powder

1/2 teaspoon baking soda

1/2 teaspoon salt

1/2 teaspoon ground cinnamon

1 teaspoon minced orange zest

1/2 cup fresh or frozen (thawed) berries (blueberries, raspberries, or sliced strawberries)

1 cup unsweetened applesauce

1 cup soy milk

3 tablespoons maple syrup

These muffins have an excellent texture and flavor but are not very sweet, so if a sweeter treat is desired, increase the maple syrup to 1/4 cup. Hearty and wholesome, each muffin contributes 4 grams of protein, as well as at least 100 fewer calories, half the sugar, and a quarter to half the fat of a comparable-sized commercial corn muffin.

1. Preheat the oven to 375°F.

2. Combine the flour, cornmeal, flaxseed meal, leavening agents, salt, cinnamon, and orange zest in a mixing bowl. Stir in the berries.

3. Make a well in the center of the flour mixture and add the applesauce, soy milk, and maple syrup. Mix gently but thoroughly until all the ingredients are completely moistened.

4. Spoon the batter into muffin tins that have been wiped with oil or lined with paper muffin cups, filling almost to the top.

5. Bake for 20 minutes or until a toothpick inserted in the center of a muffin comes out clean. Remove from the oven and allow to sit for 5 minutes. Then remove the muffins from the tin and transfer to a wire rack to cool.

Insuring Moist Muffins

When baking muffins, if there is not enough batter to fill all the cups in the muffin tin, add about 1/2 inch of water to each empty cup. This will not only prevent the pan from scorching, but will also help keep the muffins moist.

Banana Oat Bran Muffins

YIELD: 10 MUFFINS

2 cups whole wheat flour

$^1/_4$ cup oat bran

2 teaspoons baking powder

$^1/_2$ teaspoon baking soda

$^1/_2$ teaspoon salt

$^1/_3$ cup walnut pieces

1 cup mashed banana (about 2 medium bananas)

1 cup soy milk

3 tablespoons honey

1 tablespoon canola oil

These protein-rich muffins taste more of banana than honey, and are not very sweet. If a sweeter muffin is desired, increase the honey to $^1/_4$ cup.

1. Preheat the oven to 375°F.

2. Combine the flour, oat bran, leavening agents, and salt in a mixing bowl. Stir in the walnuts.

3. Make a well in the center of the flour mixture and add the mashed banana, soy milk, honey, and oil. Mix gently but thoroughly until all the ingredients are completely moistened.

4. Spoon the batter into muffin tins that have been wiped with oil or lined with paper muffin cups, filling almost to the top.

5. Bake for 20 minutes or until a toothpick inserted in the center of a muffin comes out clean. Remove from the oven and allow to sit for 5 minutes. Then remove the muffins from the tin and transfer to a wire rack to cool.

Variation

- To make Banana Wheat Germ Muffins, replace the oat bran with $^1/_4$ cup wheat germ.

HONEY-YOGURT MUFFINS

YIELD: 12 MUFFINS

2½ cups whole wheat flour

2 tablespoons wheat germ

1 teaspoon baking powder

1 teaspoon baking soda

½ teaspoon salt

3 tablespoons canola oil

¼ cup honey

2 cups plain nonfat yogurt

Although these muffins are especially tender, each one offers more than 6 grams of protein. Like other baked goods made with yogurt, they are a good source of calcium.

1. Preheat the oven to 400°F.

2. Combine the flour, wheat germ, leavening agents, and salt in a mixing bowl.

3. Make a well in the center of the flour mixture and add the liquid ingredients in the order listed. After all the liquids have been added, stir gently with a fork just until the dry ingredients are completely moistened.

4. Spoon the batter into muffin tins that have been wiped with oil or lined with paper muffin cups, filling each two-thirds full.

5. Bake for 20 minutes or until a toothpick inserted in the center of a muffin comes out clean. Remove from oven and allow to sit for 5 minutes. Then remove the muffins from the tin and transfer to a wire rack to cool.

"Animals are my friends . . . and I don't eat my friends."

–George Bernard Shaw

5. Appetizers and Hors D'Oeuvres

Appetizers and hors d'oeuvres are designed primarily to be snacked on before the meal, or to serve as a first course at the table. Many also make handy between-meal snacks or lunch choices. Keep in mind that leftover side dishes and entrées can often serve as a first course with creative presentation.

Here are some ideas for making the first course easy as well as integral to the rest of the meal:

- Coordinate your appetizers and hors d'oeuvres choices with the rest of the menu. For example, if the main dish is light on vegetables, emphasize them before the meal. Likewise, a bean-based first course can complement a vegetable-based entrée.
- Set out a plate of raw vegetables for nibbling before the meal. It can include carrot and celery sticks, cucumber slices, pepper strips, broccoli and cauliforets, fennel wedges, jicama, and the like. For added nutritional value and appeal, accompany with a dip or dressing such as Black Bean Hummus, Tofu-Mustard Dip, Superior Spinach Dip, or Roasted Green Pepper and Avocado Mayonnaise.
- Scoop up dips with lettuce, endive, or radicchio leaves.
- Make instant hors d'oeuvres by spreading celery stalks with Soy Butter, Tahini Miso Spread, or natural peanut or almond butter.
- Slice up cucumbers and create simple canapés by topping them with a dollop of Bean Guacamole, Toasted Soy Spread, Tahini Garlic Spread, or Onion Butter.
- When offering bread or crackers with spreads and dips, make it a whole grain choice.
- Set out a bowl of unsalted nuts, roasted soy nuts, or roasted chickpeas, sprinkled with freshly ground pepper, for before-meal munching.

Naturally, many of the recipes in this section can play a dual role. For example, Cold Tofu with Sesame Sauce, Tofu-Stuffed Artichokes, and Tomato Gratin make excellent entrées. Other dishes, such as Bean Bruschetta and Quick White Pita Pizzas, make suitable accompaniments to many main courses. In addition, Tofu Pâté, Deviled Tofu, Bean Guacamole, Black Bean Hummus, and Quick Grilled Tofu are excellent choices for sandwich fillings. To minimize added fat when making sandwiches, any of the spreads, from Soy Butter to Roasted Green Pepper and Avocado Mayonnaise, can be used instead of butter or mayonnaise to moisten the bread.

Bean Guacamole

YIELD: 4 TO 6 SERVINGS

1 cup cooked or canned white beans (navy, Great Northern, or cannellini)

1 large ripe avocado, peeled and pitted

1/4 cup chopped Italian plum tomato (1 medium)

2 tablespoons lemon juice

2 tablespoons finely chopped fresh cilantro or flat-leaf Italian parsley

Hot pepper sauce

Salt

A new twist on the popular Mexican avocado dip, Bean Guacamole boasts added protein, less fat, and fewer calories. Serve with Baked Tortilla Crisps below.

1. In a medium-size bowl, mash the beans completely with a potato masher. Add the avocado and mash until evenly combined.
2. Stir in the tomato, lemon juice, and cilantro or parsley. Mix well.
3. Add the hot pepper sauce and salt to taste.
4. Serve immediately or cover and store in the refrigerator for up to 2 days.

Baked Tortilla Crisps

YIELD: 4 SERVINGS

6 to 8 corn or whole wheat tortillas (6 inches each), or 4 whole wheat burrito-size tortillas

This is an easy way to make fat-free chips for hors d'oeuvres, dips, or snacking, or to make crisp tacos for use in a Mexican bean or tofu entrée.

1. Preheat the oven to 500°F.
2. Run cold water quickly over each tortilla. Let drain briefly.
3. *To prepare as chips for dipping:* Stack the tortillas and cut the 6-inch tortillas into 6 wedges, or the larger tortillas into 8 wedges. Spread in a single layer on a baking sheet. *To prepare for tacos:* Place the uncut tortillas directly on the oven rack.
4. Bake for 5 minutes. Turn and bake for 2 to 3 additional minutes, or until crisp. If the tortilla wedges stick to the baking sheet, gently loosen with a spatula.

About Avocados

Most United States-grown avocados come from California and are the Hass variety, characterized by a thick, pebbly skin that turns black when ripe. Hass avocados have a rich, buttery texture and a subtle sweet, nutty flavor. They are the foundation of guacamole, and their creaminess makes them an agreeable stand-in for butter. The less common Florida specimens are considerably larger and have bright green, smooth skins. Florida avocados contain about half the fat of California varieties and more water. This is reflected in their blander taste and firmer flesh. Unlike California avocados, which are easily mashed, Florida avocados are more suitable for slicing and dicing.

Black Bean Hummus

YIELD: 2 CUPS

- 2 cups cooked or canned black beans
- 2 tablespoons lemon juice
- 2 cloves garlic, finely minced
- 1/2 teaspoon hot pepper sauce, or to taste
- 2 tablespoons tahini (sesame seed paste)
- 2 tablespoons yogurt cheese (page 22)
- Salt

A marriage of cuisines, this dish joins traditional Mideastern hummus with black beans, and spices it up with hot sauce. This appetizer can be prepared with fresh-cooked or canned beans and served right away or made ahead and refrigerated. For best flavor, enjoy at room temperature with raw vegetables, Baked Tortilla Crisps (page 52), or whole wheat pita.

1. Drain the beans, reserving any liquid. Do not rinse.
2. Purée the beans in a blender or food processor, adding the reserved bean liquid as needed to make a smooth purée. The need for added liquid will depend on how soft the beans are and how much liquid clings to them.
3. Transfer the bean purée to a shallow bowl and use a fork to beat in the lemon juice, garlic, and hot pepper sauce. When well combined, beat in the tahini and yogurt cheese.
4. Add salt to taste if the beans were unsalted, and adjust the hot pepper sauce as needed.
5. Serve immediately or cover and store in the refrigerator for up to 3 days.

TOFU-MUSTARD DIP

YIELD: 2 CUPS

8 ounces soft tofu

1 cup diced peeled cucumber

2 tablespoons lemon juice

1 1/2 tablespoons prepared mustard

1 1/2 tablespoons light miso

1 tablespoon soy sauce

1/2 teaspoon paprika

2 large cloves roasted garlic (page 19) or 1 large clove raw garlic

When soft tofu is puréed, it forms the basis of a vegetable dip as creamy as one made with sour cream or mayonnaise. If soft tofu is not available, regular or firm tofu can be used, but you will need to add a few tablespoons of soy milk, vegetable broth, or bean cooking liquid to make the consistency suitable for dipping.

1. Combine all of the ingredients in a blender or food processor fitted with a steel chopping blade. Process until the mixture is a smooth purée.
2. Adjust the seasoning.
3. Serve immediately or cover and store in the refrigerator for up to 3 days.

SOY BUTTER

YIELD: 6 TABLESPOONS

1/2 cup cooked soybeans, drained

1 tablespoon flaxseed or olive oil

This basic spread can be jazzed up by adding crushed garlic, minced fresh herbs, or light miso to taste. Compared with butter, it has less than half the calories and one-third the fat. Moreover, each tablespoon of Soy Butter offers 2.5 grams of protein—a nutrient that is insignificant in butter.

1. Place the soybeans in a food processor and purée until well ground.
2. Add the oil to the soybeans, and continue to purée until creamy.
3. Serve immediately or cover and store in the refrigerator for up to several weeks.

Superior Spinach Dip

YIELD: 2 CUPS

1 package (10 ounces) frozen spinach, thawed

1 1/2 cups yogurt cheese (page 22)

1/4 cup chopped fresh dill

1/4 cup chopped fresh parsley

1 tablespoon lemon juice

1/2 teaspoon salt

1/4 teaspoon hot pepper sauce

2 tablespoons minced scallions

Spinach dip is a universal favorite. This version is superior to most in every way.

1. Drain the spinach and squeeze out as much liquid as possible. Chop finely and set aside.

2. Combine the yogurt cheese, dill, parsley, lemon juice, salt, and hot pepper sauce in a mixing bowl, and mix well.

3. Stir the spinach and scallions into the yogurt cheese mixture, stirring until evenly blended. If the dip seems stiff, loosen by adding some plain yogurt.

4. Serve immediately or cover and store in the refrigerator for up to 3 days.

Toasted Soy Spread

YIELD: 3/4 CUP

1 cup soy flour

2 tablespoons flaxseed, hemp, or olive oil

6 tablespoons water

2 teaspoons light miso

2 teaspoons honey

You can enjoy this delicious spread on bread or crackers, just as you would peanut or other nut butters. When compared with nut butters, Toasted Soy Spread has about half the calories and half the fat.

1. Place the soy flour in a dry heavy skillet and toast over low heat, stirring continuously, until the flour begins to lightly color. This will take about 5 minutes.

2. Remove the skillet from the heat and immediately stir in the oil.

3. Add the water, miso, and honey to the flour mixture, and mix until smooth and of spreadable consistency, adding a little more water if needed.

4. Serve immediately or cover and store in the refrigerator for up to several weeks.

Tahini Garlic Spread

YIELD: 1/2 CUP

1/2 cup tahini (sesame seed paste)

2 tablespoons lemon juice

1 tablespoon soy sauce

1 large clove garlic, crushed

Water

Tahini is a paste made by grinding sesame seeds, just as peanut butter is obtained by grinding peanuts. It is widely available in natural food stores, Middle Eastern grocery stores, and many supermarkets.

1. Place the tahini, lemon juice, soy sauce, and garlic in a small bowl, and beat with a fork to make a thick paste.
2. Gradually beat in a little water to make a smooth spread.
3. Serve immediately or cover and store in the refrigerator for up to a week.

Tahini Miso Spread

YIELD: ABOUT 3/4 CUP

1/2 cup tahini (sesame seed paste)

1/4 cup miso

About 6 tablespoons water

This basic spread can be made with any variety of miso.

1. Combine the tahini and miso in a small bowl.
2. Using a fork, gradually beat the water into the tahini mixture until you have a smooth spread.
3. Serve immediately or cover and store in the refrigerator for up to several weeks.

Roasted Sweet Red Pepper Purée

YIELD: ABOUT 3/4 CUP

1 large or 2 medium red peppers (about 10 ounces), roasted (page 20)

1 teaspoon wine vinegar

1 clove garlic, sliced

1/8 teaspoon salt

Use this delicious and versatile fat-free spread by itself on crackers or bread, or on sandwiches as you would mayonnaise, mustard, ketchup, or other condiments.

1. Cut the roasted red pepper into several pieces, and combine with the wine vinegar, garlic, and salt in a blender or food processor. Purée until smooth.

2. Serve immediately or cover and store in the refrigerator for up to 2 weeks.

Spicy Green Pepper Purée

YIELD: 1/2 CUP

1 large or 2 small to medium green peppers (8 ounces), roasted (page 20)

1 small hot pepper, roasted (page 20)

1 clove garlic, sliced

2 tablespoons lightly packed fresh cilantro leaves

1 teaspoon lemon juice

1/8 teaspoon salt

Depending on the "heat" of your hot pepper, this can be quite a spicy spread.

1. Cut the roasted peppers into several pieces, and combine with the garlic, cilantro, lemon juice, and salt in a blender or food processor. Purée until smooth.

2. Serve immediately or cover and store in the refrigerator for up to 2 weeks.

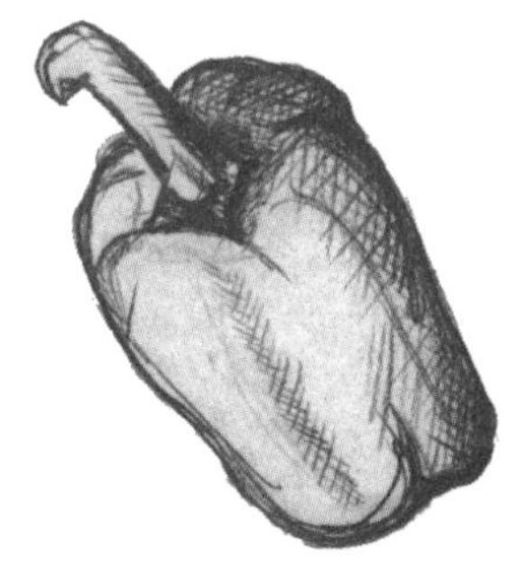

Deviled Tofu

YIELD: 1 1/2 CUPS

8 ounces regular or firm tofu

1/4 cup minced green pepper

1/4 cup minced onion

2 teaspoons prepared mustard

1/2 teaspoon soy sauce

1/8 teaspoon turmeric

Salt

1/8 teaspoon paprika

Serve this flavorful spread on cucumber rounds, sweet red or green pepper wedges, or whole grain rye crackers.

1. Place the tofu in a small bowl, and mash with a fork until crumbly. Add all of the remaining ingredients except the paprika, and mix well. Sprinkle paprika on the top before serving.

2. Use at once or cover and store in the refrigerator for up to a week.

Tofu Pâté

YIELD: ABOUT 1 1/4 CUPS

1/2 cup finely chopped onion

1/4 cup shredded carrot

1 tablespoon soy sauce

1/4 cup chopped fresh parsley

1/4 cup walnuts

6 ounces firm or extra firm tofu, diced (about 1 cup)

About 2 tablespoons water

Salt

Prepare this pâté ahead of time so it has time to chill, and serve it on crackers.

1. Combine the onion, carrot, and soy sauce in a small skillet. Cook over medium heat, stirring frequently, for 3 to 5 minutes, or until tender. Set aside to cool.

2. Combine the parsley and walnuts in a food processor or blender, and process until the parsley is finely minced. Add the tofu and process until smooth. Add water, if needed, to reach a spreadable consistency.

3. Transfer the tofu mixture to a bowl, and stir in the cooked vegetables. Season with salt to taste, and chill well before serving. Store in the refrigerator for up to a week.

Green Pepper and Avocado Mayonnaise

YIELD: 3/4 CUP

1 large or 2 small to medium green peppers (8 ounces), roasted (page 20)

1 small hot pepper, roasted (page 20)

1 clove garlic, sliced

2 tablespoons lightly packed fresh cilantro leaves

1 teaspoon lemon juice

1/4 teaspoon salt

1/2 small ripe California avocado, peeled and diced

This recipe is a variation of Spicy Green Pepper Purée (page 57). The addition of avocado to the mixture gives it the creaminess of mayonnaise without the egg or oil. In fact, it is essentially a reduced-fat guacamole that can be used as a dip for raw vegetables or on sandwiches. Omit the hot pepper if you want a milder spread.

1. Cut the roasted peppers into several pieces, and combine with the garlic, cilantro, lemon juice, and salt in a blender or food processor. Purée until smooth.

2. Add the avocado to the pepper purée and process until smooth.

3. Serve immediately or cover and store in the refrigerator for up to 3 days.

Onion Butter

YIELD: 1/2 CUP

1 tablespoon wine or sherry

8 ounces onions, thinly sliced into half rings (about 1 1/2 cups)

1 teaspoon soy sauce

2 tablespoons water

1 tablespoon soy flour

This spread is mildly sweet and mellow.

1. Place the wine or sherry in a 10- or 12-inch skillet, and cook over medium heat until warm.

2. Add the onions and soy sauce to the skillet, cover, and cook over very low heat for about 20 minutes, stirring occasionally, until the onions are soft enough to mash with a fork.

3. Using a fork or potato masher, mash the onion mixture until pulpy. Set aside.

4. In a small bowl, stir the water into the soy flour until smooth. Stir the flour mixture into the mashed onions.

5. Cook the onion butter over medium heat, stirring constantly, for 3 to 5 minutes, or until the mixture is thick and creamy and the soy flavor mellows.

6. Chill the butter before serving. Store in the refrigerator for up to a week.

Succulent Stuffed Mushrooms

YIELD: 2 TO 4 SERVINGS

1/2 cup yogurt cheese (page 22)

1 1/2 teaspoons mixed dried herbs of choice, such as oregano, parsley, basil, sage, and thyme, or your favorite seasoning mix

8 medium to large mushrooms

Allow two to four of these stuffed mushrooms per person, depending on the size of the mushrooms, on whether you're serving them as casual hors d'oeuvres or a first course, and on your guests' appetites.

1. Preheat the oven to 350°F.

2. Combine the yogurt cheese with the herbs in a small bowl. Mix well.

3. Remove the mushroom stems and reserve for another use. Clean the mushroom caps.

4. Fill each of the caps with a spoonful of the seasoned yogurt cheese.

5. Arrange the mushrooms on a baking sheet, filling side up, and bake for 15 to 20 minutes, or until tender. Remove from the oven and allow to cool briefly before serving.

Pesto-Stuffed Mushrooms

YIELD: 4 TO 6 SERVINGS

12 to 16 medium to large mushrooms, or about 24 small mushrooms

3/4 to 1 cup Chickpea Pesto (page 209) or Creamy Walnut Pesto (page 210)

Serve these savory mushrooms on a platter as a party hors d'oeuvre, or at the table as a first course.

1. Preheat the oven to 350°F.

2. Remove the mushroom stems and reserve for another use. Clean the mushroom caps.

3. Fill each of the caps with a spoonful of pesto. Large mushrooms will hold about a tablespoonful of the filling, while small ones may hold only a generous teaspoonful.

4. Arrange the mushrooms in a baking dish, filling side up, and bake for 15 minutes, or until tender. Very large mushrooms may take 5 minutes longer to cook.

Marinated Eggplant Appetizer

1 medium eggplant (1 to 1 1/4 pounds), cut into 1-inch cubes

1/2 cup white vinegar

1 clove garlic, split

1 teaspoon dried oregano

1 teaspoon dried basil

1/4 teaspoon freshly ground pepper

About 2 tablespoons olive oil

Serve this salad by itself or as part of an antipasto platter.

1. Steam the eggplant cubes for 10 to 15 minutes, or just until tender. Transfer the eggplant to a heatproof bowl and set aside.

2. Combine the vinegar, garlic, oregano, basil, and pepper in a small saucepan, and bring to a boil over high heat.

3. Pour the hot vinegar mixture over the eggplant, and allow to marinate at room temperature for several hours.

4. Chill the eggplant salad for several hours, and drizzle the olive oil over the salad just before serving. Store in the refrigerator for up to several weeks.

Tomato Gratin

YIELD: 4 SERVINGS

- ¾ cup yogurt cheese (page 22)
- 3 tablespoons chopped green or black olives
- 3 tablespoons chopped capers
- 3 large or 4 medium tomatoes (1½ pounds), sliced ¼-inch thick
- Freshly ground pepper
- 2 cloves garlic, finely chopped
- 1 tablespoon chopped fresh basil
- 2 tablespoons chopped fresh parsley
- 2 tablespoons pumpkin seeds
- 1 tablespoon wheat germ
- 1 teaspoon olive oil

This flavorful tomato-yogurt cheese casserole goes well with most cuisines. Best made with ripe, summer tomatoes, it provides modest appetizer-size servings. For 4 to 6 hearty eaters or for use as an entrée, you can double the recipe and bake it in a shallow 2-quart or 9-x-13-inch baking dish.

1. Preheat the oven to 350°F.

2. Combine the yogurt cheese, olives, and capers in a small bowl, and set aside.

3. Arrange half the tomato slices in overlapping layers in a shallow 9-inch baking dish or glass pie plate. Season generously with pepper and sprinkle with half the garlic, basil, and parsley. Top with half the yogurt cheese mixture, using a spoon to drop in dollops evenly over the tomato slices. Repeat the layers.

4. Grind the pumpkin seeds to a fine meal in a blender or food processor. Combine the ground seeds with the wheat germ, and sprinkle evenly over the top of the assembled dish. Drizzle with the olive oil.

5. Bake for 30 minutes or until heated through. Serve warm, but not piping hot.

Skewered Tempeh with Orange-Nut Crust

YIELD: 4 TO 8 SERVINGS

- 24 ounces tempeh, cut into 1-inch cubes
- 1 recipe Spicy Orange Nut Sauce (page 211)

These mini kebabs are a nice appetizer to pass around at a party or set out on an hors d'oeuvres buffet. Any extra sauce can be served on the side for dipping, or used as a dipping sauce for raw vegetables.

1. Preheat the broiler.

2. Thread the tempeh onto 8 skewers, and arrange the skewers so that the ends rest on opposite edges of a shallow baking pan with the tempeh hanging above the surface of the pan.

Coat the top of the tempeh generously with the sauce.

3. Broil for about 5 minutes, or until golden. Turn the skewers, spread more sauce over the uncooked side of the tempeh, and broil for an additional 5 minutes, or until the coating forms a crust.

QUICK GRILLED TOFU

YIELD: 4 SERVINGS

1 pound firm or extra firm tofu

1 to 2 tablespoons soy sauce

Grilled tofu strips not only make a fast hors d'oeuvre, but also can be used on main-dish salads. While nothing more than a quick seasoning with soy sauce is needed, you can add a few drops of hot sesame oil or hot pepper sauce for a more lively taste, or rub the surfaces with your seasoning mix of choice.

1. Preheat a grill, or set a wire cake rack over a gas burner.

2. Cut the tofu into 8 to 12 slices, allowing 2 to 3 per serving. Season on both sides by sprinkling with soy sauce and spreading it gently with your fingers to disperse.

3. Arrange the tofu slices on the grill or rack, and cook for a few minutes, just until the bottom is grilled to taste. Turn and grill the other side.

4. Cut the tofu into strips for easy eating.

Broiled Tofu with Parsley Dressing

YIELD: 4 SERVINGS

1 pound firm or extra firm tofu

2 tablespoons water

2 teaspoons soy sauce

1 cup lightly packed fresh parsley leaves or a combination of parsley and dill

2 large cloves garlic, sliced

2 tablespoons lemon juice

2 tablespoons wine vinegar

1 teaspoon paprika

1/8 teaspoon crushed red pepper flakes, optional

Quick and flavorful, this tofu can be cubed or cut into strips and served as an hors d'oeuvres, or left in slices and served as an entrée accompanied by a grain, cooked vegetable, and salad.

1. Preheat the broiler.

2. Slice the tofu into 8 pieces, each about 1/2 inch thick. Pat dry and set aside.

3. Combine the water and soy sauce in a shallow baking pan large enough to hold the tofu in a single layer.

4. Dip each tofu slice in the diluted soy sauce, turning so both sides are seasoned. Arrange the tofu slices in a single layer in the liquid remaining in the pan, and set aside.

5. Combine the fresh herbs and garlic in a food processor, and process until minced. Add the lemon juice, vinegar, paprika, and red pepper flakes if desired, and process until evenly blended. Spread the herb mixture thickly on top of each tofu slice.

6. Broil the tofu 4 to 6 inches below the heat for 5 to 8 minutes, or until lightly browned on top. Cut into bite-size cubes or strips as desired.

TOFU JERKY

YIELD: 12 TO 16 PIECES

1/4 cup soy sauce

1/4 cup water

2 tablespoons lemon juice

1 tablespoon grated fresh ginger

1 teaspoon honey, molasses, or maple syrup

1 clove garlic, minced

1 pound firm or extra firm tofu, sliced 1/8 inch thick

Tofu jerky makes a flavorful nibbling food or snack. The basic recipe can be spiced up by adding hot sauce or a good pinch of cayenne pepper. Chili powder makes a chili jerky; oregano and basil create pizza jerky.

1. Combine all of the ingredients except the tofu in a shallow pan (or two) large enough to hold the tofu in a single layer.

2. Arrange the tofu slices in the soy sauce marinade, turning to coat both sides. Cover the pan and allow the tofu to marinate in the refrigerator for several hours, or even overnight. Turn a few times for maximum penetration.

3. Remove the tofu the from the marinade, discarding the marinade. *For oven drying:* Set the temperature to 200°F, place the tofu pieces on a wire rack (such as a cake cooking rack or grilling rack), place the rack on a baking sheet, and place in the oven. *If drying in a dehydrator:* Place the tofu on trays and set the temperature to about 140°F. Keep the tofu in the oven or dehydrator until it is very chewy, but not yet crisp. The drying time is 4 to 6 hours, but this will vary somewhat depending on the tofu, the drying method used, and even the ambient room condition.

4. Store in airtight containers, where it will keep for months.

TOFU-STUFFED ARTICHOKES

YIELD: 4 TO 8 SERVINGS

4 medium to large artichokes

1 1/2 cups mashed tofu, any type (12 ounces)

1/3 cup dry whole grain breadcrumbs

1/4 cup sunflower seeds, ground (6 tablespoons sunflower meal)

1/4 cup chopped fresh parsley

2 tablespoons flaxseed meal (page 17)

2 tablespoons wheat germ

2 cloves garlic, minced

1 teaspoon dried oregano

1/2 teaspoon salt

Depending on the other dishes you're serving, you may want to cut the artichokes in half for appetizers. To serve Tofu-Stuffed Artichokes as the entrée, set on top of cooked brown rice or your grain of choice. In either case, serve with Agliata (page 217) as a dipping sauce or with wedges of fresh lemon.

1. To prepare the artichokes for stuffing, cut off the sharp tips, spread the inner leaves, remove the small leaves attached to the heart, and scrape out the hairy "choke." Cut off any stem so that the artichoke sits firmly upright. If there's enough stem to eat, peel, slice in half lengthwise, and cook along with the artichoke.

2. Rinse the artichokes under cold water. Invert to drain.

3. To make the filling, combine all the remaining ingredients in a medium-sized bowl. Mix well until thoroughly blended, and knead gently by hand until the mixture holds together.

4. Stuff about 1/4 cup filling into the hollow at the center of each artichoke. Pack any remaining filling between the leaves.

5. Arrange the artichokes upright in a vegetable steamer set over boiling water. Surround with any prepared leftover stems.

6. Steam the artichokes for 35 to 45 minutes, or until tender. Alternatively, pressure cook for 13 to 15 minutes.

Cold Tofu with Sesame Sauce

YIELD: 6 APPETIZER SERVINGS OR 4 ENTRÉE SERVINGS

6 tablespoons tahini (sesame seed paste)

2 tablespoons almond butter

1/4 cup white or rice wine vinegar

1/4 cup soy sauce, divided

2 to 3 tablespoons hot water or black or green tea

1 teaspoon spicy sesame oil*

1 teaspoon shredded fresh ginger

1 pound soft tofu, cut into bite-size cubes

2 scallions, thinly sliced including dark green portion

*Toasted sesame oil with a pinch of cayenne can be substituted for spicy sesame oil.

Cold tofu in a rich piquant sauce will be familiar to anyone who has eaten the popular Chinese dish of cold noodles with sesame paste. This dish is easy to assemble and requires no cooking. And besides making a great appetizer, it can also be served as an entrée.

1. In a shallow bowl, combine the tahini and almond butter. Using a fork, beat in the vinegar, followed by 2 tablespoons of the soy sauce and 2 tablespoons of the hot water or other liquid. The mixture should be the consistency of rich cream. If too thick, beat in additional liquid until the desired consistency is reached.

2. Beat the sesame oil into the tahini mixture.

3. Pour the sauce into a shallow serving dish large enough to hold the tofu in a single layer, and drizzle the remaining 2 tablespoons of soy sauce over the sauce. Scatter the ginger on top.

4. Arrange the tofu cubes in a single layer over the sauce, and cover with the scallions. Serve at room temperature.

Alan's Curry Tofu Cubes with Dipping Sauce

YIELD: 4 SERVINGS

1 pound firm or extra firm tofu

1 tablespoon curry powder

Made in a pressure cooker, these tasty cubes can be served on salads, pasta, or a cooked grain; bathed in a favorite gravy or sauce; or mixed with cooked vegetables. And, of course, they make good hors d'oeuvres with a dipping sauce such as Agliata (page 217), Spicy Orange Nut Sauce (page 211), or Tomato Almond Pesto (page 210).

1. Pat the surface of the tofu dry, and cut into ¾-inch cubes.
2. Toss the tofu in a bowl with the curry to coat.
3. Place the tofu cubes in the steamer basket of a pressure cooker and set above boiling water. Close the cooker and bring to pressure. Pressure-cook for 8 minutes.
4. Release the pressure using the pressure release valve. On older models, run under cold water to bring the pressure down.

Women who eat more than 1½ servings of red meat per day are almost twice as likely to develop hormone-related breast cancer as those who eat fewer than 3 portions per week.

–Study published in *Archives of Internal Medicine*, November 2006

QUICK WHITE PITA PIZZAS

YIELD: 4 TO 6 APPETIZERS OR 2 TO 4 ENTRÉE SERVINGS

Two 2-ounce whole wheat pita breads

$^{3}/_{4}$ cup yogurt cheese (page 22)

Vegetable Topping

2 cups shredded raw greens, such as spinach, romaine, leaf lettuce, arugula, endive, or radicchio

$^{1}/_{2}$ teaspoon crushed red pepper flakes

$^{1}/_{4}$ cup pine nuts, grated Parmesan cheese, or crumbled feta

Cut the finished pizzas into triangles for hors d'oeuvres or as part of an antipasto first course. You can also serve two full rounds per person as an entrée or one as an individual pizza to accompany a meal.

1. Preheat the oven to 400°F.

2. Use a fork to perforate the circumference of the breads. Separate each into two rounds.

3. Spread each pita round with 3 tablespoons of yogurt cheese. Then add the Vegetable Topping by sprinkling each round first with the shredded raw greens, and then with the red pepper flakes and the pine nuts or cheese.

4. Arrange the pizzas on a baking sheet and bake for 15 minutes, or until lightly browned at the edges. Allow to cool for a few minutes to set the filling before serving.

VARIATIONS

- For a Mushroom Topping, replace the Vegetable Topping with $1^{1}/_{3}$ cups thinly sliced raw mushrooms and $^{1}/_{4}$ cup frozen green peas. Scatter slivered garlic generously on top. Season each round with $^{1}/_{8}$ teaspoon dried oregano or mixed Italian seasonings.

- For an Artichoke Topping, follow the directions for the Mushroom Topping, replacing the mushrooms with $1^{1}/_{3}$ cups thinly sliced canned or cooked artichoke hearts.

- For a Sweet Red Pepper Topping, follow the directions for the Mushroom Topping, replacing the mushrooms with $1^{1}/_{3}$ cups thin strips of sweet red pepper, and the green peas with 1 tablespoon of capers.

Bean Bruschetta

YIELD: 4 SERVINGS

4 cups cut-up greens, such as Swiss chard, arugula, escarole, spinach, or beet greens (about 8 ounces)

2 teaspoons red wine vinegar

1 cup cooked or canned white beans

2 cloves garlic, minced

2 teaspoons olive oil

Salt

Freshly ground pepper

4 slices whole grain bread, or 2 whole wheat pitas separated into rounds

2 tomato heels (ends), if available

This is an excellent way to add more beans to the menu. Serve as an hors d'oeuvre, as an accompaniment to grain and vegetable entrées, for lunch with vegetable soup or a big salad, or even as a snack. The recipe is also easily multiplied for serving a crowd.

1. Combine the greens and the wine vinegar in a heavy skillet, preferably cast iron. Cook, stirring frequently, for about 5 minutes, or until wilted. When cool enough to handle, chop fine and set aside.

2. Place the beans in a small bowl and mash with a potato masher. Mix in the minced garlic and oil, and season to taste with salt and pepper.

3. Grill the bread on both sides or toast until golden. If tomato heals are available, rub on one side of the hot bread to moisten.

4. Cover the moistened side of each bread slice with $1/4$ cup of mashed beans, and top with 2 tablespoons of cooked greens.

"The greatness of a nation can be judged by the way its animals are treated."

–Mahatma Gandhi

6. Soups

Making soup is more of an art than a science. There are so many variables when it comes to ingredients, proportions, and textures, that you should feel free to improvise. While it is hard to beat the flavor of a slow-simmered soup, time limitations should not be a deterrent. As the recipes in this chapter demonstrate, a delicious soup can be made without hours of preparation and cooking.

Certainly nothing is more versatile than a soup. It can serve as a first course, as a lunch entrée, or even as a dinner entrée when coupled with a fresh salad and a loaf of hearty bread. When choosing or preparing a soup, here are some things to keep in mind:

- Select a soup recipe with an eye toward the rest of the meal. Soups that highlight beans can balance a meal that primarily features vegetables, while lighter soups are suitable when serving hearty grain- or bean-based entrées. Conversely, soups in which grains play a central role should not be paired with a pasta dinner.
- Since soups generally improve with reheating, make more than you need for one meal so that you can eat it the next day as well.
- If you pack lunches for yourself or your family, invest in a thermos so that homemade soups can be enjoyed away from home.
- To wake up the flavor of soup without adding extra fat or salt, try a dash of vinegar or lemon juice or a pinch of cayenne pepper.
- When the weather turns warm, cool down with a chilled soup like Blender Salad Soup or Cold Cucumber Yogurt Soup, or with a chilled version of one of our carrot soups.

As a final note, although homemade broth makes an indisputably rich soup base, few people take the time these days to prepare their own broths or stocks. While there are some additive-free prepared broths on the market, all too often the most affordable and easily found options rely on chemical additives and salt for their flavor. Consequently, we have formulated most of our soup recipes using water as the principal liquid. However, the substitution of vegetable stock will benefit the flavor and nutritional value of any soup. One easy way to keep a ready supply of "stock" on hand is to use ice cube trays to freeze any liquid left from cooking vegetables or draining canned tomatoes. Use these cubes to replace some or all of the water whenever the opportunity arises.

Quick Corn Chowder

YIELD: 4 TO 6 SERVINGS

4 cups soy milk

2 cups corn kernels, fresh or frozen

2 slices whole wheat or other whole grain bread (remove crusts if tough)

1 thin slice onion

2 teaspoons salt

This delicious chowder takes just minutes to prepare.

1. Combine all the ingredients in a blender or food processor, and process at high speed for 20 seconds, or until chunky.

2. Pour the soup into a 2- to 3-quart soup pot and warm through over medium heat. Avoid boiling the soup.

Quick Vegetable Bean Soup

YIELD: 4 TO 6 SERVINGS

1 small onion, chopped

2 carrots, sliced

2 stalks celery, sliced

2 cloves garlic, sliced

4 cups water mixed with any bean cooking liquid, divided

2 cups cooked or canned red, pink, or white beans

2 tablespoons tomato paste, or 1/4 cup canned crushed tomatoes

1/3 to 1/2 cup chopped fresh parsley

1 tablespoon light or dark miso

It will take you just thirty minutes to get this soup to the table.

1. Combine the onion, carrots, celery, and garlic in a 2- to 3-quart soup pot. Cover and cook over medium heat for 10 minutes, stirring occasionally to prevent sticking.

2. Add 2 cups of water or the water-bean cooking liquid mixture to the pot, and bring to a boil over high heat. Lower the heat to a simmer, cover, and cook for 10 minutes.

3. Add the beans, tomato paste, parsley, and remaining 2 cups of water to the pot, and simmer for 2 minutes.

4. Place the miso in a small bowl, and stir in some of the hot soup to melt. Stir the diluted miso into the soup pot.

5. Remove the pot from the heat, cover, and let sit for 5 minutes before serving.

Simple Miso Soup

YIELD: 4 SERVINGS

6 cups water

½ cup chopped onion or sliced scallions

2-inch strip kombu seaweed

8 ounces soft, regular, or firm tofu, cut into cubes

3 tablespoons light or dark miso

2 to 4 tablespoons sliced scallions, chopped fresh parsley, or toasted nori seaweed, optional

This light soup is a good lunch choice coupled with a sandwich or salad. For added flavor, garnish each bowl with scallions, parsley, or toasted seaweed. For a heartier lunch entrée, during the last few minutes of cooking, add up to 1 cup frozen corn or peas, or precooked carrots, squash, brown rice, or whole grain pasta.

1. Combine the water, onion or scallions, and kombu in a 3- to 5-quart soup pot, and bring to a boil over high heat.

2. Add the tofu, reduce the heat to a simmer, and cook for 5 minutes.

3. Place the miso in a small bowl, and stir in some of the hot soup to melt. Stir the diluted miso into the soup pot.

4. Reduce the heat to very low and cook gently, without boiling, for 1 to 2 minutes. Garnish each serving with scallions, parsley, or toasted nori if desired.

Portuguese Bread and Garlic Soup

YIELD: 4 SERVINGS

4½ cups water

4 to 6 slices whole grain bread (about 6 ounces), torn into small pieces

4 cloves garlic, cut in pieces

1 teaspoon salt

Freshly ground pepper

Chopped fresh parsley

This very substantial soup, made from quite modest ingredients, takes just 10 minutes to prepare.

1. Place the water in a 2- to 3-quart soup pot, and bring to a boil over high heat.

2. Reduce the heat and add the bread, garlic, and salt. Simmer for 5 minutes or until the bread is very soft.

3. Mash the soup with a spoon or fork until pulpy, and return briefly to a boil.

4. Season generously with freshly ground pepper and adjust the salt to taste if necessary. Sprinkle chopped parsley over each serving.

HEARTY MISO VEGETABLE SOUP

YIELD: 6 SERVINGS

2 large carrots, thinly sliced

2 medium potatoes, diced

1 large onion, quartered and thinly sliced

6 cups water

2 to 3 cups chopped greens, such as chard, beet greens, cabbage, or even romaine lettuce

1 cup corn kernels, fresh or frozen

1/2 cup minced fresh dill or parsley, optional

1/3 cup light miso

1/4 cup sliced scallions, optional

1 teaspoon toasted plain or spicy sesame oil, optional

The vegetables in this soup can be altered according to what's in season, what's in the pantry, and the whim of the cook. If you choose, you can add some sesame oil to make the soup more robust, or you can add hot sesame oil to give it some zing.

1. Combine the carrots, potatoes, and onion in a 3- to 5-quart soup pot. Cover, place over medium heat, and let the vegetables sweat for 5 minutes.

2. Stir the vegetables. If the onions have not wilted, replace the cover and sweat a few minutes longer.

3. Add the water to the pot and bring to boil. When boiling, add the greens, corn, and herbs, if desired. Cover and simmer gently for 10 to 15 minutes, or until the vegetables are tender.

4. Place the miso in a small bowl, and stir in some of the hot soup to melt. Stir the diluted miso into the soup.

5. Cover the pot, remove from the heat, and let rest 5 to 10 minutes before serving. If desired, garnish each bowl with some sliced scallions and season with a little sesame oil. Note that when reheating leftovers, you should avoid boiling. The enzymes in miso like to be treated gently.

How to Make a Quick Soup

Although a long-simmered soup has great depth of flavor, a quickly made soup can also be delicious and satisfying. Such a soup does not require a precise recipe and can often be prepared with any vegetables that you have on hand, along with whatever grains or pasta you keep in your pantry.

When soup is really hot, its flavor is difficult to judge. Therefore, it is best to let people adjust seasoning to taste by providing salt and pepper at the table. A generous dollop of yogurt cheese in each bowl will make any soup richer.

The following is a basic recipe for a quart of Quick Soup. Adjust it according to your preferences and what you have in your kitchen.

1. Chop up a large onion and/or a leek, if available, and place it in a soup pot with a spoonful of olive oil. Cover and cook over medium heat until soft.

2. Meanwhile, prepare additional vegetables, as listed below, and add in order as they are ready. You can include:

- 1 or 2 cloves garlic, chopped
- 1 celery stalk, sliced (with leaves if available)
- 2 carrots, diced or cut into coins
- Diced potatoes
- Cut-up string beans
- Broccoli or cauliflower florets
- Diced turnips
- Diced or sliced parsnips
- Chopped leafy vegetables such as kale, chard, beet greens, cabbage, or romaine

3. When all the vegetables have cooked in the covered pot for a few minutes to release their juices, add about a cup of water, or enough to cover, and a generous pinch of salt. Bring to a boil. Then lower the heat to a simmer, cover, and cook for 10 to 15 minutes, or until the vegetables start to soften.

4. Add 1 to 2 cups of cooked dried beans (along with some of their cooking liquid), or some diced tofu. You can also add a cup or so of cooked rice, barley, millet, or other precooked grain, or some uncooked whole wheat couscous or pasta.

5. Add 1 to 2 cups of tomato juice and 2 to 3 cups of cold water, according to your preferences regarding flavor and texture.

6. Cover and cook about 10 minutes longer, or until everything is tender. During the last minute, add some frozen peas or corn if more vegetables are desired.

Pan Asian Tomato-Rice Soup

YIELD: 4 SERVINGS

½ cup drained canned tomatoes

1 tablespoon curry powder

6 cloves garlic, cut into pieces

1 cup liquid from canned tomatoes, divided

3 cups water

½ teaspoon salt

8 ounces firm or extra firm tofu, cut into cubes

1½ cups cooked brown rice

1 tablespoon light or dark miso

2 tablespoons chopped fresh cilantro

With its multi-cultural mix of ingredients, this makes a very tasty first course. If you want to serve this soup as a main dish, double the recipe for 6 servings. To dress the soup up, float a few thin rounds of toast in each bowl.

1. Combine the tomatoes and curry in a 3- to 5-quart soup pot, and cook over medium heat for 2 minutes while mashing the tomatoes with the back of a spoon.

2. Add the garlic and ½ cup of the tomato liquid to the pot. Bring to boil over high heat, cover, and reduce the heat to a simmer. Cook for 10 minutes.

3. Transfer the tomato mixture to a blender or food processor, and purée.

4. Return the purée to the soup pot. Add the remaining tomato liquid, the water, and the salt, and bring to a boil over high heat. Add the tofu, cover, and reduce the heat to simmer gently for 10 minutes.

5. Add the rice to the pot and simmer, uncovered, for 5 to 10 minutes, or until the rice is hot.

6. Place the miso in a small bowl, and stir in some of the hot soup to melt. Stir the diluted miso into the soup pot.

7. Cover the pot, remove from the heat, and let stand for 5 minutes. Adjust the salt to taste. Garnish each serving with some chopped cilantro.

MUSHROOM BARLEY SOUP

YIELD: 6 SERVINGS

6 cups water

12 ounces mushrooms, any type, coarsely chopped (about 4 cups)

1 cup barley

1 cup chopped onion

2 tablespoons soy sauce

1 teaspoon salt

Freshly ground pepper

Pressure-cooking makes an exceptionally creamy mushroom barley soup. If you do not have a pressure cooker, follow the second set of directions for conventional stove-top cooking. With either version, let the soup rest a while before serving to enhance the richness.

1. *When using a pressure cooker:* Combine the water, mushrooms, barley, onion, and soy sauce in a pressure cooker. Cover and bring up to pressure over high heat. Reduce the heat to just maintain the pressure, and cook for 50 minutes. Remove from the heat and let sit 10 minutes before releasing the pressure and opening the pot.

   When using a stove top: Combine the water, mushrooms, barley, onion, and soy sauce in a 5-quart soup pot. Bring to a boil, cover, and reduce the heat to simmer gently for 90 minutes, or until the barley is tender.

2. Add salt and pepper to taste before serving.

"The eating of meat extinguishes the seed of great compassion."
–Buddha

Country Mushroom Soup

YIELD: 4 SERVINGS

12 ounces mushrooms, any type, quartered (about 4 cups)

2 tablespoons chopped fresh parsley

1 clove garlic, sliced

$\frac{1}{4}$ teaspoon ground nutmeg

$2\frac{1}{2}$ cups vegetable broth or water flavored with a few spoonfuls of canned crushed tomatoes, tomato purée, or tomato paste

$\frac{2}{3}$ cup fresh whole grain bread torn into pieces

$\frac{1}{2}$ teaspoon salt (omit if broth is salted)

Freshly ground pepper

$1\frac{1}{2}$ cups soy milk

This delicate mushroom soup provides an admirable first course in just half an hour.

1. Place the mushrooms in a 2-quart soup pot. Cover and cook over medium heat for 10 minutes, or until the mushroom liquid runs freely.

2. Stir the parsley, garlic, and nutmeg into the mushrooms, and cook briefly.

3. Add the broth or tomato-flavored water to the pot along with the bread, salt, and a generous amount of pepper. Bring to a boil, cover, and simmer over low heat for 10 minutes.

4. Transfer the soup to a blender or food processor fitted with a steel chopping blade. Chop coarsely so that the soup is chunky rather than smooth, with tiny pieces of mushrooms.

5. Return the soup to the pot and stir in the soy milk. Cook over gentle heat, stirring frequently, until hot. Do not boil, as this could curdle the milk, which would detract from the appearance although not the flavor. Adjust the salt and pepper to taste before serving.

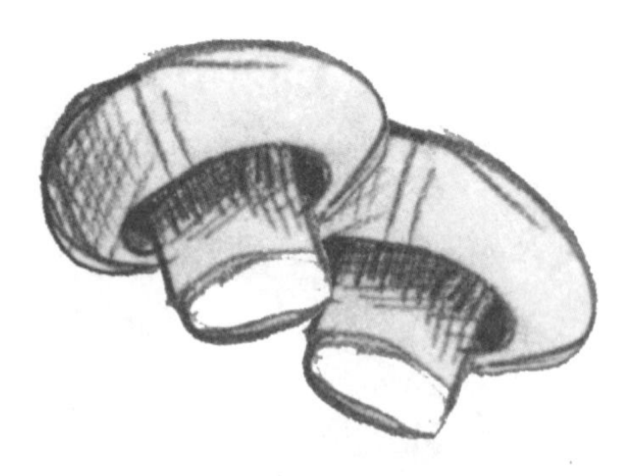

Carrot Soup with Tomato Ginger Cream

YIELD: 4 TO 6 SERVINGS

2 cups tomato juice

6 medium carrots, sliced (about 3 cups)

1 shallot, sliced, or 1/4 cup chopped sweet Vidalia or red onion

1 cup water

3/4 cup orange juice

1 teaspoon slivered orange zest

1 teaspoon honey, if needed

Tomato Ginger Cream

6 tablespoons yogurt cheese (page 22)

2 tablespoons tomato juice

1 teaspoon orange juice

1 teaspoon grated fresh ginger, or 1/4 teaspoon dried ground ginger

Tomatoes, carrots, and orange make a surprisingly good soup that is even more delectable with swirls of Tomato Ginger Cream. In hot weather, prepare this dish in advance and serve chilled.

1. Bring the tomato juice to a boil in a 2-quart soup pot. Add the carrots and the shallot or onion, and reduce the heat so the liquid is barely simmering. Cover and cook for 15 minutes.

2. Add the water, orange juice, and orange zest to the pot. Cover and simmer for 15 minutes, or until the carrots are tender.

3. While the soup is cooking, combine all of the Tomato Ginger Cream ingredients in a small bowl, and beat with a fork until smooth. Refrigerate the cream until ready to serve.

4. Transfer the soup to a blender or food processor and process until evenly blended but still somewhat rough textured.

5. Return the soup to the pot and taste. If the flavor is a bit sharp or acidic, add the honey to taste.

6. Simmer the soup, uncovered, for 5 minutes. Top each serving with a generous spoonful of Tomato Ginger Cream and swirl into the soup. Pass any remaining cream at the table.

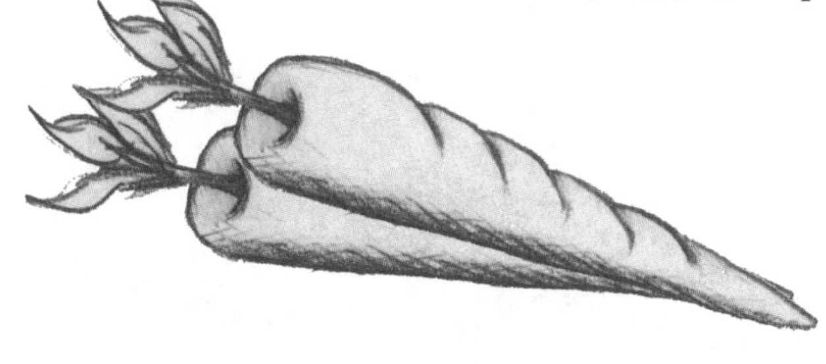

CARROT BISQUE

YIELD: 4 TO 6 SERVINGS

3 cups water

6 medium carrots, sliced (about 3 cups)

1/2 cup chopped onion

1/2 cup sliced celery (include a few leaves if available)

1 tablespoon chopped fresh ginger

1/2 teaspoon salt

1/4 teaspoon ground cinnamon

1 bay leaf

2 tablespoons almond butter

1 tablespoon soy sauce

1 cup soy milk

Freshly ground pepper

This is another carrot soup that is excellent either hot or cold. If the soup needs to be reheated, avoid boiling.

1. Combine the water, carrots, onion, celery, ginger, salt, cinnamon, and bay leaf in a 2- to 3-quart soup pot, and bring to a boil. Cover and simmer over medium-low heat for 15 minutes, or until the carrots are tender. Let cool slightly.

2. Transfer about half the soup to a blender or food processor. Add the almond butter and soy sauce and purée until smooth. If there is room in the blender, add the remaining soup. Otherwise, purée the soup in batches.

3. Return all of the carrot purée to the soup pot and add the soy milk. Place over medium heat and warm through without boiling.

4. Season generously with freshly ground pepper to taste.

"I have no doubt that it is part of the destiny of the human race in its gradual improvement to leave off eating animals."

–Henry David Thoreau

MINESTRONE

Minestrone is the classic Italian vegetable soup. The vegetables can be varied according to what is available. Green beans, fresh green peas, turnips, and fennel are among those that can be added to or substituted for the vegetables included here.

YIELD: 6 TO 8 SERVINGS

1 small onion, chopped

2 cloves garlic, chopped

1 tablespoon olive oil

4 cups water

3 cups tomato juice

8 ounces potatoes, diced

2 carrots, diced

1 stalk celery, diced

1 tablespoon chopped fresh parsley

1 tablespoon chopped fresh basil or 1 teaspoon dried basil

1 teaspoon salt

2½ cups shredded greens, such as spinach, Swiss chard, chicory, or romaine

2 cups cooked or canned red or white kidney beans

½ cup whole wheat elbow macaroni, small shells, or broken spaghetti

1 small zucchini, diced

1. Combine the onion, garlic, and oil in a 5-quart soup pot, and cook for a few minutes over medium heat until softened.

2. Add the water, tomato juice, potatoes, carrots, celery, parsley, basil, and salt, and bring to a boil over high heat. Lower the heat to a simmer, cover, and cook for 20 minutes.

3. Add all of the remaining ingredients, cover, and simmer for an additional 20 to 30 minutes, or until the vegetables are quite tender.

Hot Borscht

YIELD: 4 TO 6 SERVINGS

3 cups water

1 cup tomato purée or pulp (seeded, peeled tomato)

1 onion, diced

1 cup peeled and shredded or finely chopped carrots

1 cup peeled and shredded or finely chopped beets

1 cup shredded or finely chopped potatoes

2 cups thinly shredded cabbage

2 teaspoons salt

1 tablespoon lemon juice

Serve this Russian vegetable soup with plenty of yogurt cream (page 22) to spoon into each bowl.

1. Combine the water and tomato in a 3- to 5-quart soup pot, and bring to a boil over high heat.

2. Add the vegetables and salt, cover, and reduce the heat to a simmer. Cook for about 30 minutes, or until the vegetables are tender.

3. Stir in the lemon juice before serving.

Leek and White Bean Soup

YIELD: 4 TO 6 SERVINGS

9 cups water

2 cups dried white beans

1 pound leeks

1 teaspoon salt

2 tablespoons chopped fresh sage, or 1/4 cup chopped fresh parsley

Freshly ground pepper

This is a rich potage with a southern French-Italian flair. To complete the dish, float rounds of toasted whole grain bread thickly spread with roasted garlic in each bowl. You might also offer additional cloves of roasted garlic on the side.

1. Combine the water and beans in a 3- to 5-quart soup pot and let soak for 8 hours. Alternatively, bring to a boil for 2 minutes, remove from the heat, cover, and let soak for 1 to 2 hours.

2. Return the beans to a boil, cook for 5 minutes, cover, and simmer gently over low heat for 20 minutes, or until partially tender.

3. While the beans are cooking, prepare the leeks by trimming off the dark green portion and the root, cutting in half lengthwise, and running under cold water to remove any dirt lodged between the layers. Then cut crosswise into thin slices. You should have between 2½ and 3 cups.

4. Add the leeks and salt to the partially cooked beans. Replace the cover and continue to cook for 30 minutes, or until the beans are very tender.

5. Using a potato masher, mash the beans to a pulpy consistency. Simmer for 5 minutes.

6. Season the soup by adding the sage or parsley and the freshly ground pepper. Adjust the salt to taste.

Black Bean Soup

This bean soup hails from South America. We often serve it as an entrée, setting out brown rice, yogurt, chopped green pepper, and chopped raw onion on the side for everyone to add as they please. We complete the menu with a tossed green salad and either warm corn tortillas or a crusty whole grain bread.

YIELD: 4 SERVINGS

- 3½ cups water
- 1 cup dried black beans
- 1 small onion, chopped
- ½ medium green pepper, chopped
- 1 bay leaf
- 1 clove garlic, chopped
- 1 teaspoon dried oregano
- 2 tablespoons wine vinegar
- 1 teaspoon salt
- ½ teaspoon hot pepper sauce, or to taste

1. Combine the water and beans in a 3-quart soup pot and let soak for 8 hours. Alternatively, bring to a boil for 2 minutes, remove from the heat, cover, and let soak for 1 to 2 hours.

2. Add the onion, green pepper, bay leaf, garlic, and oregano to the pot and bring to a boil over high heat. Reduce the heat to a simmer, cover, and cook for 1 hour, or until the beans are tender.

3. Add the vinegar, salt, and hot pepper sauce to the pot, and cook for 5 additional minutes. Taste for seasoning and adjust if necessary.

4. Remove about half of the beans from the pot and purée in a blender or food processor. Stir the puréed beans back into the soup and cook for a few more minutes, or until slightly thickened. If the soup is too thick, add up to ½ cup water.

Mom's Thick Split Pea Soup

YIELD: 8 SERVINGS

8 cups water

2 cups dried split peas

2 medium onions, chopped

4 carrots, chopped

4 to 6 leafy celery tops, chopped

1 large bay leaf

1 1/2 teaspoons salt

Freshly ground pepper

Split pea soup is a time-honored favorite at our house, handed down from Nikki's mother. It reheats well and can also be successfully frozen.

1. Combine the water and split peas in a 3- to 5-quart soup pot, and bring to a boil over high heat.

2. Add the vegetables, bay leaf, and salt, and reduce the heat to a simmer. Cover and cook for 1 to 1 1/2 hours, or until the peas are very soft.

3. Mash the pea mixture with a fork or purée in a food mill, blender, or food processor.

4. If the soup was removed from the pot, return it and simmer, uncovered, for a few minutes to thicken. Season generously with freshly ground pepper.

Greek Lentil Soup

YIELD: 6 TO 8 SERVINGS

1 tablespoon olive oil

2 medium onions, chopped

8 1/2 cups water

2 cups dried lentils

2 stalks celery, chopped

2 tablespoons tomato paste

1 bay leaf

4 cups shredded spinach or other dark leafy greens

1 1/2 teaspoons salt

2 to 3 tablespoons lemon juice

This is another soup that we serve quite often, sometimes varying it through the addition of cooked brown rice or small whole wheat shells or macaroni. We always top each serving with a generous amount of yogurt.

1. Place the oil in a 5-quart soup pot, and heat over medium heat. Add the onions and sauté for about 3 minutes, or until limp.

2. Add the water, lentils, celery, tomato paste, and bay leaf to the pot, and bring to a boil over high heat. Reduce the heat to a simmer, cover, and cook for about 45 minutes, or until the lentils are just tender.

3. Add the greens and salt to the pot, cover, and cook for 15 minutes, or until the beans are completely tender. The consistency should be fairly thick, but if the soup appears to be too dry, add a little water.

4. When fully cooked, add the lemon juice to taste.

Blender Salad Soup

YIELD: 6 SERVINGS

4 medium-size ripe tomatoes, quartered

1 small cucumber, peeled and sliced

½ medium onion, sliced

½ large green pepper, sliced

1 clove garlic

3 tablespoons wine vinegar

½ cup ice water

2 tablespoons olive oil

1 teaspoon salt

¼ teaspoon hot pepper sauce

6 ice cubes

Similar to a classic gazpacho, this chilled soup is made in a blender or food processor, and is ready in just a few minutes.

1. Working in batches if necessary, place all of the ingredients except the ice cubes in a blender or food processor fitted with a steel blade. Process quickly so that the vegetables are finely chopped but not reduced to a purée.

2. Spoon the soup into bowls and place an ice cube in each one so it becomes very cold.

Borscht with Cucumber

YIELD: 4 TO 6 SERVINGS

4 medium beets (about 2 pounds), peeled and chopped (3½ to 4 cups)

4 cups water

1 cup chopped onion

1½ teaspoons salt

1 tablespoon honey

1 tablespoon lemon juice

8 to 12 thin cucumber slices

There are many ways to prepare this soup, which is a Jewish classic. Typical garnishes include chopped hard-cooked eggs, boiled potatoes, scallions, and fresh dill.

1. Combine the beets, water, onion, and salt in a 3- to 5-quart soup pot and bring to a boil over high heat. Reduce the heat to a simmer, cover, and cook for 35 minutes or until the beets are tender.

2. Remove the pot from the heat and stir in the honey and lemon juice. Chill thoroughly.

3. Ladle the soup into individual bowls, float a few cucumber slices in each serving, and add the garnishes of your choice.

Cold Cucumber Yogurt Soup

YIELD: 6 SERVINGS

1/2 cup fine bulgur* (cracked wheat) or whole wheat couscous

1 cup boiling water

2 medium cucumbers, peeled and cut into chunks (about 3 cups)

1/4 cup chopped onion

1/4 cup chopped fresh dill

2 cups plain nonfat or low-fat yogurt

Salt

Freshly ground pepper

1/3 cup coarsely chopped walnuts

6 lemon wedges

* Bulgur, also known as cracked wheat, comes in several textures. If the fine bulgur called for in this recipe is not available, reduce coarse varieties to a fine grind in the blender or food processor, or use whole wheat couscous instead.

This is a warm weather favorite.

1. Place the bulgur or couscous in a heatproof bowl and cover with the boiling water. Let soak for 15 to 20 minutes, or until the grains are soft and the liquid has been absorbed.

2. While the grain soaks, combine the cucumbers, onion, and dill in a blender or food processor, and process to a thick purée. Transfer to a bowl.

3. Add the yogurt to the cucumber purée and mix well. Stir in the soaked grain.

4. Season to taste with salt and pepper, and cover and refrigerate until ready to serve.

5. Ladle the soup into individual bowls, garnish with the chopped walnuts, and set a lemon wedge on the rim of each bowl. Each person should squeeze the lemon juice into the soup before eating.

"If you have men who will exclude any of God's creatures from the shelter of compassion and pity, you will have men who will deal likewise with their fellow men."

–Saint Francis of Assisi

7. Salads and Salad Dressings

Infinitely adaptable, a salad can make a nourishing, satisfying lunch entrée; a light dinner entrée; or a refreshing side dish. This chapter offers a wealth of creative salads regardless of whether you're looking for a main dish or just a healthful side salad.

As you know, at its simplest, the salad can be composed of nothing more than greens. When creating your own salads, we recommend starting with a base of looseleaf or romaine lettuce. Then, if you choose, you can jazz up your simple greens with some of the suggestions that follow:

- For more color, flavor, and texture, add arugula, endive, radicchio, mesclun (mixed baby greens), mizuna, escarole, chicory, watercress, and such.
- To add more interest to your salad, toss in some sprouts, carrot and cucumber slices, strips of red or green pepper, diced celery, raw mushrooms, tomato wedges, grated red cabbage, or raw beets.
- Garnish your salad with leftover cooked vegetables or a handful of cooked beans.
- Make your salad impressive with little effort by adding a few olives, capers, walnuts, or toasted pine nuts or pumpkin seeds.
- Boost your salad's flavor and nutritional value by throwing in cubes or slices of cooked tofu or tempeh.

With so many distinctive ingredients, your salad may not need any dressing at all. But since the salad dressing recipes in this chapter are good in every sense of the word—tasty, packed with nutrients, and made with only healthful fats—you should feel free to dress your salads amply. In general, for side-dish salads, plan on about two tablespoons of dressing per serving; for main-dish salads, allow at least a quarter cup of dressing per serving.

SALADS

Creamy Miso Mustard Coleslaw

YIELD: 4 TO 6 SERVINGS

1 1/2 pounds cabbage, shredded (about 7 cups)

3/4 cup Creamy Miso Mustard Dressing (page 105)

Like most coleslaw recipes, this one can be varied by adding shredded carrots, slivered green pepper, or minced celery.

1. Combine the cabbage and dressing in a serving bowl, mixing until the dressing is evenly and thoroughly blended with the cabbage.

2. Serve immediately or refrigerate for up to 2 days.

Brussels Slaw

YIELD: 4 SERVINGS

1 pint (10 ounces) Brussels sprouts

1/2 cup plain nonfat or low-fat yogurt

1 slightly rounded tablespoon grainy mustard

1 tablespoon flaxseed or hemp oil

1/4 cup walnut pieces

Although often disliked due to their strong sulfurous odor when cooked, Brussels sprouts make excellent eating when served raw in a coleslaw-type salad. A member of the same family as cabbage and broccoli, Brussels sprouts are one of the most nutrient-rich vegetables available.

1. Slice the Brussels sprouts into thin shreds. You should have a little more than 3 cups. Set aside.

2. In serving bowl, mix the yogurt and mustard until evenly blended. Using a fork, beat in the oil.

3. Add the shredded Brussels sprouts and walnut pieces to the dressing, and mix well.

4. Serve immediately or refrigerate for up to 2 days.

Cucumber Tomato Salsa

YIELD: 6 SERVINGS

1 cup chopped plum tomatoes

2 cups chopped cucumber

1/4 cup minced scallions

1/4 cup minced fresh cilantro or flat-leaf Italian parsley

1 jalapeño pepper, seeded and finely chopped

1 tablespoon lemon juice

1/2 teaspoon salt

For a lively hors d'oeuvre, spoon this spicy salsa on Baked Tortilla Crisps (page 52) and top with yogurt cheese (page 22) seasoned lightly with tomato juice. The salsa can be made with less hot pepper for a milder salsa, or prepared entirely without the pepper. Parsley can be used if you don't care for cilantro's distinctive taste.

1. Combine all the ingredients in a serving bowl, tossing well to mix.
2. Serve immediately or refrigerate for up to 3 days.

Moroccan Carrot Slaw

YIELD: 4 SERVINGS

2 cups shredded carrots (4 to 5 medium carrots)

1/2 cup loosely packed chopped fresh cilantro and/or flat-leaf Italian parsley

3 tablespoons orange juice

1 tablespoon flaxseed, hemp, or olive oil

1/2 teaspoon paprika

1/4 teaspoon ground cumin

1/8 teaspoon cayenne pepper

1/8 teaspoon salt

This shredded carrot salad has a real kick.

1. Place the carrots in a serving bowl and set aside.
2. Combine all of the remaining ingredients in a blender or food processor and purée.
3. Pour the dressing over the carrots and toss well to mix.
4. Serve at once, hold for 1 to 2 hours at room temperature, or refrigerate for up to 2 days.

YOGURT CUCUMBER SALAD

YIELD: 4 SERVINGS

1 cup plain nonfat or low-fat yogurt

1/2 to 1 tablespoon crushed dried mint

1 1/2 cups thinly sliced peeled cucumber

Small lemon wedge

This cooling salad works in almost any menu. Although simple to put together at the last minute, if the salad is prepared half an hour or more before serving, the flavors have a chance to blend and develop. If prepared more than an hour before serving, be sure to refrigerate.

1. Place the yogurt in a serving bowl, and beat the mint in with a fork, gauging the amount by personal taste.
2. Stir in the cucumber and squeeze in a little lemon juice.
3. Serve immediately or store in the refrigerator for up to 2 days.

VARIATIONS

- Substitute 2 to 4 tablespoons of fresh mint, parsley, or dill for the dried mint.
- Substitute 1/2 teaspoon of ground cumin for the mint.
- Add 2 thinly sliced scallions and/or a minced clove of garlic.

"When you see the golden arches you are probably on your way to the pearly gates."

–William Castelli, MD
Medical Director of the Framingham Cardiovascular Institute

Roasted Corn Salad

YIELD: 4 TO 6 SERVINGS

4 ears corn

2 long hot peppers, roasted and chopped (page 20)

1/2 cup chopped cucumber

2 scallions, thinly sliced

4 cloves garlic, roasted and mashed (page 19)

1/4 cup orange juice

1 teaspoon minced orange zest

1/4 teaspoon salt

Dry-roasted corn enhances the flavor of this salad, which depends on fresh corn. Admittedly, it is time-consuming to roast all the components of this dish. To save steps, roast the peppers and garlic together in the oven. This salad is a good choice with bean, tofu, or tempeh entrées, or as a lively accent on a mixed vegetable plate.

1. Cut the kernels off the cob. You should have about 4 cups. Place a large heavy cast-iron skillet over high heat. When hot, add the corn kernels and roast, tossing frequently, until the kernels are lightly colored and starting to pop. This should take 15 to 20 minutes. Do not crowd the corn in the pan. If you do not have a large enough skillet (15 inches at least), roast in two batches. When cooked, transfer the corn to a serving bowl.

2. Add the peppers, cucumber, scallions, garlic, orange juice, orange zest, and salt to the corn, and mix well.

3. Serve at once or let sit at room temperature until serving time. Extra salad can be kept for several days in the refrigerator, but bring to room temperature before serving.

Carrot Raita

YIELD: 4 SERVINGS

2 carrots, coarsely grated

2 cups plain nonfat or low-fat yogurt

1/2 teaspoon salt

1/2 teaspoon cumin

1/4 teaspoon cayenne pepper

Grated carrots and yogurt unite in this salad, which is soothing and spicy at the same time.

1. Place the carrots in a serving bowl and stir in the yogurt and salt until well mixed.

2. Sprinkle the cumin and cayenne pepper over the top of the salad, and serve immediately.

Spur-of-the-Moment Carrot Salad

YIELD: 4 SERVINGS

1 1/2 cups coarsely shredded carrots (3 medium carrots)

1/4 cup slivered green pepper

1/4 cup Orange Parsley Dressing (page 101), Tomato Basil Dressing (page 101), or Piquant Mustard Tomato Dressing (page 102)

1 tomato, cut into thin wedges

Shredded carrots mixed with a favorite dressing provide a great last-minute accompaniment to almost any meal.

1. Combine the carrots and green pepper in a mixing bowl.

2. Add the dressing of choice, and toss well to mix.

3. Divide the salad among four serving plates, and garnish each serving with a few tomato wedges. Serve immediately.

Orange Arame Salad

YIELD: 4 SERVINGS

1 cup arame

1 cup orange juice

A few red onion slices

2 small oranges

1/2 cup coarsely chopped walnuts

Arame is a shredded, dark brown sea grass with a mild aroma and flavor. It is a good introduction to sea vegetables, as it tastes the least strongly of the sea.

1. Combine the arame and orange juice in a small saucepan, and set aside for 5 to 10 minutes to soften. Then bring to a boil and simmer for 5 minutes.

2. Remove the saucepan from the heat and add the onion slices. Set aside to cool to room temperature.

3. Using a sharp paring knife, peel and segment each orange over a bowl to catch any juices. (See the inset on page 93.)

4. Transfer the arame mixture to a shallow serving bowl and top with the orange segments. Sprinkle the walnuts on top of the salad and serve immediately.

Fennel and Orange Salad

YIELD: 4 TO 6 SERVINGS

1 large fennel bulb

2 navel oranges

½ small red onion, thinly sliced

12 black olives

Splash of balsamic vinegar

Freshly ground pepper

This is a refreshing salad to pair with grain, pasta, or bean entrées.

1. Remove the stalks and feathery leaves (fronds) from the fennel. Discard the stalks. Set aside about 1 tablespoon of the chopped fronds, and reserve the remainder for another use.

2. Cut the fennel bulb in half lengthwise. Slice into thin wedges. Arrange on a serving plate.

3. Using a sharp paring knife, peel and segment each orange over the fennel plate to catch any juices. (See the inset below.)

4. Intersperse the orange segments with the fennel, and scatter the onion slices over all. Garnish as desired with the olives.

5. Dress with a splash of balsamic vinegar and a generous amount of freshly ground pepper. Scatter the reserved tablespoon of fennel fronds on top, and serve immediately at room temperature.

Segmenting an Orange

A segmented orange makes an attractive addition to many salads. To begin, peel the orange using a sharp paring knife. First remove a slice of peel from the top. Then go around the orange in a circular fashion, removing the peel and the white pith below it in a continuous motion. When done, you will have a spiral of peel and a skinless, pithless orange.

To divide the orange into segments, slip the paring knife between the segments, just under the thin membrane that separates them, and lift out the segments, which should be free of both pith and membrane. Do this over a bowl to catch any juices. With a little practice, you will be able to segment an orange quickly and easily. If desired, wrap the peel and freeze it to use in recipes that call for orange peel or zest.

Warm Mushroom Salad

YIELD: 4 SERVINGS

2 cups sliced mushrooms, any type (6 ounces)

2 tablespoons chopped shallots or scallions

2 tablespoons balsamic vinegar

1 large clove garlic, minced

1 cup diced tomato

1/4 teaspoon salt

4 to 6 cups mixed greens

For a salad that is both economical and flavorful, a combination of half white button and half "exotic" mushrooms works well. Of course, you can also prepare this dish using only the exotics: cremini, shiitake, portobello, oyster, and chanterelle. Or it can be made exclusively with common button mushrooms.

1. Combine the mushrooms, shallots or scallions, vinegar, and garlic in a large skillet. Sauté over medium heat for 5 minutes, or until the mushroom juices run freely.

2. Remove the skillet from the heat and stir in the tomato and salt.

3. Arrange the greens on four serving plates. Top with the warm mushroom-tomato mixture, spooning the juices in the pan over all. Serve immediately.

Curried Tomato and Cucumber Salad

YIELD: 4 TO 6 SERVINGS

2 teaspoons curry powder

1/2 teaspoon ground cumin

1 1/2 cups diced tomatoes

1 1/2 cups diced peeled cucumber

2 cloves garlic, minced

3 tablespoons chopped fresh cilantro

1/4 teaspoon salt

1 cup plain nonfat or low-fat yogurt

The seasoned vegetables for this salad can be prepared in advance and held at room temperature for about an hour or refrigerated for several hours. But wait until just before serving to add the yogurt.

1. Place the curry powder and cumin in a dry skillet. Set over low heat and stir for about 1 minute, or just until aromatic. Remove from the heat.

2. Combine the tomatoes, cucumbers, garlic, and cilantro in a serving bowl. Add the skillet-toasted seasonings and salt, and mix well.

3. Stir in the yogurt just before serving.

RICE SALAD

YIELD: 4 TO 6 SERVINGS

3 cups cooked brown rice, warm or at room temperature

1 cup Orange Parsley Dressing (page 101), Piquant Mustard Tomato Dressing (page 102), or Tomato Basil Dressing (page 101)

Sunflower seeds, toasted pumpkin seeds, capers, radishes, halved cherry tomatoes, and/or peeled orange segments as garnishes

Rice salad can be made many different ways. Here is a model to guide you. For visual appeal, use the garnishes best suited to your chosen dressing to decorate the dish.

1. Combine the rice and dressing of choice in a large serving bowl, mixing well.

2. Cover the dish and allow to marinate for 30 minutes to 2 hours at room temperature.

3. Just before serving, decorate with the garnishes of your choice. If desired, store in the refrigerator for up to 3 days.

BASIL BEAN SALAD

YIELD: 4 SERVINGS

2 cups cooked or canned chickpeas, white beans, pink beans, or black beans, well drained

1/2 cup chopped celery or red or green pepper

1/2 cup Tomato Basil Dressing (page 101)

This basic recipe can be prepared with almost any bean and with different dressings, as well. Like most bean salads, it can also be refrigerated and held for several days.

1. Combine all the ingredients in a serving bowl.

2. Cover the dish and allow to marinate at room temperature for 1 hour.

3. Serve immediately or refrigerate for up to 4 days.

VARIATION

- For a more elaborate salad, add 1/2 cup cooked fresh or thawed frozen corn kernels.

Black Bean Salsa

YIELD: 4 SERVINGS

2 cups cooked or canned black beans, rinsed and drained

1 cup diced tomato

1/2 cup minced green pepper

1/4 cup minced sweet onion such as Vidalia, Walla Walla, or Maui, or red onion

1/4 cup minced fresh cilantro or parsley

1 large clove garlic, minced

3 tablespoons lime juice

1 tablespoon minced hot pepper

1 teaspoon ground cumin

Salt

Serve this salsa as a side dish or as a topping for grains or vegetables. When choosing a hot pepper, use a jalapeño for a spicy salsa, and a Serrano for a less spicy dish. If preferred, omit the fresh hot pepper and season to taste with hot pepper sauce.

1. Combine all the ingredients in a serving bowl, seasoning with hot pepper and salt to taste.

2. Cover the dish and allow to sit at room temperature for at least 30 minutes to give the flavors a chance to fully develop.

3. If prepared more than a few hours ahead, chill. If the salad has been chilled, return to room temperature to serve. Store in the refrigerator for up to 4 days.

Tofu Sandwich Salad

YIELD: 4 SERVINGS

8 ounces firm or extra firm tofu (about 1 1/2 cups mashed)

1/2 cup chopped celery or green or red pepper

2 tablespoons chopped mild onion or scallions, optional

1 1/2 tablespoons light miso

1 tablespoon lemon juice

2 teaspoons prepared mustard

1/2 teaspoon paprika

This dish is great as part of a salad plate, as a spread for crackers, or as a sandwich filling. It is also excellent when arranged on a bed of lettuce and surrounded by sliced tomato, cucumber, raw onion, and sprouts.

1. *To blend by hand:* Mash the tofu with a fork or potato masher, and mix in the remaining ingredients. Then knead gently with your hands to form an evenly blended, cohesive mass. *To prepare in a food processor:* Combine all the ingredients in a food processor and pulse until the vegetables are finely chopped. Do not allow to turn into a purée.

2. Serve immediately or refrigerate for up to 3 days.

Tofu "Tuna"

YIELD: 4 SERVINGS

12 ounces firm or extra firm tofu (2 cups mashed)

3 tablespoons tahini (sesame seed paste)

Wedge of lemon

2 teaspoons soy sauce

1/3 cup shredded carrot

1/3 cup chopped celery, red or green pepper, or cucumber

A great choice for a salad plate, crackers, or sandwiches, Tofu "Tuna" is a bit more substantial in texture than Tofu Sandwich Salad (page 96).

1. Place the tofu in a serving bowl, and mash it well using a potato masher or fork.

2. Mix the tahini into the tuna. Then squeeze in the lemon juice and add soy sauce to taste. Finally, fold in the vegetables.

3. Serve immediately or refrigerate for up to 3 days.

Spinach-Yogurt Salad

YIELD: 4 SERVINGS

8 ounces fresh spinach

1 cup plain nonfat or low-fat yogurt

2 tablespoons lemon juice

1/4 teaspoon salt

1 teaspoon dried mint

You can hold this salad at room temperature for about an hour in cool weather, but if made well in advance or in hot weather, you'll want to refrigerate it until ready to serve.

1. Wash the spinach well and drain to remove as much water as possible. Discard any tough stems.

2. Place the spinach in a medium-size pot, cover, and cook over medium heat for 5 to 10 minutes, or until the leaves have wilted.

3. Allow the spinach to cool enough to handle. Squeeze out as much moisture as possible, and chop. (The liquid can be saved for soup stock.) You should have about 1 cup.

4. In a serving bowl, combine the chopped spinach with the yogurt, lemon juice, and salt, mixing well. Then sprinkle the mint on top and serve.

WARM BULGUR SALAD

YIELD: 4 TO 6 SERVINGS

1 1/2 cups strong peppermint tea

1 cup bulgur (cracked wheat)

1/4 cup sunflower seeds

1/3 cup chopped Vidalia, Maui, or other sweet onion, or red onion

1/2 cup lightly packed chopped fresh parsley

2 tablespoons chopped capers

2 tablespoons lemon juice

Salt

Serve this salad in a shallow bowl and encourage diners to scoop it up with lettuce leaves.

1. Combine the tea, bulgur, and sunflower seeds in a 1-quart pot, and bring to a boil over high heat. Lower the heat to a simmer, cover, and cook for 10 minutes.

2. Remove the pot from the heat and stir in the onion. Allow to sit uncovered for about 10 minutes, or until all the liquid has been absorbed.

3. Transfer the bulgur mixture to a serving bowl and use a fork to mix the parsley, capers, and lemon juice into the salad. Season with salt to taste.

4. Serve warm or at room temperature, fluffing the salad with a fork before serving to separate the grains. If desired, store in the refrigerator for up to 3 days.

VARIATION

- To make Cinnamon Scented Cracked Wheat Salad, omit the capers and add 2 tablespoons of currants or chopped raisins to the pot along with the onion. Season with 1/2 teaspoon cinnamon when adding the parsley and lemon juice.

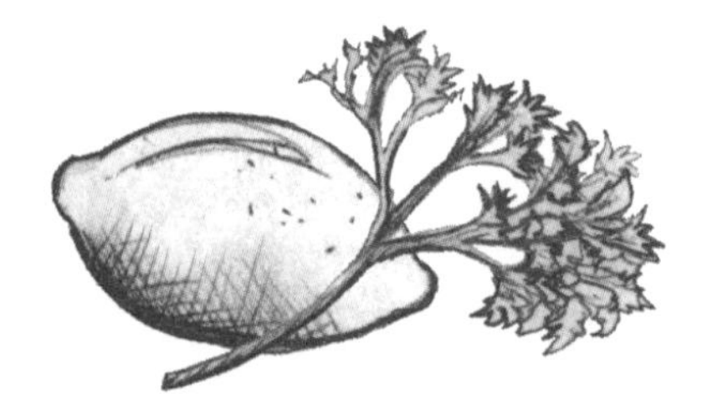

THAI SALAD

YIELD: 4 SERVINGS

$^{1}/_{2}$ cup fresh lime juice

$^{1}/_{4}$ cup soy sauce

2 teaspoons grated fresh ginger

2 cloves garlic, crushed

$^{3}/_{4}$ teaspoon crushed red pepper flakes

12 ounces firm tofu, cut into thin strips

$^{1}/_{2}$ cup diced red or green pepper

1 medium cucumber, peeled and thinly sliced

$^{1}/_{4}$ cup sliced scallion or diced sweet onion

$^{1}/_{4}$ cup chopped fresh cilantro

6 cups mixed salad greens torn into bite-size pieces

$^{1}/_{2}$ cup sprouts, such as bean, sunflower, radish, or alfalfa, optional

$^{1}/_{2}$ cup fresh green peas, sliced edible pod peas, or sliced radishes, optional

$^{1}/_{4}$ cup chopped peanuts

Toasted sesame oil, optional

This pretty salad makes a good warm weather entrée, and also offers a lot of room for creativity. For example, instead of garnishing with sprouts and peas, you can arrange fresh steamed green beans around each salad, creating the appearance of a nest, or you can surround the salad with freshly steamed broccoli buds. Rice cakes make a good accompaniment.

1. Combine the lime juice, soy sauce, ginger, garlic, and red pepper flakes in a medium-size bowl. Add the tofu strips and gently mix.

2. Add the green pepper, cucumber, scallion or onion, and cilantro to the tofu mixture, and mix again. Do not worry if the tofu falls apart somewhat. Cover and refrigerate until serving time.

3. Arrange the greens on four serving plates. Top with the marinated tofu and vegetables. Pour any remaining dressing over the salad and, if desired, surround with the sprouts and peas. Sprinkle 1 tablespoon of chopped peanuts on top of each salad.

4. Serve immediately, passing a bottle of toasted sesame oil for those who wish to sprinkle a little on their salad to temper the intense lime flavor.

Indonesian Tempeh Salad

YIELD: 4 SERVINGS

$^1/_4$ cup pumpkin seeds, toasted (page 19)

$^1/_4$ cup peanuts

1 large Vidalia or other sweet onion, sliced into half rings, divided

$^1/_3$ cup water

2 large cloves garlic

3 tablespoons soy sauce

2 tablespoons lemon juice

1 tablespoon molasses

$^1/_2$ teaspoon cayenne pepper

12 ounces tempeh, sliced into $^1/_8$-inch strips

6 cups mixed salad greens torn into bite-size pieces

1 medium cucumber, peeled and sliced

Lemon wedges

This is a generous main dish salad. For added color, garnish with a few red pepper strips, radishes, or tomato wedges. Accompany with lightly toasted rice cakes. To go along with the salad, try corn on the cob or grilled or oven-roasted sweet potatoes.

1. Place the pumpkin seeds, peanuts, 1 slice of the onion, and all of the water, garlic, soy sauce, lemon juice, molasses, and cayenne pepper in a blender or food processor. Purée to a make a sauce that is evenly blended but not quite smooth.

2. Transfer the sauce to a large skillet, and add the remaining onion and the tempeh strips. Mix to coat the onion and tempeh with the sauce, cover, and cook over medium heat for 5 minutes. Stir the tempeh, recover the pot, and cook for 5 additional minutes.

3. Pile $1^1/_2$ cups of greens on each of four serving plates. Surround the greens with the cucumber slices, and mound the tempeh mixture on top of the greens. Use a spoon to scrape any sauce that clings to the pan and pour it over the salads. Garnish with lemon wedges for individual seasoning at the table, and serve immediately.

DRESSINGS

TOMATO BASIL DRESSING

YIELD: ¾ CUP

1 cup loosely packed basil leaves

½ cup tomato juice or vegetable juice cocktail, such as V-8

1 clove garlic

1 tablespoon balsamic vinegar

1 teaspoon French-style or grainy mustard

This tasty fat-free dressing is perfect on green salads or on thick slices of fresh summer tomatoes, hot steamed potatoes, green beans, or cauliflower. It is also a good dressing choice for cooked beans. (See the Basil Bean Salad on page 95.)

1. Combine all of the ingredients in a blender or food processor, and purée until the basil is finely chopped and the dressing is well blended.

2. Use immediately or store for up to 1 week in the refrigerator. If prepared in advance, beat with a fork or shake to recombine before serving.

ORANGE PARSLEY DRESSING

YIELD: 1 CUP

1 cup loosely packed fresh parsley leaves

½ cup orange juice

¼ cup red wine vinegar

2 tablespoons hemp, flaxseed, or olive oil

¼ teaspoon salt

¼ teaspoon cayenne pepper

While 2 tablespoons of this dressing contain just 3.5 grams of fat, a 2-tablespoon serving of typical bottled dressing ranges from 12 to 16 grams of fat.

1. Combine all of the ingredients in a blender or food processor, and purée until the parsley is finely chopped and the dressing is well blended.

2. Use immediately or store for up to 1 week in the refrigerator. If prepared in advance, beat with a fork or shake to recombine before serving.

Piquant Mustard Tomato Dressing

YIELD: $^3/_4$ CUP

- $^1/_2$ cup cider vinegar
- $^1/_4$ cup unsweetened or fruit juice-sweetened (natural) ketchup
- 3 tablespoons orange juice
- 1 teaspoon prepared mustard
- 1 teaspoon maple syrup
- 1 clove garlic, minced
- $^1/_2$ teaspoon paprika

As the name implies, this is a tangy dressing.

1. Combine all of the ingredients in a small bowl, and beat with a fork or whisk until blended.

2. Use immediately or store for up to 1 week in the refrigerator. If prepared in advance, beat with a fork or shake to recombine before serving.

Creamy Italian Dressing

YIELD: $^3/_4$ CUP

- $^1/_3$ cup red wine vinegar
- $^1/_3$ cup water
- 4 canned artichoke hearts, drained
- 2 scallions, thinly sliced
- 1 clove garlic, split
- 1 tablespoon olive oil
- 1 teaspoon honey
- $^1/_2$ teaspoon dried basil or 1 tablespoon chopped fresh basil
- $^1/_2$ teaspoon dried oregano
- Freshly ground pepper

In addition to good taste, this dressing provides just 2 grams of fat in each 2-tablespoon serving, versus the 15.5 grams provided by most bottled creamy Italian dressings.

1. Combine all of the ingredients except the pepper in a blender or food processor, and purée until smooth. Transfer to a bowl, and add freshly ground pepper to taste.

2. Use immediately or store for up to 4 days in the refrigerator. If prepared in advance, beat with a fork or shake to recombine before serving.

Lemon Tahini Dressing

YIELD: 1 CUP

1/4 cup tahini (sesame seed paste)

1/4 cup lemon juice

1/4 cup water

1/3 cup plain nonfat or low-fat yogurt

1 teaspoon soy sauce

1/4 teaspoon salt

This is a basic dressing that can be modified in a number of ways. For example, you can add 1 tablespoon of minced fresh dill or parsley and/or a chopped clove of garlic. Or you can add a few vegetables and prepare it in a blender or food processor. (See the Variation at the end of the recipe.)

1. Place the tahini in a small bowl, and use a fork or whisk to beat the lemon juice into the tahini.

2. Gradually beat the water into the tahini mixture until creamy. Then stir in the yogurt, soy sauce, and salt.

3. Use immediately or store for up to 1 week in the refrigerator.

Variation

- To add vegetables to the dressing, combine all the ingredients except the yogurt in a blender or food processor. Add 1 scallion or 1 onion slice, 1 small celery stalk with leaves, and 1 wedge of green pepper. Process until the vegetables are integrated into the dressing. Stir in the yogurt.

"We all love animals.
Why do we call some 'pets' and others 'dinner'?"

–k.d. lang

YOGONAISE

YIELD: ABOUT $^2/_3$ CUP

$^1/_2$ cup plain nonfat yogurt

1 tablespoon grainy mustard

2 tablespoons flaxseed, hemp, or canola oil

Yogonaise can be used as a salad dressing, as a dipping sauce for steamed vegetables, in potato salad, and in any other dish that calls for mayonnaise. In return, when made with nonfat yogurt, this dressing provides less than half the sodium and one-third the fat of regular mayonnaise, and contains only 35 calories per tablespoon.

1. Place the yogurt and mustard in a small bowl and use a fork to beat the ingredients together until evenly blended. Then beat in the oil.

2. Use immediately or store for up to 1 week in the refrigerator.

TOFU MAYONNAISE

YIELD: 1 CUP

8 ounces soft tofu

2 tablespoons lemon juice

1 tablespoon cider vinegar

2 teaspoons prepared mustard

2 teaspoons light miso

Pinch salt

Soft tofu makes a surprisingly creamy and tasty "mayonnaise." Moreover, this extremely low-fat dressing supplies a mere 10 calories per tablespoon.

1. Combine all the ingredients in a blender or food processor, and purée until creamy.

2. Use immediately or store for up to 1 week in the refrigerator.

Creamy Miso Mustard Dressing

YIELD: 3/4 CUP

- 1/3 cup tahini (sesame seed paste)
- 1 tablespoon prepared mustard
- 1 tablespoon dark miso
- 3 tablespoons cider vinegar
- 1/4 to 1/3 cup water

This is a good dressing for a mixed salad, coleslaw, or a creamy bean salad.

1. Place the tahini, mustard, and miso in a small bowl, and use a fork to beat until well blended.
2. Beat the cider vinegar into the tahini mixture. Then gradually beat in the water to make a creamy, pourable dressing.
3. Use immediately or store for up to 1 week in the refrigerator.

Creamy Tofu Russian Dressing

YIELD: 2 CUPS

- 8 ounces soft tofu
- 1/2 cup diced peeled cucumber
- 2 tablespoons lemon juice
- 1 tablespoon cider vinegar
- 2 teaspoons dark miso
- 1 teaspoon prepared mustard
- 1/2 cup soy milk
- 1/2 cup unsweetened or fruit juice-sweetened (natural) ketchup
- 1/4 teaspoon hot pepper sauce or to taste

Due to variations in texture between different brands of tofu, the amount of soy milk in this recipe may have to be adjusted to reach the desired pourable consistency. While the flavor and texture of soft tofu is preferred, the dressing can be made with firm tofu as well, although additional soy milk will be needed.

1. Combine the tofu, cucumber, lemon juice, cider vinegar, miso, and mustard in a blender or food processor, and purée until evenly blended.
2. Gradually add the soy milk and process to a smooth consistency.
3. Add the ketchup and hot sauce, and process briefly to incorporate. Add additional soy milk, if necessary, to obtain a rich, pourable dressing.
4. Use immediately or store for up to 4 days in the refrigerator.

Creamy Tofu Ranch Dressing

YIELD: 1¾ CUPS

8 ounces soft tofu

½ cup diced peeled cucumber

2 tablespoons lemon juice

1 tablespoon cider vinegar

1 tablespoon prepared mustard

2 teaspoons light miso

½ teaspoon turmeric

1 clove garlic

½ cup soy milk

As when making Creamy Tofu Russian Dressing (page 105), you may need to add more or less soy milk, depending on the density of the tofu used.

1. Combine all the ingredients except the soy milk in a blender or food processor, and purée until evenly blended.
2. Gradually add the soy milk and process to a smooth, creamy, pourable consistency.
3. Use immediately or store for up to 4 days in the refrigerator.

Cucumber Yogurt Dressing

YIELD: ABOUT 1 CUP

¾ cup plain nonfat or low-fat yogurt, divided

½ cup diced peeled cucumber

1 clove garlic, sliced

1 tablespoon fresh dill

1 tablespoon lemon juice

1 tablespoon tahini (sesame seed paste)

1 tablespoon flaxseed, hemp, or olive oil

¼ teaspoon salt

This cool and refreshing dressing will add a protein and calcium boost to any salad.

1. Combine ¼ cup of the yogurt and all of the remaining ingredients in a blender or food processor, and purée until smooth.
2. Transfer the mixture to a small bowl and beat in the remaining ½ cup of yogurt with a fork.
3. Use immediately or store for up to 5 days in the refrigerator.

8. ENTRÉES

The entrée, or main dish, is generally the focal point of a meal. Entrées also tend to be the primary source of protein, although with proper menu planning, this is not essential.

Many people find that the most difficult part of following a vegetarian diet—or of simply adding more vegetarian fare to their lives—is coordinating the entrée with the other dishes in the meal to insure adequate protein. Here are some tips:

- Fill your kitchen with the basic foods that make vegetarian meals convenient, as described in Chapter 2.
- Rely on entrées that feature beans, soy, eggs, or dairy to provide the protein you need.
- When a main dish is mostly composed of vegetables, add an appetizer, salad, and/or side dish that features beans, soy, eggs, or dairy for added protein.
- When the main dish seems ample, don't feel that you have to prepare complicated side dishes as well. It often takes nothing more than a loaf of whole grain bread and a tossed salad to complete the meal.
- Realize that as an alternative to a single entrée, you can combine bean and grain side dishes to provide the protein component of the meal.
- Don't hesitate to use the main dishes in this chapter as side dishes if that works best in your menu. To serve an entrée from this section as an accompaniment, figure on getting one and a half to two times the servings indicated. In other words, a dish that serves four people as an entrée will generally serve six or even eight people as a side dish.

As you explore the recipes in this chapter, you will discover that many of them include menu suggestions. To give you a preview, on page 108, we have provided six dinners that illustrate how varied and tempting meat-free dining can be.

Sample Dinner Menus

Savory Baked Tofu (page 118)
Tomato Couscous (page 199)
Sesame Green Beans (page 178)
Warm Mushroom Salad (page 94)

Maple Pecan Tempeh (page 131)
Louisiana Sweet Potatoes (page 189)
Country Greens (page 181)

Cold Cucumber Yogurt Soup (page 86)
White Beans with Swiss Chard (page 142)
Moroccan Carrot Slaw (page 89)
Whole grain bread with Tahini Garlic Spread (page 56)

Cowboy Beans (page 154)
Golden Biscuits (page 46)
Creamy Miso Mustard Coleslaw (page 88)

Superior Spinach Dip (page 55) with raw vegetables
Portobello Pasta (page 161)
Fennel and Orange Salad (page 93)

Portuguese Bread and Garlic Soup (page 73)
Multicultural Rice, Beans, and Greens (page 165)
Assorted oven-roasted or grilled vegetables of choice

VERY VEGETABLE ENTRÉES

CHILI RELLENOS

YIELD: 4 SERVINGS

Eight 4- to 6-inch poblano chilies, Anaheim chilies, or Italian frying peppers, roasted (page 20)

$1\frac{1}{2}$ cups yogurt cheese (page 22)

$1\frac{1}{2}$ cups fresh or frozen corn kernels

$\frac{1}{3}$ cup thinly sliced scallions

4 cups Quick Spicy Mexican Tomato Sauce (page 213) or other tomato sauce of choice

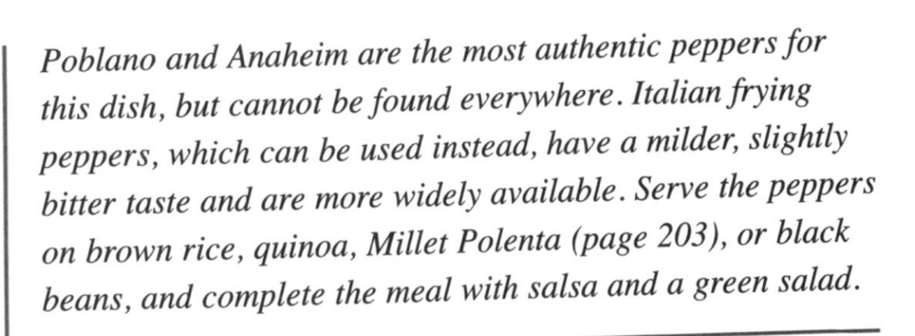

Poblano and Anaheim are the most authentic peppers for this dish, but cannot be found everywhere. Italian frying peppers, which can be used instead, have a milder, slightly bitter taste and are more widely available. Serve the peppers on brown rice, quinoa, Millet Polenta (page 203), or black beans, and complete the meal with salsa and a green salad.

1. Cut a slit in the side of each roasted pepper and carefully remove any seeds. Pat the inside of the peppers with a paper towel to absorb the moisture.

2. Combine the yogurt cheese, corn, and scallions in a medium-size bowl, and spoon the mixture into the peppers. If the surface of the peppers gets messy during filling, wipe with a damp paper towel when finished.

3. Pour the tomato sauce into a skillet large enough to hold the peppers in a single layer. Arrange the peppers slit side up in the sauce. The sauce should generously surround the peppers but not reach as high as the slit.

4. Bring the sauce to a boil over medium heat. Lower the heat so the sauce gently simmers, and partially cover the pot, leaving the lid slightly ajar to allow steam to escape. Cook for 20 minutes or just until the peppers are tender, and serve hot.

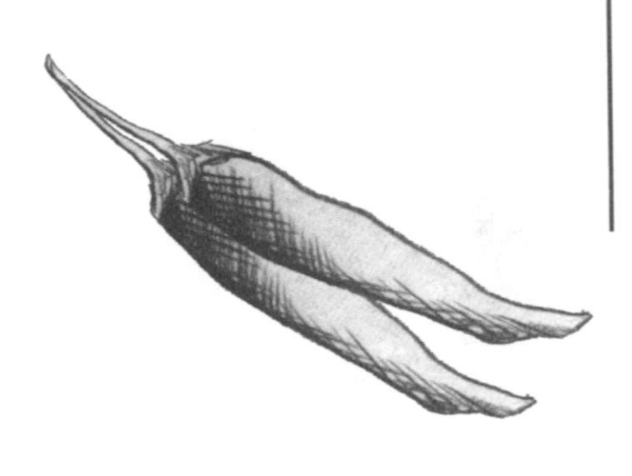

MUSHROOM RAGOUT

YIELD: 4 TO 6 SERVINGS

8 ounces white mushrooms

8 ounces mixed mushrooms of choice, such as portobello, cremini, shiitake, and chanterelle

1/2 cup thinly sliced shallots

1/4 cup sherry or dry wine

2 teaspoons soy sauce

1/2 cup yogurt cheese (page 22)

1/2 teaspoon salt

Freshly ground pepper

This creamy mushroom melange can be served over toast, baked potatoes, kasha, rice, or bow-tie noodles.

1. Cut the mushroom caps and stems into bite-size pieces. You should have about 3 cups.

2. Combine the mushrooms, shallots, sherry or wine, and soy sauce in a medium-size skillet. Cook over medium heat, stirring frequently, for 8 to 10 minutes, or until the mushrooms release their juices and are tender.

3. Remove the skillet from the heat and stir in the yogurt cheese and salt. Return to low heat and cook, stirring continuously, for 1 to 2 minutes, or until the mixture is creamy and warm. Do not boil.

4. Season the mushroom mixture with freshly ground pepper to taste and spoon over toast, potatoes, or your grain or pasta of choice.

IRISH STEW

YIELD: 4 SERVINGS

1 medium onion, cut into small chunks

1 pound Yellow Finn, Yukon Gold, red bliss, or new potatoes, cut into bite-size pieces

2 large carrots, peeled and sliced

1/2 to 2/3 cup chickpea cooking liquid or water

1/2 teaspoon ground turmeric

2 cups cooked or canned chickpeas

Salt

This recipe employs the technique of braising, or cooking in just enough liquid to keep the food moist. Keep the heat moderate, as cooking quickly on high heat will cause the vegetables to become dry. This is a homey dish that goes nicely with Savory Oat Biscuits (page 47) or whole grain bread and a cucumber or cabbage salad.

1. Place the onion in a heavy 3-quart pot and cook over medium heat, stirring frequently, for about 3 minutes or until wilted.

2. Add the potatoes to the pot and cook for 1 to 2 minutes.

3. Add the carrots, $^1/_2$ cup of the cooking liquid, or enough to generously cover the bottom of the pot, and the turmeric. Cover and cook over medium heat for 10 minutes, stirring occasionally to keep the cooking even, and adding more liquid if needed. The liquid should be the consistency of rich gravy.

4. Stir in the chickpeas and add salt to taste. Cover and continue to cook for about 5 minutes, or until the potatoes and carrots are fork tender. Serve hot.

Zucchini Pasta

YIELD: 4 SERVINGS

Sauce

2 tablespoons sherry or red wine

1 medium zucchini, diced small

2 large cloves garlic, minced

4 plum tomatoes, diced (about 2 cups)

2 tablespoons minced fresh parsley

2 tablespoon minced fresh basil

2 tablespoons capers

Freshly ground pepper

"Pasta"

4 medium zucchini (about 10 ounces each)

$^1/_4$ to $^1/_2$ cup crumbled feta cheese or grated Parmesan

Crisp zucchini cut into strips makes a delightful pasta alternative. Prepared with a lightly cooked zucchini-tomato sauce, this dish is crisp and colorful. Pair with a bean salad.

1. To prepare the sauce, place the sherry or wine in a large skillet and cook over medium heat until hot. Add the zucchini and garlic and cook for 5 minutes, stirring occasionally.

2. Add the tomatoes, parsley, basil, and capers to the skillet, and cook for 2 to 3 minutes, or until heated through. Season generously with pepper.

3. To prepare the "pasta," bring a large pot of salted water to a boil. Trim the ends from the zucchini and cut each lengthwise into halves. Place the zucchini halves cut side down on a cutting board and slice them lengthwise into thin strips.

4. Add the zucchini to the boiling water and cook for 3 minutes. Do not overcook. Drain well.

5. Combine the zucchini "pasta" with the sauce and serve hot, topping each portion with 1 to 2 tablespoons of cheese.

QUICK MIXED ITALIAN VEGETABLES IN TOMATO JUICE

YIELD: 4 TO 6 SERVINGS

- 1 ½ pounds mixed vegetables and beans of choice, such as green beans, broccoli or cauliflower, cabbage, carrots, corn, zucchini, summer squash, asparagus, snow peas, mushrooms, potatoes, chickpeas, kidney beans, etc., cut into bite-size pieces (6 to 8 cups)
- ½ cup coarsely chopped onion
- ½ cup diced green pepper
- 2 tablespoons minced hot chili pepper, optional
- 2 tablespoons dry wine or sherry
- 1 cup tomato juice
- 3 cloves garlic, chopped
- 2 tablespoons chopped fresh basil, or 1 teaspoon dried basil
- 1 teaspoon dried oregano
- ¼ cup chopped fresh parsley
- 1 tablespoon balsamic vinegar

This Italian-style vegetable dish can easily become an Indian or Mexican entrée with just a few alterations. (See the Variations at the end of the recipe.) A generous topping of yogurt would provide additional protein, but this can be supplied by an accompanying dish. For example, Quick White Pita Pizzas (page 69) would be a natural complement to the Italian version.

1. Combine your vegetables of choice, onion, green pepper, chili pepper, and wine or sherry in a large saucepan. Cook over medium high heat, stirring occasionally, for 2 minutes.

2. Add the tomato juice, garlic, basil, and oregano to the pan, and stir to blend. Reduce the heat, cover, and cook for 12 to 15 minutes, or until the vegetables are tender, stirring occasionally to promote even cooking.

3. Remove the saucepan from the heat and stir in the parsley and vinegar. Serve hot, just warm, or at room temperature.

VARIATIONS

- For Quick Mixed Indian Vegetables, omit the basil, oregano, parsley, and balsamic vinegar. Instead, add 1 dried chili pepper or ¼ teaspoon red pepper flakes, and ½ teaspoon ground turmeric in Step 1. Then add 2 teaspoons grated fresh ginger and 1 teaspoon ground cumin in Step 2. Finally, add ¼ cup chopped fresh cilantro in Step 3. Serve with Channa Dahl (page 194), rice, and Curried Tomato and Cucumber Salad (page 94).

- For Quick Mixed Mexican Vegetables, omit the basil, oregano, parsley, and balsamic vinegar. Instead, add 1 dried chili pepper or ¼ teaspoon red pepper flakes, plus 2 teaspoons chili powder in Step 1. Then add 1 teaspoon ground cumin in Step 2. Serve with brown rice, black beans, and corn tortillas.

BAKED STUFFED ONIONS

YIELD: 4 SERVINGS

- 4 medium red onions or Vidalia onions
- 1 cup bulgur (cracked wheat)
- 2 cups boiling water or mint tea*
- 2 tablespoons pine nuts or pumpkin seeds, toasted (page 19)
- 2 tablespoons minced fresh mint, or 1/4 cup minced fresh parsley*
- 1/2 teaspoon salt
- 1/4 cup balsamic vinegar

* If you do not have access to fresh mint, prepare the grain with mint tea and use fresh parsley in the filling. For an extra minty taste, use both the mint tea and the fresh mint.

Baking brings out the onion's natural sugar and provides a sweet receptacle for this delicate grain filling. For an elegant meal, begin with raw vegetables paired with Green Pepper and Avocado Mayonnaise (page 59) or Superior Spinach Dip (page 55). Then serve the onions with Zucchini Pasta (page 111), a tossed green salad, and whole grain French bread.

1. Preheat the oven to 375°F.

2. Remove the outer papery layer from the onions and cut in half crosswise. Remove the centers from each onion half, leaving the outer 2 to 3 layers of rings and the bottom intact to form a small bowl. (A grapefruit spoon is a good tool for this job.) If there is a hole in the bottom, place a piece of the scooped-out onion over it to cover.

3. Chop enough of the scooped-out onion to make 1 cup. Reserve the rest for another use.

4. Place the chopped onion and the cracked wheat in a 1-quart heatproof bowl, and cover with the hot water or mint tea. Let sit for 10 minutes. Then drain off any liquid that has not been absorbed.

5. Stir the pine nuts or pumpkin seeds, mint or parsley, and salt into the wheat mixture. Then divide the mixture among the onion bowls, pressing the mixture with your hands and mounding to fill tightly.

6. Arrange the onions in a baking pan or ovenproof skillet that holds them snugly. Cover and bake for 30 minutes.

7. Remove the cover from the dish and continue baking for about 15 minutes, or until the onions are tender. Remove the onions from the pan and arrange on a serving dish. Set aside.

8. Add the balsamic vinegar to the baking pan. Place on the stove and cook over medium heat for 2 to 3 minutes, stirring to mix any pan juices and dislodge any filling that's sticking to the pan. When slightly thickened and syrupy, remove from the heat and spoon on top of each onion. If the pan does not come clean, stir in a little water and spoon this, too, over the onions. Serve hot or at room temperature.

Creamy Greek-Style Garden Vegetables

YIELD: 4 SERVINGS

4 cups vegetables of choice, such as asparagus, broccoli stalks, carrots, cauliflower, celery, corn, fennel, green beans, leeks, shredded greens, sweet red or green pepper, snow peas, and zucchini, cut into 1- to 2-inch strips or bite-size pieces

2 cups coarsely chopped mushrooms, any type

1 small onion, cut into thin crescents

$^{1}/_{4}$ cup minced fresh dill

2 tablespoons sherry

1 cup yogurt cheese (page 22)

$^{1}/_{3}$ cup crumbled feta cheese

Freshly ground pepper

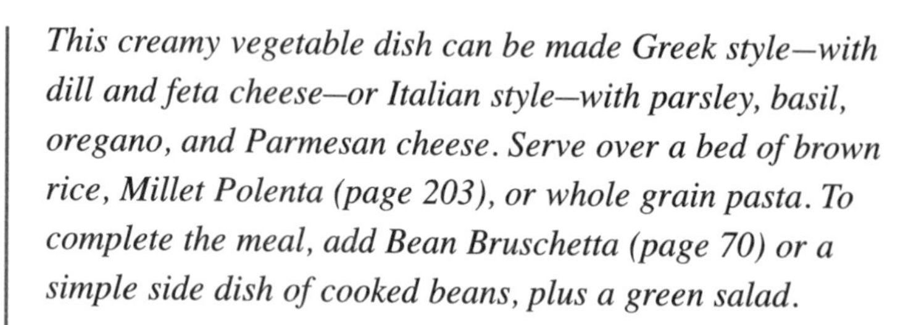

This creamy vegetable dish can be made Greek style—with dill and feta cheese—or Italian style—with parsley, basil, oregano, and Parmesan cheese. Serve over a bed of brown rice, Millet Polenta (page 203), or whole grain pasta. To complete the meal, add Bean Bruschetta (page 70) or a simple side dish of cooked beans, plus a green salad.

1. Combine the mixed vegetables, mushrooms, onion, dill, and sherry in a large heavy skillet. Cover and cook over moderate heat for 10 minutes, or until the vegetables are just tender and the mushroom liquid runs freely.

2. Remove the skillet from the heat and stir in the yogurt cheese. Place the skillet over low heat and cook, stirring continuously, until the yogurt cheese melts and the sauce is creamy. Do not boil.

3. Stir the feta cheese into the vegetable mixture and remove from the heat. Season generously with freshly ground pepper and serve hot.

Variation

- To make Creamy Italian-Style Garden Vegetables, omit the dill and the feta cheese. Instead of the dill, add $^{1}/_{4}$ cup chopped flat-leaf Italian parsley, 2 tablespoons chopped fresh basil or $^{1}/_{2}$ teaspoon dried basil, and 1 teaspoon dried oregano. Instead of the feta, use $^{1}/_{3}$ cup grated Parmesan or romano cheese. For best flavor, buy a high-quality cheese and grate just before using.

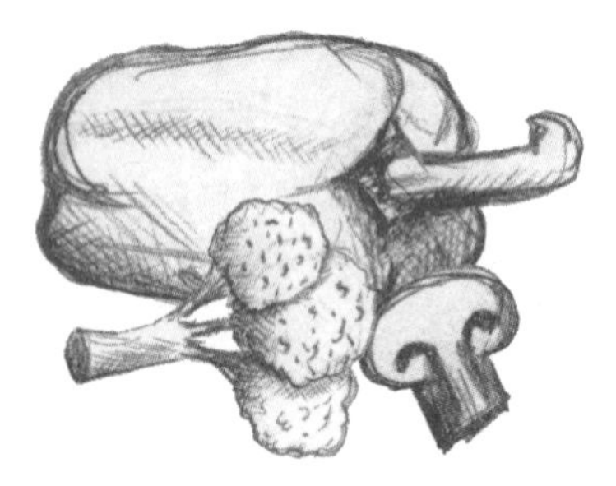

Rare Root Stew

YIELD: 4 SERVINGS

2 good-size parsnips (at least 8 ounces), peeled and cut into 1-inch pieces

2 good-size carrots (at least 8 ounces), peeled and cut into 1-inch pieces

2 medium turnips (at least 8 ounces), peeled, quartered, and cut into 1-inch chunks

1 large leek, cut lengthwise, rinsed to remove any dirt, and cut into 1-inch segments

1 fennel bulb, stalks and fronds removed, cut into wedges

1 small celery root, peeled and cut into wedges, optional

1 stick cinnamon, broken in half

2 large cloves garlic, sliced

1 tablespoon minced fresh ginger

1 medium onion, sliced into rings

1/3 cup apple juice

3 cups cooked or canned red kidney beans, lightly drained

1/2 teaspoon salt

1/4 cup chopped fresh parsley

This dinner stew features several uncommonly eaten vegetables, such as parsnips, turnips, and—if you can find it—celery root (celeriac). Each serving provides about one pound of vegetables, generously surpassing the daily recommended minimum. Just be sure to cut all the vegetables the same size so that they will finish cooking at the same time.

1. Place the parsnips, carrots, turnips, leek, fennel, and celery root, if using, in a large heavy pot with a tight-fitting lid. Bury the cinnamon in the vegetables, scatter the garlic and ginger over the top, and cover with the onion rings. Pour the apple juice over all.

2. Bring the vegetables to a boil over high heat. Then reduce the heat to a gentle simmer, cover, and cook for 15 to 20 minutes, or until the vegetables start to give a little but are not yet tender. Stir a few times to promote even cooking.

3. Add the beans and salt to the pot, mixing well. Then replace the cover and continue to cook for 10 additional minutes, or until the vegetables are tender. If necessary, add more apple juice or other liquid to prevent the stew from becoming dry.

4. When done, sprinkle the stew with parsley and replace the cover to wilt. Serve hot.

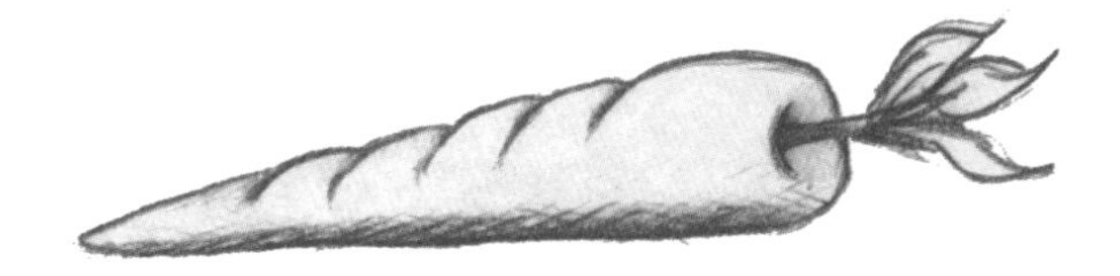

Mixed Vegetable Curry with Chickpeas

YIELD: 4 TO 6 SERVINGS

4 cups coarsely chopped, lightly packed leafy greens, such as spinach, kale, and Swiss chard

1 large onion, coarsely chopped

2 cloves garlic, minced

1 tablespoon grated fresh ginger

1 teaspoon ground cumin

1 teaspoon ground turmeric

1/2 teaspoon ground cinnamon

1/4 teaspoon crushed red pepper flakes

2 cups cooked or canned chickpeas

1 1/2 cups chickpea cooking liquid or water

1 1/2 cups diced potatoes

1 cup cauliflower florets

1 cup diced zucchini

1 cup green beans cut into 1-inch segments, or 1 cup fresh or frozen green peas

1/2 cup canned crushed tomatoes

1/2 teaspoon salt (reduce if cooking liquid is salted)

2 tablespoons almond butter or cashew butter

2 tablespoons chopped fresh cilantro

This mild but flavorful curry has an appealing mixture of vegetables, but feel free to change the selection if necessary. For example, zucchini can be replaced with extra cauliflower or winter squash, sweet potatoes can replace white potatoes, and so on. Accompany with Curried Tomato and Cucumber Salad (page 94) and brown rice or bread to sop up the juices.

1. Combine the greens, onion, garlic, ginger, cumin, turmeric, cinnamon, and red pepper flakes in a 15-inch skillet or large pot. Cook over medium heat, stirring frequently, for 5 minutes.

2. Add the chickpeas, cooking liquid or water, vegetables, and salt to the pot. If using frozen green peas, wait until the last few minutes of cooking to add them. Bring to a boil over high heat. Lower the heat to a simmer, cover, and cook for 20 to 30 minutes, or until the potatoes are tender.

3. In a small bowl, stir a little of the hot curry into the almond or cashew butter to melt. Return the liquid to the skillet and simmer over medium heat, stirring continuously, for 3 to 5 minutes, or until the sauce is creamy.

4. Adjust the salt to taste, if necessary, and sprinkle with the cilantro. Serve immediately to retain the creaminess.

TOFU AND TEMPEH ENTRÉES

BAKED TOFU STICKS

YIELD: 6 SERVINGS

2 pounds firm tofu

2 eggs, lightly beaten

1/2 cup cornmeal

1/2 cup wheat germ

1/4 cup finely chopped walnuts

1 teaspoon salt

1 teaspoon paprika

Generous pinch cayenne pepper

Baked Tofu Sticks are flavorful and fun to eat. Serve with lemon wedges and Better Than Ketchup (page 211) or Salsa Cruda (page 212) for dipping. For a complete meal, begin with grapefruit and accompany with corn on the cob and Creamy Miso Mustard Coleslaw (page 88) or a green salad.

1. Preheat the oven to 400°F.

2. Cut the tofu into sticks 3/4 inch thick and about 3 inches long. You should have 24 sticks. Pat dry with paper towels and set aside.

3. Place the eggs in a shallow bowl and set aside.

4. Combine the cornmeal, wheat germ, walnuts, salt, paprika, and cayenne pepper on a plate, mixing well.

5. Dip the tofu sticks in the beaten egg. Then roll the tofu in the dry mixture to coat. Transfer to a wire rack and let sit while preparing the remaining tofu. This recipe can be prepared up to a day in advance to this point and refrigerated. In fact, this will give the coating a chance to set.

6. Arrange the tofu in a single layer on an oiled baking sheet, and bake for 15 to 20 minutes, or until the coating is golden. Serve hot.

Baked Italian Tofu

YIELD: 4 SERVINGS

1 cup canned crushed tomatoes

2 large cloves garlic, minced

1 tablespoon balsamic vinegar

1 teaspoon dried oregano

1 teaspoon dried basil

1/4 teaspoon salt

1 pound firm or extra firm tofu, sliced 1/4 inch thick

In this dish, tofu has a thick coating, making it a flavorful entrée or sandwich filling. This dish can be enjoyed hot from the oven or at room temperature, and it reheats well.

1. Preheat the oven to 375°F.

2. Combine all of the ingredients except the tofu in a small bowl. Then spread half of the sauce over the bottom of a 9-x-13-inch baking dish or other shallow casserole large enough to hold the tofu in a single layer.

3. Arrange the tofu slices in a single layer over the tomato mixture. Spoon the remaining sauce over the tofu, spreading so that all surfaces are well coated.

4. Bake uncovered for 30 minutes, or until the sauce is quite hot and beginning to bubble. Serve hot or at room temperature.

Savory Baked Tofu

YIELD: 4 SERVINGS

1/4 cup soy sauce

1/4 cup water

1 large clove garlic, split

1 tablespoon lemon juice

1 teaspoon grated fresh ginger, or 1/4 teaspoon ground ginger

1 pound firm or extra firm tofu, sliced 1/4 inch thick

These firm, well-seasoned tofu slices are terrific as a dinner entrée accompanied by a grain or potatoes, in sandwiches, or simply eaten out of hand. Serve right from the oven, at room temperature, or chilled.

1. Preheat the oven to 350°F.

2. In a 9-x-13-inch baking dish or other shallow casserole large enough to hold the tofu in a single layer, combine all the ingredients except the tofu.

3. Arrange the tofu slices in a single layer over the soy sauce mixture and allow to sit for at least 5 minutes. Then turn the tofu so that both sides are coated with the mixture. If time permits, allow the tofu to marinate for 30 minutes or so.

4. Bake uncovered for 30 minutes, or until the tofu is dry and nicely browned. Serve hot, at room temperature, or chilled.

BAKED MEXICAN TOFU

YIELD: 4 SERVINGS

1 1/2 cups canned crushed tomatoes

1 large clove garlic, minced

1 tablespoon red or white wine vinegar

2 teaspoons chili powder

1 teaspoon ground cumin

1/2 teaspoon salt

1/4 teaspoon cayenne pepper

1 pound firm or extra firm tofu, sliced 1/4 inch thick

This recipe gives baked tofu Mexican flair. Serve on a bed of rice, or roll it inside tortillas. Like Baked Italian Tofu (page 118), this savory dish can be eaten hot from the oven or at room temperature, and reheats perfectly.

1. Preheat the oven to 375°F.

2. Combine all of the ingredients except the tofu in a small bowl. Then spread half of the sauce over the bottom of a 9-x-13-inch baking dish or other shallow casserole large enough to hold the tofu in a single layer.

3. Arrange the tofu slices in a single layer over the tomato mixture. Spoon the remaining sauce over the tofu, spreading so that all surfaces are well coated.

4. Bake uncovered for 30 minutes, or until the sauce is quite hot and beginning to bubble. Serve hot or at room temperature.

VARIATION

- For Baked Mexican Tempeh, substitute tempeh for the tofu and cut it into 1/4-inch-thick patties or strips.

SWEET AND SOUR TOFU AND VEGETABLES

YIELD: 4 SERVINGS

1 cup orange juice

1/4 cup canned crushed tomatoes

2 tablespoons soy sauce

1 small onion, cut into crescents

1/2 red pepper, cut into strips

1 tablespoon minced fresh ginger

4 cups mixed vegetables, such as carrots, cauliflower, broccoli, fennel, green beans, snow peas, and turnips, cut into 1- to 2-inch strips or bite-size pieces

1 pound firm or extra firm tofu, cut into 1-inch strips

1/2 cup frozen green peas, optional

1/4 cup white wine or rice vinegar

1 1/2 teaspoons prepared mustard

Serve this dish with brown rice or rice pasta. For extra flavor, drizzle a little toasted sesame oil over the grain.

1. Combine the orange juice, crushed tomatoes, and soy sauce in a small bowl. Pour 1/4 cup of this mixture into a large skillet, along with the onion, red pepper, and ginger. Cover and cook over medium heat for 5 minutes.

2. Add the mixed vegetables and tofu to the skillet, along with the remaining orange juice mixture. Bring to a boil over high heat. Then reduce the heat to a gentle simmer, cover, and cook for 10 to 15 minutes, or until the vegetables are just tender.

3. Add the green peas, if desired, and the vinegar and mustard to the skillet, stirring to mix well. Simmer uncovered for 5 minutes.

4. Taste for seasoning, adding more mustard if necessary, and serve hot.

"If you step back and look at the data, the optimum amount of red meat you eat should be zero."

–Dr. Walter Willet
Harvard School of Public Health

Simmered Soft Tofu with Vegetables

YIELD: 4 SERVINGS

$^{2}/_{3}$ cup water

$^{1}/_{4}$ cup soy sauce

1 small onion, diced

$^{1}/_{2}$ cup diced red pepper

1 hot pepper, minced, optional

3 cups snow peas or green beans cut into 1-inch pieces, or 3 cups frozen green peas

1 pound soft tofu

$^{1}/_{3}$ cup minced fresh parsley

$^{1}/_{4}$ cup sliced scallions

This delicate tofu-vegetable combination can stand on its own or be served over buckwheat soba, whole wheat linguini, brown rice, or another cooked grain.

1. Combine the water and soy sauce in a small bowl. Pour $^{1}/_{4}$ cup of this mixture into a large skillet, along with the onion and both the red and hot peppers. Bring to a simmer, cover, and cook over medium heat for 5 minutes.

2. Add the snow peas or green beans, if using, to the skillet along with the remaining soy sauce mixture. Cover and cook over medium heat for 8 to 10 additional minutes, or until the vegetables are just tender. If using frozen green peas, do not add until later.

3. Drain the tofu if necessary and pat dry. Using a spoon, break the tofu into generous bite-size chunks.

4. Add the tofu to the skillet along with the frozen green peas, if using, and the parsley and scallions. Simmer uncovered for 5 to 8 minutes, or until the tofu is hot, and serve immediately.

Variation

- For a more robust dish, add $^{1}/_{2}$ cup of sliced portobello mushrooms or soaked dried porcini mushrooms to the skillet along with the snow peas or green beans.

Smothered Tofu with Peas

YIELD: 4 SERVINGS

- 3 large Vidalia, Maui, or Spanish onions, halved and thinly sliced
- 3/4 cup water, divided
- 2 tablespoons soy sauce
- 1 pound firm or extra firm tofu, cut into bite-size cubes
- 1 tablespoon paprika
- Generous pinch cayenne pepper
- 1 cup fresh or frozen green peas

In this dish, slow-cooked onions form a sweet gravy that smothers the tofu. High-quality paprika makes a big difference in the flavor, as it is the predominant seasoning. A bit more cayenne than indicated will provide a lift if the paprika is too bland. Serve with your favorite grain, pasta, or crusty whole grain bread, and add a cooked vegetable and salad.

1. Combine the onions, 1/4 cup of the water, and the soy sauce in a large heavy skillet. Cover and cook over medium-low heat, stirring occasionally, for 15 minutes, or until the onions are soft.

2. Add the tofu, paprika, cayenne pepper, and another 1/4 cup of water to the skillet. Mix well, cover, and continue to cook for another 15 minutes, stirring occasionally. If using fresh peas, add them after 5 minutes, allowing 10 minutes for them to cook. If using frozen peas, wait until cooking is almost complete before adding.

3. Gradually add the remaining 1/4 cup of water to produce a rich gravy. The dish is done when the onions are very soft and almost sauce-like in consistency. Serve while still warm.

Soy Balls

YIELD: 4 SERVINGS

- 1 pound firm tofu
- 1/2 cup wheat germ
- 1 large clove garlic, minced
- 3 tablespoons minced onion
- 1 teaspoon dried oregano
- 1 tablespoon soy sauce
- 2 to 3 cups sauce of choice

The character of these Soy Balls is determined largely by the sauce. You could choose an Italian- or Mexican-style tomato sauce, or you could choose something creamy, such as Creamy Mushroom Gravy (page 215). Serve over pasta, brown rice, barley, or kasha, or arrange on whole grain bread for a hot sandwich. Round out the menu with a cooked vegetable and salad.

1. Preheat the oven to 375°F.

2. Pat the tofu dry, cut into chunks, and place in a mixing bowl. Then mash with a fork or potato masher.

3. Add all of the remaining ingredients except the sauce to the tofu. Using your hands, knead the mixture until it is evenly combined and holds together when compressed.

4. Using generous tablespoonfuls, shape the tofu mixtures into 16 balls, each about 1½ inches in diameter, and arrange on an oiled baking sheet.

5. Bake for 20 minutes or until firm and golden.

6. While the Soy Balls are baking, heat your sauce of choice in a large pot. Add the baked Soy Balls, warm through, and serve hot.

Creamed Tofu with Peas

YIELD: 4 SERVINGS

- ¼ cup soy sauce, plus additional soy sauce for seasoning
- 3 tablespoons cornstarch
- 3 cups soy milk
- 8 ounces frozen tofu, thawed (see inset on page 124)
- 1 teaspoon poultry seasoning
- 8 ounces firm tofu, cut into ½-inch cubes
- 1 cup fresh or frozen green peas

This makes a homey meal when served over a grain such as brown rice, wild rice, kasha, millet, or quinoa, or when spooned over whole grain English muffins or toast.

1. Combine ¼ cup of soy sauce and the cornstarch in a 1½- to 2-quart saucepan and stir until smooth. Gradually stir in the soy milk. Place over medium heat and cook, stirring constantly, until the gravy thickens and just comes to a gentle boil.

2. Squeeze the moisture from the defrosted frozen tofu, place in a bowl, and sprinkle lightly with soy sauce. Squeeze to distribute the flavoring evenly. Then tear the tofu into bite-size pieces.

3. Stir the poultry seasoning into the gravy. Add the cubed fresh tofu, thawed tofu, and peas. Simmer gently, stirring continuously, for about 2 minutes or until the tofu is heated through and the vegetables are tender. Serve hot.

Variation

- Replace the peas with fresh or frozen corn kernels or tiny broccoli florets.

Freezing Tofu

A wonderful illustration of tofu's versatility is that it can be frozen for long-term keeping. Moreover, freezing dramatically changes the texture of tofu—so much so that it is like an entirely different food in terms of taste and use. While fresh tofu is soft and dense, frozen tofu is chewy with an open, coarse texture. Some people compare it to chicken; in fact, it can be torn into small pieces and used in chicken salads and many other recipes that call for poultry. Freezing also increases tofu's sponge-like ability to absorb flavors. Firm tofu is the preferred choice for freezing.

To Freeze Tofu:

1. Slice the tofu into ½-inch-thick pieces, each weighing about 2 ounces.

2. Wrap each piece in freezer-proof paper or foil. This individual packaging keeps the tofu pieces from sticking together and makes it easy to remove them as needed and defrost them quickly. As an alternative, the tofu pieces can be packaged in a single bundle by laying them out next to one another and building layers, if need be, with a piece of freezer-proof paper between them.

3. Freeze and use within six months.

To Defrost Frozen Tofu:

1. Remove the freezer packaging and place the tofu in a heatproof bowl.

2. Pour boiling water over the tofu until it is submerged. Allow to sit about 10 minutes, or until the water is cool enough to touch.

3. Remove the tofu and if not completely defrosted, repeat the process.

4. When completely thawed, press the tofu firmly between your palms to expel all moisture. It is now ready to use.

TOFU A LA KING

YIELD: 4 SERVINGS

12 ounces frozen tofu, thawed (see inset on page 124)

1 cup cold water

2 tablespoons soy sauce

1/4 cup sherry, divided

1 medium onion, chopped

1/2 cup chopped red pepper

2 cups diced mushrooms, any type

1/4 cup whole wheat flour

1 1/2 cups soy milk

1/2 teaspoon salt

Hot pepper sauce

1/4 cup chopped fresh parsley

Serve this rich, flavorful dish over Golden Biscuits (page 46), whole grain toast, or rice.

1. Squeeze the moisture from the thawed tofu and place in a bowl. Combine the cold water and soy sauce and pour the mixture over the tofu. Allow the tofu to marinate while you cook the sauce.

2. In a 1 1/2-quart saucepan, combine 2 tablespoons of the sherry with the onion, red pepper, and mushrooms. Cover and cook over medium heat for about 8 minutes, or until the mushrooms are soft and have released their liquid.

3. Stir the flour into the mushroom mixture. Then gradually stir in the soy milk. Cook over medium heat, stirring continuously, for 5 to 8 minutes, or until the mixture is thick and begins to boil.

4. Remove the tofu from the soy sauce marinade and press once again to expel the moisture. Tear into bite-size pieces.

5. Add the tofu to the mushroom mixture along with the remaining 2 tablespoons of sherry, the salt, and the hot pepper sauce to taste. If the sauce seems too thick, gradually stir in a little more soy milk. Continue to cook and stir for a few minutes to heat through. Adjust the seasonings to taste.

6. Garnish with the parsley after spooning over biscuits, toast, or rice.

TOFU CHILI

YIELD: 4 SERVINGS

1 pound frozen tofu, thawed (see inset on page 124)

$1\frac{3}{4}$ cups Quick Spicy Mexican Tomato Sauce (page 213)

This quickly made chili can be served on corn bread, on Three-Grain Polenta Bread (page 203), or with rice and tortillas.

1. Squeeze the moisture from the thawed tofu and tear into bite-size pieces with your hands.

2. Combine the tofu with the sauce in a 1- to $1\frac{1}{2}$-quart pot and simmer for 5 minutes, or until heated through. Serve hot.

ROSANNE'S WATERCRESS TOFU

YIELD: 4 SERVINGS

$\frac{1}{2}$ cup thinly sliced scallions

2 tablespoons soy sauce, divided

1 pound soft tofu, cut into bite-size cubes

$\frac{1}{4}$ cup sunflower seeds

2 tablespoons chopped fresh ginger

$\frac{3}{4}$ cup water

2 good-size bunches watercress, trimmed of tough stems (12 ounces, or 8 cups loosely packed)

1 teaspoon toasted sesame oil, optional

While any style tofu can be used, we prefer soft tofu in this dish. If watercress is not available, substitute fresh spinach, arugula, or a combination of these greens. This tofu dish is excellent served over brown rice mixed with up to a third kamut or barley.

1. Combine the scallions with 1 tablespoon of the soy sauce in a wok or large skillet. Cook over medium heat, stirring continuously, for a few minutes.

2. Add the remaining tablespoon of soy sauce and the tofu, sunflower seeds, and ginger to the wok. Continue to cook and stir for about 5 minutes, gradually adding water as the pan becomes dry.

3. Add any remaining water along with the watercress, and continue cooking and stirring for 5 to 10 minutes, or until the greens wilt and become tender.

4. Remove the wok from the heat, stir in the sesame oil, if using, and serve hot.

Fajitas

YIELD: 4 SERVINGS

1 pound frozen tofu, thawed (see inset on page 124)

1/2 cup fresh lime juice (2 to 3 limes)

2 tablespoons soy sauce

2 teaspoons chili powder

2 hot peppers, minced

2 cloves garlic, minced

2 medium onions, sliced into thin crescents

2 medium zucchini (8 to 10 ounces each), cut into sticks 2 inches long and 1/4 inch thick

1 large red or green pepper, cut into strips

8 corn tortillas, or 4 large whole wheat tortillas

1 avocado, peeled and diced as garnish

Plain nonfat or low-fat yogurt as garnish, optional

Fajitas are a popular Mexican dish that you eat by scooping or rolling up a filling in pieces of tortilla. This version features frozen tofu, but can be varied by substituting strips of tempeh. Because marinating is involved, preparation should begin at least an hour before cooking. Accompany the fajitas with brown rice and Cucumber Tomato Salsa (page 89).

1. Squeeze the moisture from the thawed tofu and cut it into thin strips.

2. Combine the lime juice, soy sauce, chili powder, hot peppers, and garlic in a large container or bowl. Add the tofu strips and marinate for 1 hour at room temperature, or longer in the refrigerator.

3. Place a 15-inch skillet, wok, or large pot over high heat. Add the onions, zucchini, red or green pepper, marinated tofu, and any remaining marinade to the skillet and cook, stirring often, for about 10 minutes, or until the vegetables are cooked but still crisp.

4. To prepare the tortillas, if you have a gas stove, cook one at a time by holding with tongs and warming briefly over a burner. Then transfer to a cloth napkin and wrap to keep warm and pliable, piling up the tortillas until they are all hot. Alternatively, stack the tortillas together, wrap in foil, and heat in a 350°F to 400°F oven for about 10 minutes, or until steamy.

5. Serve each person a portion of the tofu mixture accompanied by the hot tortillas, avocado, and yogurt, if desired. To eat, scoop the tofu-vegetable mixture into a tortilla and top with the avocado and yogurt.

EGGPLANT ROLLATINI

**YIELD:
4 AMPLE SERVINGS**

2 medium eggplants (1 to 1½ pounds each)

Olive oil

1 pound firm tofu

2 tablespoons lemon juice

2 tablespoons tahini (sesame seed paste)

2 tablespoons light miso

1 clove garlic, minced

1 (10-ounce) package frozen chopped spinach, thawed, or 1 cup finely chopped, pressed fresh spinach

4 cups Puttanesca Sauce (page 214) or tomato sauce of choice

Rolled filled eggplant slices are similar to manicotti or cannelloni, with the vegetable serving the same purpose that the pasta does in the familiar Italian dishes. This entire dish can be assembled in advance and refrigerated for later baking. It also reheats well, but freezing is not recommended.

1. Preheat the broiler.

2. Peel the eggplants and cut lengthwise into ¼-inch-thick slices to make 16 slices.

3. Generously oil a large baking sheet with olive oil. Arrange the eggplant slices in a single layer on the sheet, then turn them over so both sides are lightly coated with oil.

4. Broil 6 inches below the heat for about 5 minutes on each side, or until lightly browned. You may have to do this in two batches. Set aside.

5. To prepare the filling, purée the tofu in a food processor or mash thoroughly with a potato masher. Mix in the lemon juice, tahini, and miso. Add the garlic. Squeeze the spinach to remove all moisture, and stir into the tofu until evenly combined.

6. Preheat the oven to 350°F.

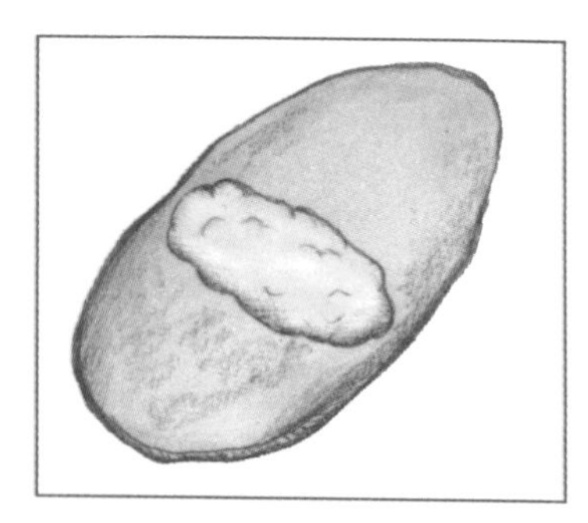
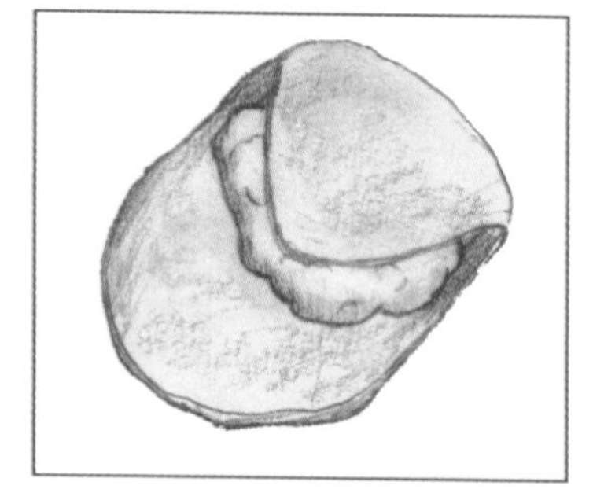
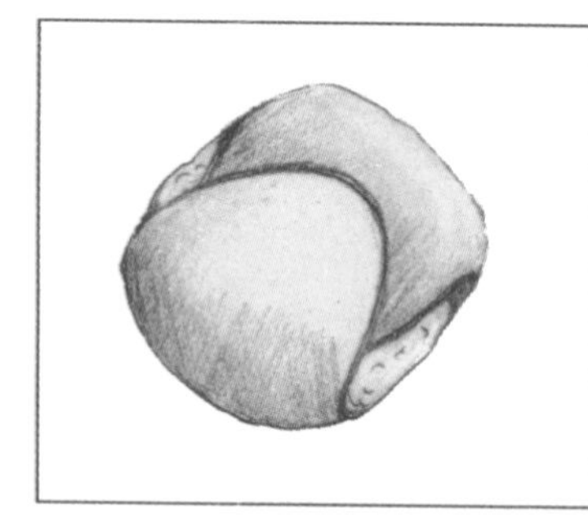

Filling and Folding an Eggplant Slice

7. Place a sausage-like strip of filling across the center of each eggplant slice, using about 2 tablespoons of filling per slice. Fold the bottom and top of the slice over the filling.

8. Pour half the sauce into a 9-x-13-inch baking pan, spreading the sauce to cover the bottom. Arrange the eggplant rolls side by side in the sauce, and pour the remaining sauce over all.

9. Cover and bake for 20 minutes. Remove the cover and bake for 10 additional minutes, or until the eggplant is easily pierced with a fork. Allow to sit for about 10 minutes before serving.

Individual Tofu Loaves

YIELD: 4 SERVINGS

1 pound firm or extra firm tofu

1/4 cup oat bran

1/4 cup chopped walnuts

2 tablespoons miso, any type

2 teaspoons poultry seasoning

1/2 teaspoon ground ginger

If desired, you can cover these Individual Tofu Loaves with a generous blanket of sauce. We think they make an especially good match with Sweet Onion Gravy (page 217), Creamy Mushroom Gravy (page 215), or Tahini-Mushroom Gravy (page 216). You can also serve them with a rich tomato sauce.

1. Preheat the oven to 375°F.

2. Pat the tofu dry, cut into chunks, and place in a mixing bowl. Then mash with a fork or potato masher.

3. Add all of the remaining ingredients to the tofu and knead with clean hands until the mixture is well blended and holds together when compressed. Shape into 4 mounds and arrange on an oiled baking sheet.

4. Bake for 20 minutes, or until the surface of the loaves is browned. Serve warm.

Variation

■ For Tofu Burgers, shape the mixture into 8 flat patties instead of 4 mounds. Bake as directed above and serve on whole wheat buns with your favorite accompaniments, such as ketchup, onion, tomato slices, sprouts, lettuce, or a spicy salsa.

Tofu-Stuffed Sweet Red Peppers

YIELD: 4 SERVINGS

4 large red peppers (about 8 ounces each)

1 1/2 pounds regular or firm tofu

2/3 cup dry whole grain breadcrumbs

1/2 cup sunflower seeds, ground (3/4 cup sunflower meal)

1/2 cup chopped fresh parsley

1/4 cup flaxseed meal (page 17)

1/4 cup wheat germ

3 large cloves garlic, minced

2 teaspoons dried oregano

1 teaspoon salt

While these peppers make a great entrée, they can also be used as an appetizer. Just place half a pepper on a bed of fresh salad greens and top with Agliata (page 217).

1. Cut the peppers in half lengthwise, through the stem. Remove the seeds and any tough ribs, and set the peppers aside.

2. Place the tofu in a bowl and mash with a potato masher or fork. Add all of the remaining ingredients and mix well to thoroughly blend. Then knead gently by hand until the mixture holds together.

3. Pack about 1/2 cup of filling into each pepper half. Arrange the pepper halves, filling up, in a vegetable steamer set over boiling water. Steam for 20 minutes or just until the peppers are tender, and serve warm.

Tempeh Burgers

YIELD: 2 SERVINGS

8 ounces tempeh

1/3 cup water

2 tablespoon soy sauce

Serve these burgers on whole wheat hamburger rolls or toasted whole grain English muffins, and load on the sprouts, sliced fresh tomato, onion, and Better Than Ketchup (page 211).

1. Cut the tempeh into 2 burger-size squares. You can leave them the thickness of the tempeh or slice each through the middle to make 2 thinner patties.

2. Combine the water and soy sauce in a small dish.

3. Heat a heavy skillet, preferably cast iron, over medium heat. Add the tempeh patties and about half the diluted soy sauce to the skillet, cover, and cook for 5 minutes, or until the tempeh starts to color on the bottom.

4. Turn the tempeh over, add the remaining liquid, and cover. Cook for 5 additional minutes.

5. Remove the cover and continue to cook the patties until the liquid is gone and the tempeh is nicely colored on both sides. Serve hot.

Maple Pecan Tempeh

YIELD: 4 SERVINGS

1 pound tempeh

3 tablespoons prepared mustard

1/3 cup cornmeal

3 tablespoons soy sauce

3 tablespoons maple syrup

1/4 cup chopped pecans

1/4 cup water

These tempeh cutlets have a sweet nutty topping. Serve them as a focal point of a "Southern" meal that includes Louisiana Sweet Potatoes (page 189)—or plain baked or mashed sweet potatoes—and cooked greens.

1. Cut the tempeh into 8 "cutlets," each about 1/4 inch thick.

2. Spread a thin coating of mustard on both sides of each tempeh cutlet. Then dredge with the cornmeal.

3. Wipe a large heavy skillet with oil to coat, and place over medium heat. Add the tempeh and cook for 3 to 5 minutes on each side, or until browned.

4. Combine the soy sauce, maple syrup, and pecans in a small bowl, and spoon evenly over the tempeh.

5. Reduce the heat to low and pour the water into the bottom of the skillet, standing back, as the water will sputter. Cover the pan and cook for 5 additional minutes, or until the liquid is absorbed and the tempeh is coated with the sauce and nuts. Serve warm.

STUFFED PEPPERS

YIELD: 4 SERVINGS

3 cups tomato juice

2 carrots, peeled and chopped

1 small hot pepper, optional

2 cloves garlic, minced

4 green peppers

1 pound regular or firm tofu

2 cups cooked grain, such as kasha, millet, barley, oat groats, or short grain brown rice

1/4 cup chopped onion

1 tablespoon soy sauce

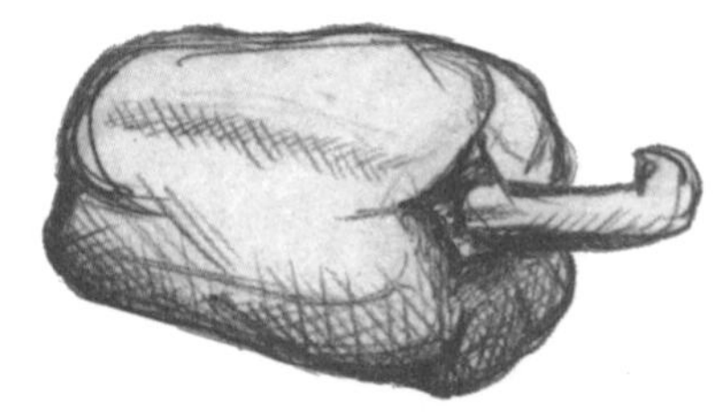

This is a great way to use leftover cooked grains.

1. In a large skillet or broad pot that will hold the pepper halves in a single layer, combine the tomato juice, carrots, hot pepper, and garlic. Bring to a boil over high heat. Then reduce the heat to low and simmer gently while you prepare the peppers and tofu.

2. Cut the peppers in half lengthwise, through the stem. Remove the seeds and any tough ribs, and set the peppers aside.

3. Place the tofu in a bowl and mash with a potato masher or fork. Add the grain, onion, and soy sauce, and mix well.

4. Divide the tofu mixture among the pepper halves, packing it into the peppers. Then arrange the peppers, filling side up, in the gently simmering sauce.

5. Spoon a little sauce over each pepper, cover, and cook for 30 minutes, or until the peppers are just tender and the carrots in the sauce are soft.

6. Remove the peppers from the pot. Using a potato masher, mash the carrots into the sauce, creating a coarse consistency. If preferred, the sauce can be transferred to a blender and puréed.

7. Spoon the sauce over the peppers to serve. If you do not wish to serve immediately, return the peppers to the sauce and reheat briefly before eating.

Baked Corn-Tempeh Hash

YIELD: 4 SERVINGS

8 ounces tempeh, crumbled or coarsely chopped (2 cups)

1 medium green pepper, chopped

1 medium onion, chopped

2 tablespoons sherry or dry wine

2 medium tomatoes, diced, or 2 cups drained canned tomatoes

1/2 teaspoon salt

1/4 teaspoon ground nutmeg

1/4 teaspoon cayenne pepper

1/2 cup crumbled whole grain bread

1/2 cup soy milk

1 cup fresh or frozen corn kernels

Hash is generally regarded as a "family" dish, and this one is quite tasty. For more elegant fare, stuff the hash inside tomatoes or peppers, as described in the Variation found at the end of the recipe.

1. Preheat the oven to 350°F.

2. Combine the tempeh, green pepper, onion, and sherry or wine in a large skillet. Cover and cook over medium heat for 8 to 10 minutes, or until the onion has softened.

3. Add the tomatoes, salt, nutmeg, and cayenne pepper to the skillet. Increase the heat to medium-high and cook, stirring frequently, for about 5 minutes, or until the tomato softens. Remove the skillet from the heat.

4. While the tempeh cooks, combine the crumbled bread and soy milk in a small bowl. When the tomato mixture is finished cooking, mash the bread and add to the skillet along with any unabsorbed soy milk and the corn. Mix well.

5. Transfer the hash mixture to an oiled 9-inch baking pan or shallow 1-quart casserole. Bake for 30 minutes or until the hash is piping hot, but still a bit moist. If the hash seems to be drying out during baking, pour a little soy milk over the surface as it cooks. Serve hot.

Variation

- For a more elegant meal, stuff the unbaked hash into 8 medium-size hollowed-out tomatoes or blanched peppers (remove the tops and steam for 5 minutes), or a combination of the two. Plan on 2 stuffed vegetables per serving. Bake as directed above, placing the tomatoes in an oiled baking dish, and the peppers in a baking dish surrounded by hot water to a depth of 1 inch.

PICADILLO

YIELD: 4 SERVINGS

1 pound tempeh, cut into thin strips
1 small onion, chopped
1 medium green pepper, chopped
2 cloves garlic, minced
3 tablespoons water
1 tablespoon soy sauce
1 1/2 cups canned crushed tomatoes or tomato sauce
1/4 cup currants or chopped raisins
2 tablespoons capers
1 tablespoon molasses
1 tablespoon cider vinegar
1 teaspoon ground cumin
1 teaspoon ground cinnamon
2 tablespoons chopped olives, any type

Picadillo is a classic Latin American dish—a cross between hash and Sloppy Joes. While the recipe varies with the country of origin, the seasonings create a surprising interplay of sweet, salty, aromatic, and astringent flavors. Serve with brown rice, Glazed Plantains (page 183), and a tossed salad. Or simply roll up in warm corn or whole wheat tortillas.

1. Combine the tempeh, onion, green pepper, garlic, water, and soy sauce in a 3- to 4-quart pot. Cover and cook over low heat, stirring occasionally, for 10 minutes.

2. Add all of the remaining ingredients except for the olives to the pot. Cover and continue to cook for 10 to 15 minutes, or until quite hot.

3. Stir in the olives and serve hot.

"As we talked of freedom and justice one day for all, we sat down to steaks. I am eating misery, I thought, as I took the first bite. And spit it out."

–Alice Walker

TEMPEH-MUSHROOM STEW

YIELD: 4 TO 6 SERVINGS

2 pounds thin-skinned potatoes (about 6 medium)

1 pound asparagus or green beans, trimmed and broken into pieces (4 cups)

8 ounces mushrooms, any type, sliced (3 cups)

1 large onion, cut into crescents

12 ounces tempeh, cut into 1-inch cubes

2/3 cup water

1 tablespoon soy sauce

2 cups soy milk

1 teaspoon dried thyme

3 tablespoons capers

2 tablespoons lemon juice

Salt

Freshly ground pepper

Ground nutmeg

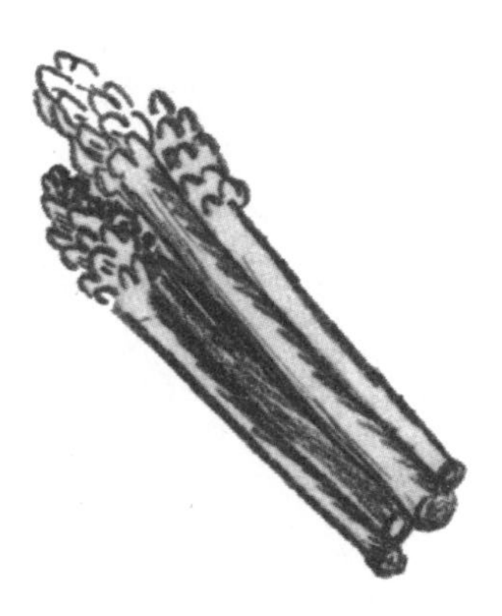

This classic stew can be served with a grapefruit appetizer, a large salad, and crusty bread.

1. Cut the potatoes into quarters if small to medium in size, or sixths if medium to large. Steam for 15 to 20 minutes, or until tender.

2. While the potatoes are steaming, combine the asparagus or green beans, mushrooms, and onion in a 3- to 5-quart pot. Cover and cook over medium heat, stirring occasionally, for about 10 minutes, or until the onion is translucent and the mushrooms begin to give up their liquid.

3. Add the tempeh, water, and soy sauce to the mushroom mixture. Cover and cook for about 10 minutes, or until the vegetables are tender.

4. Remove a third of the cooked potatoes and combine with the soy milk in the blender. Purée until smooth. (The skins can be left on the potatoes or not, according to your preference.) Cut the remaining potatoes into 1-inch pieces.

5. Add the puréed potatoes, the cut-up potatoes, and the thyme to the mushroom mixture. Heat through, stirring gently, for 5 to 8 minutes, or until the sauce is thick. If the sauce is too thick, add additional soy milk to obtain the desired consistency.

6. Remove the pot from the heat and stir in the capers and lemon juice. Season to taste with salt and pepper, and grate some fresh nutmeg over the top. Serve hot.

ASIAN GRILL

YIELD: 4 SERVINGS

$^1/_3$ cup lime or lemon juice

$^1/_3$ cup soy sauce

1 tablespoon molasses, or 2 tablespoons fruit juice-sweetened orange marmalade

1 teaspoon minced orange zest

2 cloves garlic, minced

1-inch segment fresh ginger, peeled and grated

1 pound tempeh or tofu, sliced $^1/_3$ inch thick

Marinated tofu and tempeh are both excellent grilled. If you want to include some vegetables as well, just make twice as much marinade and you will have enough for 6 to 8 mushroom caps and some broccoli, eggplant, cauliflower, or sweet potato slices. (See the Variation at the end of the recipe.)

1. Prepare the marinade by combining everything but the tempeh or tofu in a pan large enough to hold the food in a single layer.

2. Arrange the tempeh or tofu in the pan with the marinade. Turn to coat, cover, and marinate for 1 to 2 hours at room temperature or longer in the refrigerator, turning the tempeh or tofu occasionally in the marinade.

3. Cook over hot coals or a gas grill for about 5 minutes per side, or until the surface is nicely browned, using any remaining marinade as a basting sauce while cooking. Serve warm.

VARIATION

- If desired, marinate and cook your vegetables along with the tempeh or tofu. Just double the marinade and include thin broccoli trees, cauliflower florets, $^1/_4$-inch-thick rounds of eggplant, clean mushrooms caps, thick rounds or wedges of onion, and $^1/_4$-inch-thick slices of sweet potato.

Barbecued Tofu

YIELD: 4 SERVINGS

1/4 cup soy sauce

1/4 cup orange juice

2 tablespoons tomato paste

1 tablespoon chopped garlic

1 1/2 teaspoons olive oil

1 1/2 teaspoons lemon juice

1/2 teaspoon dried oregano

Freshly ground pepper

1 pound firm or extra firm tofu, sliced 1/2 inch thick

Cook the tofu on an outdoor or stove-top grill, and serve it with lots of vegetables, a grain, and a green salad.

1. Prepare the marinade by combining everything but the tofu in a pan large enough to hold the tofu in a single layer. Be sure to add a generous amount of pepper.

2. Arrange the tofu in the pan with the marinade. Turn to coat, cover, and marinate for 1 to 2 hours at room temperature or longer in the refrigerator, turning the tofu occasionally in the marinade.

3. Cook over hot coals or a gas grill for about 8 to 10 minutes per side, or until the surface is firm and lightly charred. Use any remaining sauce to baste the tofu while cooking. Serve warm.

Tempeh Kebabs

YIELD: 2 TO 4 SERVINGS

1/2 cup water

2 tablespoons soy sauce

12 ounces tempeh, cut into 16 cubes

Vegetables of choice, including onion wedges, chunks of red or green pepper, tomato wedges, and whole mushrooms, optional

Depending on what else is on the menu, and whether the kebabs contain just tempeh or vegetables as well, plan on one to two skewers per person.

1. Combine the water and soy sauce in a bowl. Add the tempeh cubes and allow to soak for 15 minutes, or until the tempeh has absorbed the liquid.

2. Thread 4 cubes of tempeh on each of 4 skewers, alternating with pieces of vegetable, if desired. Cook over hot coals or a gas grill for about 5 minutes on each side, or until the tempeh is nicely browned. Serve warm.

SHISH KEBAB IN A BAG

YIELD: 4 SERVINGS

$\frac{1}{2}$ cup water

2 tablespoons soy sauce

12 ounces tempeh, cut into 1-inch cubes

1 small eggplant (about 1 pound), cut into small chunks

2 small tomatoes or 4 plum tomatoes, cut into small chunks

1 green pepper, cut into strips

1 small onion, cut into thin rings

2 medium potatoes (about 12 ounces), thinly sliced

4 large mushrooms, thinly sliced

1 teaspoon dried oregano

1 lemon, cut into 8 wedges

These individual packets of tempeh and vegetables are designed to cook directly in hot coals, making them ideal for cookouts, campfires, or even fireplace cooking. The packets can be assembled ahead of time and held in a cooler or refrigerator until it is time to cook.

1. Combine the water and soy sauce in a bowl. Add the tempeh cubes and marinate while preparing the remaining ingredients.

2. Prepare four 12-inch squares of heavy-duty aluminum foil or double layers of regular foil. Divide the vegetables and tempeh into 4 even portions, and place 1 portion in the center of each sheet. Fold up the edges to form a bowl around the vegetables.

3. Season each packet with $\frac{1}{4}$ teaspoon oregano, the juice from 1 lemon wedge, and any leftover soy marinade. Enclose completely in the foil, folding the edges several times to seal.

4. Place the packets directly on the hot coals of a grill or in the embers of a campfire or fireplace, and cook for 20 minutes.

5. Lift the packets carefully from the heat with long-handled tongs or a long spatula. Open one to test for doneness. When done, the vegetables will be tender.

6. Distribute the packets and let everyone eat directly from the foil dish, or transfer the contents to plates. Be sure to let the food cool a bit before tasting, as it will be very hot. Serve the remaining lemon wedges on the side along with salt and pepper for individual seasoning.

MOSTLY BEAN ENTRÉES

BRAISED FENNEL WITH WHITE BEANS

YIELD: 4 GENEROUS SERVINGS

1 large or 2 medium bulbs fennel (1 pound)

1/2 cup bean cooking liquid or water

1 1/2 cups diced red or new potatoes

1 large clove garlic, minced

1/2 teaspoon salt (omit if beans are salted)

1/4 teaspoon crushed red pepper flakes

1 cup diced fresh plum tomatoes or drained canned tomatoes

1 tablespoon lemon juice

2 cups cooked or canned white beans, drained

2 tablespoons chopped black olives

Fennel has a delicate licorice flavor that goes especially well with white beans. Either home-cooked or canned beans can be used in this dish. For the rest of the meal, consider grilled portobello mushrooms, Quick White Pita Pizzas (page 69) with cooked greens, or crusty bread with Onion Butter (page 59) or Tahini Garlic Spread (page 56).

1. Trim the stem and feathery leaves from the fennel. Discard the stalk. Mince the leaves to make 1 tablespoon. Reserve the remaining leaves for another use.

2. Cut the fennel bulb in half lengthwise. Remove the core and discard. Slice the fennel into thin wedges. You should have about 4 cups.

3. Bring the bean cooking liquid or water to a boil in a medium-size saucepan. Add the fennel leaves, fennel wedges, potatoes, garlic, salt, and red pepper flakes. Lower the heat to a simmer, cover, and cook for about 10 minutes, or until the potatoes are tender but still hold their shape.

4. Add the tomatoes and lemon juice to the saucepan and mix well. Stir in the beans and olives and cook, uncovered, for 2 to 3 minutes, or until heated through. Serve warm.

White Beans and Carrots with Pesto

YIELD: 4 SERVINGS

1 cup sliced carrots

4 cups cooked or canned white beans or black-eyed peas

3/4 cup Creamy Walnut Pesto (page 210) or Tomato Almond Pesto (page 210)

Pesto sauce is a versatile flavoring that should not be regarded solely as a pasta sauce.

1. Steam the carrots or cook in a small amount of boiling water for 5 to 8 minutes, just until tender.

2. Transfer the carrots to a medium-size pot, add the beans, and place over medium heat until heated through.

3. Just before serving, remove the pot from the heat and stir in the pesto. Mix gently until the beans and carrots are completely covered with the sauce. Serve hot.

Cabbage with White Beans

YIELD: 4 SERVINGS

12 ounces cabbage, cut into 1/4-inch-thick strips (4 to 5 cups)

1 1/2 cups bean cooking liquid, vegetable broth, or water

3 cloves garlic, sliced

3 cups cooked or canned cannellini or other large white beans

1 generous tablespoon caraway seeds

Salt

Freshly ground pepper

Both home-cooked and canned beans work well in this dish. If the bean cooking liquid is insufficient, you can add water or vegetable broth. Serve with a flavorful grain, such as Kasha with Stewed Onions (page 200).

1. Combine the cabbage, cooking liquid, and garlic in a large pot. Cover and stew over medium heat for 10 minutes, or until tender.

2. Add the beans and caraway seeds to the pot and cook uncovered for about 10 minutes, stirring occasionally, until a rich gravy forms.

3. Season to taste with salt and pepper, and serve hot.

UNSTUFFED CABBAGE

YIELD: 4 SERVINGS

2 cups tomato juice

1/3 cup chopped prunes (5 large or 8 medium pitted prunes)

2 cloves garlic, minced

2 tablespoons lemon juice

1 tablespoon molasses

1 tablespoon minced fresh ginger

2-inch piece cinnamon stick

1 1/2 pounds cabbage, cut into 1/2-inch strips (about 8 cups)

3 cups cooked or canned cannellini or other large white beans, well drained

This dish is similar to stuffed cabbage, but requires much less work. While home-cooked dried beans are preferred, canned can be substituted for an easy last-minute meal. For maximum appeal, top each serving with a generous amount of yogurt cheese (page 22) and accompany with brown rice, quinoa, millet, or cracked wheat.

1. Combine the tomato juice, prunes, garlic, lemon juice, molasses, ginger, and cinnamon stick in a large pot, and bring to a boil over high heat.

2. Add the cabbage to the pot, cover, and reduce the heat to a simmer. Cook over gentle heat for 10 minutes, or until the cabbage is tender.

3. Add the beans to the cabbage. (If using canned beans, be sure to rinse them in a strainer to remove all traces of canning liquid first.) Simmer uncovered for 3 to 5 minutes, or just until heated through.

4. Remove the cinnamon stick before serving. For best flavor, serve warm but not piping hot.

"Until he extends the circle of compassion to all living things, man will not himself find peace."

–Albert Schweitzer

White Beans with Swiss Chard

YIELD: 4 TO 6 SERVINGS

1 cup dried white cannellini or Great Northern beans

3 cups water

1 large onion, chopped

2 stalks celery, thinly sliced

2 carrots, diced

5 cloves garlic, minced

12 ounces plum tomatoes, chopped (about 2 cups)

1/4 teaspoon cayenne pepper

1 pound Swiss chard, coarsely chopped

1/2 cup dry red wine

1 teaspoon salt

This dish has a noticeable bite, but those who like their food mild can reduce or omit the cayenne. A suggested menu includes baked or grilled winter squash, whole wheat pita bread, and some olives, carrot sticks, and red pepper wedges. If a grain is desired, barley makes a hearty choice, while millet is lighter.

1. Combine the beans and water in a large pot. Bring to a boil for 2 minutes. Then cover, remove from the heat, and let soak for 1 hour or longer.

2. Return the beans to a boil for 5 minutes, cover, and simmer gently for 20 minutes.

3. Meanwhile, in a separate 5-quart pot, combine the onion, celery, carrots, and garlic. Cover and stew over medium heat for about 10 minutes, or until the onions are translucent.

4. Add the tomatoes and cayenne pepper to the onion mixture and cook over medium-high heat, mashing with a spoon until the tomatoes start to soften.

5. Add the Swiss chard to the onion mixture, stirring to wilt. Then add the wine, salt, and partially cooked beans along with any cooking liquid. Cover and simmer gently for about 45 minutes, or until the beans are quite tender.

6. Remove the pot from the heat and let sit at least 10 minutes before serving. For best flavor, serve lukewarm or at room temperature.

Serving Temperatures

Pay attention to any advice the recipes provide regarding serving temperature. Sometimes, eating foods warm, rather than piping hot, maximizes their flavor.

White Bean Ratatouille

YIELD: 6 SERVINGS

1 pound eggplant

3/4 teaspoon salt, divided

1 cup dried Great Northern, navy, or pea beans, cooked and drained (page 22)

3 cloves garlic, minced, divided

2 stalks celery, sliced into 1/4-inch pieces

1 medium green pepper (about 5 ounces), cut into small strips

2 medium yellow crookneck squash (5 to 6 ounces each), sliced into 1/4-inch-thick rounds

1 medium onion, thinly sliced

2 cups chopped Italian plum tomatoes

2 tablespoons capers

2 tablespoons red or white wine vinegar

Salt, optional

Freshly ground pepper

This casserole of beans and vegetables is typical fare in the south of France. Although the recipe seems long, it is very easy to execute and produces a generous amount. Leftovers can be kept in the refrigerator for about a week and make a good sandwich filling on whole wheat Italian bread or another crusty whole grain loaf.

1. Peel the eggplant and cut into 1/2-inch cubes. Place in a strainer or colander, sprinkle with 1/4 teaspoon of the salt, and allow to sit while preparing the remaining vegetables. During assembly, preheat the oven to 400°F.

2. Arrange the beans in an oiled 9-x-13-inch baking dish or 3-quart casserole. Stir in 1/4 teaspoon of the salt and scatter a third of the garlic over the top.

3. Layer the remaining ingredients over the beans in the following order: celery, eggplant, a third of the garlic, green pepper, squash, onion, tomatoes, capers, remaining 1/4 teaspoon of salt, and remaining garlic. Drizzle the vinegar over all.

4. Cover and bake for 1 hour, or until the vegetables are tender.

5. Remove the cover and cool for 10 minutes. Add salt if needed, and season with freshly ground pepper to taste. For best flavor, serve lukewarm or at room temperature.

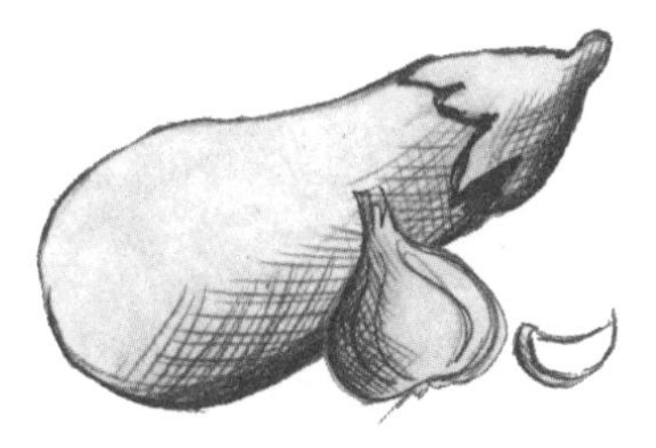

BLACK-EYED PEAS, CORN, AND GREENS

YIELD: 4 TO 6 SERVINGS

1 1/2 cups dried black-eyed peas

3 cups water

1 hot pepper, chopped, or 1/2 teaspoon crushed red pepper flakes

1/2 teaspoon salt

1 large sweet onion, such as Vidalia, Walla Walla, or Maui, chopped

1 pound kale or collard greens, coarsely chopped

2 cups fresh or frozen corn kernels

3 tablespoons red or white wine vinegar

2 tomatoes, diced, as garnish

This colorful dish has a nice bite. Adjust the spiciness by using your preferred hot pepper and/or adding more or less crushed red pepper flakes.

1. Combine the black-eyed peas and water in a large pot. Bring to a boil for 2 minutes. Then cover, remove from the heat, and let soak for 1 hour or longer.

2. Return the beans to a boil for 5 minutes, cover, and cook over low heat at a gentle simmer for 20 minutes, or until partially done.

3. Add the hot pepper or red pepper flakes and the salt to the beans, and continue cooking for 15 to 20 additional minutes, or until the beans are tender.

4. Add the onion, greens, and corn to the pot. Raise the heat to medium and cook until the greens are wilted.

5. Cover the pot, lower the heat to a simmer, and cook for 10 to 15 minutes, or until the greens are tender. Season with the vinegar, mix well, and remove from the heat.

6. Place in a serving bowl, garnish with the diced tomatoes, and serve.

The Best Antioxidant Vegetables

According to a U.S. Department of Agriculture study of the relative antioxidant capability of vegetables, the top eight, starting with the most potent, are kale, garlic, spinach, Brussels sprouts, alfalfa sprouts, broccoli florets, beets, and red bell pepper. The antioxidant rating of kale is three times that of the red pepper.

French-Style Lentils with Vegetables

YIELD: 8 SERVINGS

$2\frac{1}{2}$ cups water

1 cup dried lentils

2 medium red potatoes (12 ounces), peeled or unpeeled, cut into $\frac{1}{2}$-inch cubes

1 teaspoon salt, divided

1 cup diced onion

1 medium zucchini (10 ounces), quartered lengthwise and cut across into $\frac{1}{4}$-inch strips

$1\frac{1}{2}$ cups diced plum tomatoes

2 stalks celery, cut on the diagonal into $\frac{1}{4}$-inch slices

1 green pepper, diced

3 cloves garlic, minced

$\frac{1}{4}$ cup minced fresh parsley

3 to 4 tablespoons lemon juice

Freshly ground pepper

This dish is a good choice for a buffet, since the recipe makes a lot and the dish should be eaten at room temperature. Do not attempt this when you are in a rush, as a fair amount of chopping is involved. Leftovers can be diluted with liquid from canned tomatoes or tomato juice plus water for an excellent soup.

1. Place the water and lentils in a medium-size saucepan and bring to a boil over high heat. Reduce the heat to a simmer, cover, and cook for 15 minutes.

2. Add the potatoes and $\frac{1}{2}$ teaspoon of the salt to the pot. Replace the cover and cook for 15 to 20 minutes, or until the potatoes are tender but still hold their shape.

3. Meanwhile, combine the onion, zucchini, tomatoes, celery, green pepper, and garlic in a large skillet. Cook over medium heat, stirring frequently, for 8 to 10 minutes, or until the vegetables are crisp-tender. Do not overcook. Season with the remaining $\frac{1}{2}$ teaspoon of salt.

4. In a large serving bowl, combine the lentil-potato mixture with the vegetable mixture, including any cooking juices. Toss gently to combine.

5. Add the parsley, lemon juice, and pepper, and mix well. Taste and adjust the seasonings if necessary. This is best served at room temperature.

WINTER STEW

YIELD: 4 TO 6 SERVINGS

3 cups water

1 cup dried lentils

1 large onion, chopped

1 tablespoon grated fresh ginger

1 pound orange squash, such as acorn, butternut, or pumpkin, peeled and cut into bite-size pieces (3 cups)

1/2 teaspoon ground cumin

8 ounces kale, Swiss chard, mustard greens, spinach, arugula, or other dark greens, chopped (about 6 cups lightly packed)

3/4 teaspoon salt

1 lemon, cut into wedges

Lentils, squash, and cooked greens are a warming combination on a cold fall or winter evening.

1. Combine the water, lentils, onion, and ginger in a large saucepan, and bring to a boil over high heat. Reduce the heat to a simmer, cover, and cook for 20 minutes.

2. Add the squash and cumin to the lentil mixture. Replace the cover and simmer for about 20 minutes longer, or until both the lentils and the squash are tender.

3. Add the greens and salt to the lentils. Cover and cook for about 5 minutes, or until the greens wilt.

4. Let cool slightly before serving with fresh lemon wedges.

TWO BEANS, GREEK STYLE

YIELD: 4 SERVINGS

1/2 cup dry white wine

1 pound green beans, trimmed

1 small onion or 4 scallions, chopped

Large bunch dill, chopped (at least 1/2 cup)

1 cup chickpea cooking liquid or water

2 1/2 cups cooked or canned chickpeas, divided

1/2 teaspoon salt

1/2 lemon

Freshly ground pepper

When cooking vegetables for a substantial length of time in just a small amount of liquid, as you do here, it is very important to choose a heavy pot with a tight-fitting lid, as this will conserve the juices. Serve the resulting soft beans and gravy over cracked wheat or Mashed Potatoes with Garlic (page 186).

1. Pour the wine into a 3- to 5-quart pot, and place over medium heat until warm.

2. Add the green beans, onion or scallions, and dill to the

pot. Cover and cook over low heat for about 45 minutes, or until the green beans are soft and almost falling apart. Stir occasionally to promote even cooking. If the pan seems dry, add more wine or water.

3. Combine the cooking liquid or water and $^{3}/_{4}$ cup of the chickpeas in a blender or food processor, and purée until smooth. Add this purée, the remaining chickpeas, and the salt to the pot, adjusting the salt according to whether the chickpeas were presalted.

4. Bring to a boil over medium heat. Then reduce the heat to a simmer and cook, stirring frequently, for about 5 minutes, or until the gravy thickens and the chickpeas are heated through.

5. Remove the pot from the heat. Squeeze in the juice from the lemon half and season liberally with freshly ground pepper. Serve warm.

Garden Chili

YIELD: 4 SERVINGS

1 cup diced zucchini
$^{1}/_{2}$ cup chopped onion
$^{1}/_{2}$ cup chopped celery
$^{1}/_{2}$ cup diced red or green pepper
$^{1}/_{2}$ cup bulgur (cracked wheat)
2 tablespoons minced hot pepper, or $^{1}/_{2}$ teaspoon crushed red pepper flakes
1 tablespoon chili powder
1 teaspoon dried oregano
2 cups water
1 $^{1}/_{2}$ cups canned crushed tomatoes
1 cup dried lentils
$^{1}/_{2}$ teaspoon salt

The seasonings of this hearty chili are geared to a mild to moderate level of spiciness. If you like hot food, choose the hottest peppers and a strong chili powder. To soften the impact (and add to the nutrition) place a generous spoonful of yogurt on top of each serving. Serve with warm tortillas and a salad.

1. Combine the zucchini, onion, celery, and red or green pepper in a 5-quart pot. Cover and cook over medium heat for 5 minutes, or until the vegetables start to soften.

2. Add the bulgur wheat, hot pepper or pepper flakes, chili powder, and oregano to the pot. Cook, stirring continuously, for 1 minute.

3. Add the water, crushed tomatoes, lentils, and salt to the pot, and bring to a boil over high heat. Reduce the heat to low, cover, and cook for about 50 minutes, or until the lentils are tender. Serve hot.

BLACK BEAN CHILI

YIELD: 4 SERVINGS

1/4 cup apple juice, divided

1 medium onion, chopped

1/2 cup chopped red or green pepper

2 cloves garlic, minced

1 1/2 tablespoons chili powder

1 hot chili pepper, minced, or 1/4 teaspoon crushed red pepper flakes

1 teaspoon ground cumin

1 1/2 cups canned crushed tomatoes

1 cup green beans, cut into 1-inch pieces

3 cups cooked or canned black beans, lightly drained but not rinsed

1 cup fresh or frozen corn kernels

Serve this chili with a generous topping of yogurt cream (page 22). This chili goes well with Three-Grain Polenta Bread (page 203), slices of avocado, and either shredded lettuce or Spur-of-the Moment Carrot Salad (page 92).

1. Combine 2 tablespoons of the apple juice with the onion, red or green pepper, and garlic in a 3-quart pot. Cook over medium heat for about 3 minutes, stirring occasionally, until the onion softens.

2. Add the chili powder, chili pepper or pepper flakes, and cumin to the pot, and cook for 30 seconds.

3. Add the crushed tomatoes, green beans, and remaining 2 tablespoons of apple juice to the pot. Cover and simmer over low heat for 10 minutes, or until the green beans are almost tender.

4. Add the black beans and corn to the pot and cook, uncovered, for 10 minutes, stirring occasionally. Serve hot.

"A diet higher in whole grains and legumes and lower in beef and other meat is not just healthier for ourselves but also contributes to changing the world system that feeds some people and leaves others hungry."

–Dr. Walden Bello
Executive Director of Focus on the Global South, and 2003 winner of The Right Livelihood Award

TEMPEH BEAN CHILI

YIELD: 4 TO 6 SERVINGS

2 medium onions, chopped

1 medium green pepper, chopped

2 cloves garlic, chopped

8 ounces soy or mixed grain tempeh, coarsely chopped or crumbled (2 cups)

2 tablespoons chili powder

1 teaspoon ground cumin

1 teaspoon dried oregano

1/4 teaspoon cayenne pepper

4 cups cooked or canned kidney or pinto beans, lightly drained

3 cups chopped fresh or drained canned tomatoes

2 tablespoons dark miso

Garnishes of choice, such as chopped fresh cilantro, chopped jalapeño peppers, diced green pepper, diced cucumber, and yogurt

This is a hot, but not fiery chili. Those who like their chili spicy can add fresh chopped jalapeño peppers to taste, along with any of the other garnishes suggested in the recipe. Serve with corn or whole wheat tortillas and shredded lettuce doused with fresh lemon juice.

1. Combine the onions, green pepper, and garlic in a 3-quart pot. Cover and cook over medium heat for 5 minutes, or until the vegetables start to soften.

2. Add the tempeh, chili powder, cumin, oregano, and cayenne pepper to the pot, and cook, stirring continuously, for about 2 minutes.

3. Add the kidney beans and tomatoes to the pot. Cover and simmer gently for 20 minutes.

4. In a small bowl, combine a little of the hot chili with the miso, and stir to melt the miso. Return the mixture to the pot, cover, and let stand off the heat for about 5 minutes, allowing the flavors to develop.

5. Ladle into bowls and let each person add their garnishes of choice.

Caribbean Black Beans

YIELD: 4 SERVINGS

$^1/_2$ cup chopped onion

2 large cloves garlic, minced

2 tablespoons sherry or dry red wine

$^1/_2$ cup orange juice

$^1/_2$ teaspoon ground cumin

2 cups cooked or canned black beans, drained but not rinsed

$^1/_2$ cup diced tomatoes

1 rounded tablespoon tomato paste

1 orange, peeled and cut into bite-size pieces

Spicy Onion Topping

1 cup thinly sliced Spanish or sweet onion, such as Vidalia, Walla Walla, or Maui

Boiling water

2 tablespoons fresh lime juice

$^1/_2$ teaspoon hot pepper sauce

Paprika

Spoon these black beans over Millet Polenta Patties (page 204) or Three-Grain Polenta Bread (page 203), and serve alongside a refreshing salad that includes yogurt, such as Yogurt Cucumber Salad (page 90).

1. To make the Spicy Onion Topping, place the onions in a heatproof bowl and cover with boiling water. Let stand for 5 minutes, drain, rinse with cold water, and pat dry.

2. Return the onions to the bowl. Add the lime juice and hot pepper sauce and mix well. Let sit at room temperature for at least 15 minutes to develop the flavor. If prepared several hours ahead, store in the refrigerator, and return to room temperature before using. Sprinkle liberally with paprika just before serving.

3. While the onions are marinating, combine the chopped onion, garlic, and sherry or wine in a 2- to 3-quart saucepan. Cook over medium heat, stirring occasionally, for about 5 minutes, or until the onion softens and starts to color.

4. Add the orange juice and cumin to the saucepan and bring to a boil over high heat. Lower the heat to a simmer.

5. Add the beans and any liquid that clings to them to the pot, along with the diced tomatoes and tomato paste. Mix well and simmer, uncovered, for 10 minutes.

6. To serve, place the beans in a serving bowl. Arrange the orange pieces and Spicy Onion Topping over the beans.

Quick Cuban-Style Black Beans

YIELD: 4 SERVINGS

1 small onion, chopped

1/2 cup chopped green pepper

2 tablespoons orange juice

2 large cloves garlic, chopped

3 cups canned or cooked black beans, undrained

2 roasted pimientos, cut into strips

3 tablespoons red or white wine vinegar

1 teaspoon dried oregano

Salt

This quick bean-laden chili can be spooned over baked sweet potatoes, brown rice, millet, or cornbread. Top each serving with a generous dollop of yogurt or yogurt cheese (page 22) and provide hot sauce at the table for additional seasoning. For a really fast meal, the beans can be served over whole grain bread.

1. Combine the onion, green pepper, orange juice, and garlic in a medium skillet or saucepan. Cook over medium heat, stirring continuously, for 5 minutes.

2. Add the beans, pimientos, vinegar, and oregano to the skillet, and bring to a boil over high heat. Lower the heat to a simmer and cook for 5 minutes, or until quite hot.

3. Add salt to taste and serve hot.

Two Beans with Pesto

YIELD: 4 SERVINGS

1/4 cup dry white wine or water

1 pound green beans, trimmed and broken into 2-inch lengths

3 cups cooked or canned chickpeas

3/4 cup Creamy Walnut Pesto (page 210) or Tomato Almond Pesto (page 210)

1 large tomato, cut into wedges

Like White Beans and Carrots with Pesto (page 140), this dish combines beans, a vegetable, and pesto. Because of different beans and a different vegetable, though, this version has its own unique character.

1. Pour the wine or water into a large skillet, and place over medium heat until warm.

2. Add the green beans to the skillet, cover, and cook for 10 minutes, or until the green beans are tender but still crisp.

3. Add the chickpeas to the skillet and heat through.

4. Just before serving, remove the skillet from the heat and stir in the pesto. Garnish with the tomato wedges and serve.

PHYTO FUSION

YIELD: 4 TO 6 SERVINGS

1 cup white wine

1 small to medium cauliflower (1 to 1 1/2 pounds), broken into florets

2 medium sweet potatoes or yams (about 1 1/2 pounds), peeled and cut into 1-inch cubes

1 medium onion, chopped

1/4 cup chopped fresh parsley

3 cups cooked or canned adzuki beans, red kidney beans, black beans, or black-eyed peas, drained

1/2 cup cooking liquid from beans or water, if needed

1/2 teaspoon salt

1/4 teaspoon hot pepper sauce

This rich fusion of vegetables and beans unites several notable phytochemicals—natural components of plant-based foods that play many important roles in promoting health. For a phyto feast, serve with a green salad garnished with tomatoes and Golden Biscuits (page 46).

1. Pour the wine into a 3- to 5-quart pot, and place over medium heat until warm.

2. Add the cauliflower, sweet potatoes, onion, and parsley to the pot. Cover and cook over low heat for about 20 minutes, or until the vegetables are tender. Stir occasionally to promote even cooking.

3. Add the beans, cooking liquid or water, salt, and hot pepper sauce to the pot, adjusting the seasonings as necessary. Simmer, stirring frequently, for about 5 minutes, or until the gravy thickens slightly around the vegetables and the beans are heated through. Serve hot.

"Whether industrialized societies . . . can cure themselves of their meat addictions may ultimately be a greater factor in world health than all the doctors, health insurance policies, and drugs put together."

–The China-Oxford-Cornell Project on Nutrition

BEANS BOURGUIGNON

YIELD: 4 GENEROUS SERVINGS

1 large onion, cut into crescents

12 ounces mushrooms (preferably a mix of portobello or cremini and common white mushrooms), sliced (about 4 cups)

1 pound waxy boiling potatoes, such as red, new, Yukon Gold, or Yellow Finn, cut into 1 1/2-inch chunks

1 cup sliced carrots

1/2 cup drained canned tomatoes

3/4 cup liquid from canned tomatoes

2 cloves garlic, sliced

1 bay leaf

3 cups cooked or canned red kidney beans, lightly drained

1/3 cup dry red wine

1/4 teaspoon salt (omit if beans are salted)

Freshly ground pepper

1 to 2 tablespoons miso, any type, optional

This stew combines root vegetables with hearty red beans in a smooth, mellow mushroom-wine sauce. You may want to serve this in shallow bowls so that diners can sop up the gravy with whole grain bread.

1. Combine the onion and mushrooms in a 3- to 5-quart pot and cook over medium heat, stirring frequently, for 5 to 8 minutes, or until the mushrooms release their juices.

2. Add the potatoes, carrots, tomatoes, tomato liquid, garlic, and bay leaf to the pot. (If the tomato liquid is in the form of a thick purée, rather than a broth, dilute with bean cooking liquid or water.) Bring to a boil over high heat, reduce the heat to a simmer, cover, and cook gently for about 15 minutes, or until the potatoes begin to yield but are not yet tender.

3. Add the beans, wine, and salt to the pot. (If the beans were salted, omit the salt.) Simmer gently, uncovered, for an additional 10 minutes, or until the potatoes are tender.

4. Remove the bay leaf, season generously with freshly ground pepper, and adjust the salt to taste. For a richer gravy, combine up to 2 tablespoons of miso with a little of the hot sauce in a small bowl. Stir until the miso melts into the sauce, and return the sauce to the pot. Allow to sit for a few minutes before serving.

Cowboy Beans

YIELD: 4 SERVINGS

3 cups water

1 1/2 cups dried pinto or pink kidney beans

1 medium onion, chopped

1 medium red pepper, chopped

1 jalapeño pepper, chopped

2 carrots, peeled and diced

1 stalk celery, chopped

2 cloves garlic, chopped

1/2 cup tomato juice

1 teaspoon ground cumin

1/2 teaspoon dried oregano

1 cup fresh or frozen corn kernels

1/4 cup minced fresh cilantro or flat-leaf Italian parsley

1/2 teaspoon salt

If using conventional stove-top cooking, you will need to begin this recipe several hours ahead. But if you use a pressure cooker (see the Variation at the end of the recipe), the dish will be ready in 45 minutes, demonstrating how practical this tool is when it comes to preparing beans.

1. Combine the water and beans in a large pot. Bring to a boil for 2 minutes. Then cover, remove from the heat, and let soak for 1 hour or longer.

2. Return the beans to a boil for 5 minutes. Then reduce the heat to a simmer, cover, and cook for 1 hour.

3. Add the onion, red pepper, jalapeño pepper, carrots, celery, garlic, tomato juice, cumin, and oregano to the pot. Cover and cook for about 45 minutes, or until the beans and vegetables are tender.

4. Add the corn, cilantro or parsley, and salt to the pot, and cook for 5 additional minutes. Serve hot.

Variation

■ To prepare Cowboy Beans in a pressure cooker, combine the dried beans, water, and all the remaining ingredients except the corn, cilantro or parsley, and salt in the cooker. Bring to a boil, close the cooker, bring up to pressure, and cook for 35 minutes. Let the pressure cooker sit off the heat for 5 minutes before gradually releasing the pressure and opening. Add the corn, cilantro or parsley, and salt, and simmer for 5 minutes.

CHICKPEA ROAST

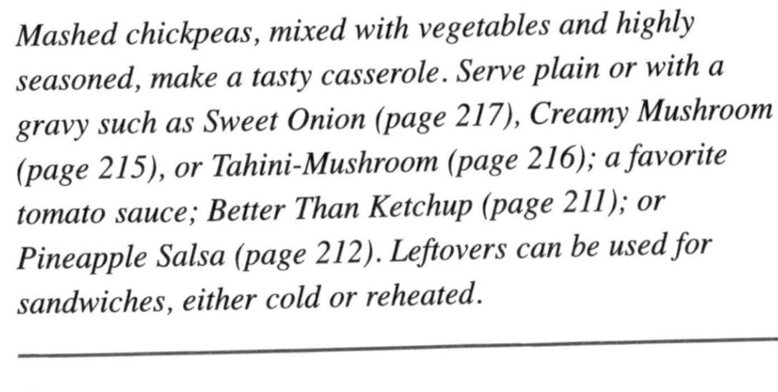

Mashed chickpeas, mixed with vegetables and highly seasoned, make a tasty casserole. Serve plain or with a gravy such as Sweet Onion (page 217), Creamy Mushroom (page 215), or Tahini-Mushroom (page 216); a favorite tomato sauce; Better Than Ketchup (page 211); or Pineapple Salsa (page 212). Leftovers can be used for sandwiches, either cold or reheated.

YIELD: 4 TO 6 SERVINGS

4 cups cooked or canned chickpeas

2 onions, chopped

3 cloves garlic, chopped

2 tablespoons soy sauce

2 stalks celery, chopped

1 carrot, peeled and grated

1/2 teaspoon ground cumin

1/4 teaspoon ground turmeric

1/4 teaspoon salt (omit if beans are salted)

2 tablespoons tahini (sesame seed paste)

Paprika

1. Preheat the oven to 375°F.

2. In a large bowl, mash the chickpeas with a potato masher, and set aside.

3. Combine the onions, garlic, and soy sauce in a skillet. Cook over medium heat for 5 minutes.

4. Add the celery, carrot, cumin, turmeric, and salt to the skillet, and cook for 5 additional minutes, or until the vegetables are crisp-tender.

5. Add the cooked vegetables and tahini to the chickpeas, and mix well.

6. Oil a 1-quart baking dish and fill with the chickpea mixture. Sprinkle liberally with paprika and bake for about 40 minutes, or until firm and nicely browned. Serve warm.

North African Chickpeas

YIELD: 4 SERVINGS

1 medium onion, thinly sliced

2 tablespoons red wine or sherry

1 tablespoon minced garlic

1 tablespoon minced fresh ginger

1 teaspoon ground cumin

1 teaspoon ground cinnamon

1 teaspoon paprika

1/2 teaspoon crushed red pepper flakes

1 cup water or chickpea cooking liquid

2 medium sweet potatoes (1 1/2 pounds), peeled and cut into bite-size pieces

1/4 cup diced dried apricots

1/2 teaspoon salt (reduce if cooking liquid is salted)

2 cups cooked or canned chickpeas

1/4 cup dark raisins

2 tablespoons lemon juice

1/4 cup sliced almonds

This unusual dish has a nice bite, but those who like foods really spicy may want to double the red pepper flakes. Serve over a cooked grain such as whole wheat couscous, bulgur, barley, or quinoa, and complete the meal with a cooling yogurt-based side dish such as Spinach-Yogurt Salad (page 97) and whole wheat chapatis.

1. In a medium saucepan, combine the onion, wine or sherry, garlic, and ginger. Cover and sweat over low heat for 5 minutes.

2. Add the cumin, cinnamon, paprika, and red pepper flakes to the saucepan, and cook, uncovered, 1 minute longer.

3. Add the water or cooking liquid, sweet potatoes, apricots, and salt to the saucepan, and bring to a boil over high heat. Then reduce the heat to a simmer, cover, and cook for about 15 minutes, or until the sweet potatoes are just tender.

4. Add the chickpeas, raisins, and lemon juice to the saucepan. Cook, stirring occasionally, for about 5 minutes, or until the chickpeas are hot. Stir in the sliced almonds and serve warm.

"Your choice of diet can influence your long term health prospects more than any other action you might take."

–Dr. C. Everett Koop
Former Surgeon General of the United States

MAINLY GRAIN ENTRÉES

PASTA WITH FRESH TOMATOES, BASIL, AND ROASTED GARLIC

YIELD: 4 SERVINGS

10 cloves garlic, roasted (page 19)

12 ounces tomatoes

¼ cup coarsely chopped fresh basil

1 tablespoon chopped capers

1 tablespoon best-quality olive oil

1 tablespoon balsamic vinegar

8 ounces small whole wheat pasta, such as spirals, penne, ziti, bow ties, or radiatore

No-cook tomato sauces such as this should be made with flavorful ripe tomatoes and the best quality olive oil. Pair this pasta with a dish that features beans and/or yogurt cheese. Suitable choices include Black Bean Hummus (page 53), Superior Spinach Dip (page 55), Pesto-Stuffed Mushrooms (page 61), or a simple dish of chickpeas seasoned with lots of freshly ground pepper.

1. Peel the roasted cloves of garlic, and place on a flat surface. Smash gently with the flat side of a knife and set aside.

2. Dice the tomatoes and place in a large bowl, retaining the tomato juices. You should have about 2 cups.

3. Add the roasted garlic, basil, capers, olive oil, and balsamic vinegar to the tomatoes, and mix well. Allow to sit for at least 20 minutes for flavors to blend.

4. While the tomato mixture is marinating, cook the pasta in a large pot of boiling water until al dente, or according to personal preferences. Drain and add immediately to the tomato mixture, tossing to blend. Serve warm or at room temperature.

Ravioli and Beans

YIELD: 4 SERVINGS

10 sun-dried tomatoes

Hot water

16 vegetable-, cheese-, or soy-filled ravioli

1 1/2 cups bean cooking liquid or vegetable broth, divided

2 large cloves garlic, sliced

1 cup lightly packed, coarsely chopped fresh parsley

1 teaspoon salt (omit if beans are salted)

4 cups cooked or canned white or black beans

In this dish, plump pillows of ravioli are nestled on a bed of beans. The various elements can be made expressly for this dish, or it can be quickly assembled if you plan ahead by preparing extra ravioli and beans for a previous meal.

1. Place the sun-dried tomatoes in a shallow heatproof bowl, and pour in hot water to just submerge. Let soften while assembling the remaining ingredients.

2. Cook the ravioli in a large pot of boiling water until tender. Drain well and set aside.

3. In a large pot, bring 1/2 cup of the cooking liquid or broth to a gentle boil. Add the garlic and simmer for about a minute.

4. Drain the softened sun-dried tomatoes, reserving the soaking liquid. Slice the tomatoes and add to the pot of cooking liquid along with the reserved cooking liquid, the parsley, and the salt. Simmer for 5 minutes.

5. Add the beans and ravioli to the pot and heat through.

6. Spoon onto serving plates, giving each person a generous portion of beans and 4 ravioli. Serve hot.

Italian Pasta and Vegetable Stew

YIELD: 4 SERVINGS

1 cup chickpea cooking liquid or water

1 pound small new or red potatoes, cut into 1-inch pieces

8 ounces green beans, trimmed and broken in half if large

2 large cloves garlic, sliced

1 tablespoon chopped fresh basil, or 1 teaspoon dried basil

1 teaspoon dried oregano

1 small hot pepper, minced, optional

2 tablespoons tomato paste

2 cups small whole grain pasta, such as spirals, penne, rigatoni, wagon wheels, or small shells

4 to 6 canned artichoke hearts or bottoms, drained and quartered

½ teaspoon salt

2½ cups water

3 cups cooked or canned chickpeas

¼ cup chopped fresh parsley

Freshly ground pepper

Here is a one-pot meal that is quick and easy to make with precooked or canned chickpeas. Serve with Succulent Stuffed Mushrooms (page 60) and a green salad.

1. Place the cooking liquid or water in a 3- to 5-quart pot, and bring to a boil over high heat. Add the potatoes, green beans, garlic, basil, oregano, and hot pepper, if desired, to the pot. Cover and simmer over medium heat for 15 minutes.

2. Stir the tomato paste into the vegetable mixture. When dissolved, add the pasta, artichoke hearts or bottoms, salt, and just enough of the water to cover. Mix well to submerge the pasta.

3. Cover and simmer gently for 10 minutes, checking halfway through the cooking time to see if more water is needed. The mixture should be neither soupy nor dry.

4. Add the chickpeas and parsley to the pot. Cover and continue to cook, stirring occasionally, for 5 to 10 minutes, or until the pasta and vegetables are tender and the gravy is thick and rich. Remember to keep an eye on the liquid and to add more water if necessary.

5. Season with freshly ground pepper and adjust the salt to taste. Serve as is or with grated cheese.

VEGETABLE PASTA WITH CHEESE

YIELD: 4 SERVINGS

1 pound asparagus, cauliflower, or broccoli

1 pound vegetable-, cheese-, or tofu-filled tortellini

1/4 cup chopped fresh parsley

1/4 cup grated Parmesan cheese

1 tablespoon olive, flaxseed, or hemp oil

Salt

Freshly ground pepper

An easy way to add more vegetables to the menu is to toss them in with pasta during the last few minutes of cooking, as done here.

1. Prepare your vegetables of choice by cutting the asparagus into 1-inch lengths, or breaking the cauliflower or broccoli into small florets.

2. Cook the pasta in a large pot of boiling water until al dente, or according to personal preferences. Add the vegetables during the last 2 minutes of cooking.

3. Drain the pasta and vegetables. Do not rinse. Transfer the mixture to a serving bowl and while still hot, toss with the parsley, cheese, and oil, mixing well.

4. Season the pasta mixture with salt and lots of freshly ground pepper. Serve additional cheese at the table for those who want it.

VARIATION

- If desired, replace the fresh vegetable with 2 cups of frozen peas. Add the peas at the very end of the cooking time, just long enough to heat through.

"I forced myself to acknowledge the fact that every time I ate a hamburger, a cow had ceased to breathe and moo and walk around."

–Moby

PORTOBELLO PASTA

YIELD: 4 GENEROUS SERVINGS

3 cups sliced portobello mushrooms (about 8 ounces)

8 cloves garlic, sliced

1/3 cup water

2 tablespoons soy sauce

1 small red onion, cut into crescents

12 ounces dark leafy greens, such as arugula, escarole, broccoli rabe, Swiss chard, spinach, or romaine, cut into bite-size pieces (about 8 cups)

2 cups cooked or canned chickpeas or white cannellini beans, drained, or 1 pound firm tofu, cut into strips

1 cup bean cooking liquid, water, or vegetable broth

1/2 cup canned crushed tomatoes

2 tablespoons balsamic vinegar, divided

12 ounces whole wheat, kamut, spelt, or brown rice angel hair pasta, linguini, or other pasta of choice

2 tablespoons pine nuts or pumpkin seeds, toasted (page 19)

We jokingly call this OsteoPasta, as it is a good source of calcium, vitamin K, and estrogenic phytochemicals that all promote good bones. Serve this hearty pasta-vegetable combo in shallow bowls so the flavorful broth is not lost, and pair it with Fennel and Orange Salad (page 93).

1. Combine the mushrooms, garlic, 1/3 cup water, and soy sauce in a 15-inch skillet or large pot. Cover and cook over low heat for 10 minutes.

2. Add the red onion, greens, beans or tofu, cooking liquid, crushed tomatoes, and 1 tablespoon of balsamic vinegar to the pot. Mix well, cover, and cook over medium heat, stirring occasionally, for about 10 minutes, or until the greens are tender. Set aside.

3. Cook the pasta in a large pot of boiling water until al dente, or according to personal preferences. Drain the pasta, reserving about 1/4 cup of the cooking water.

4. Add the hot pasta, toasted pine nuts or pumpkin seeds, and remaining tablespoon of balsamic vinegar to the vegetables. Mix well and cook for just a few minutes, or until very hot. If needed, stir in the reserved pasta water to help create a broth.

5. Transfer the mixture to serving bowls, making sure that the vegetables and broth are evenly divided among them.

BAKED MACARONI AND CORN

YIELD: 6 SERVINGS

4 cups whole grain or wheat-free spirals, small shells, or elbow macaroni

2 cups diced soft or regular tofu (12 to 16 ounces)

2 cups soy milk

3 tablespoons tahini (sesame seed paste)

1 1/2 teaspoons salt

3 cups fresh or frozen corn kernels

Paprika

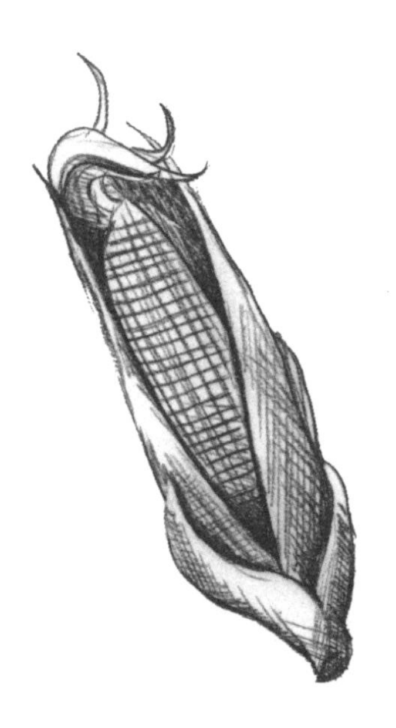

Here is a nondairy alternative to classic baked macaroni and cheese. It can be made with either whole wheat or wheat-free pastas, such as quinoa, rice, corn, kamut, or spelt. Take advantage of the hot oven and serve with baked winter squash. Complete the menu with a green salad.

1. Preheat the oven to 350°F.

2. Cook the pasta in a large pot of boiling water until slightly underdone. Monitor the cooking time closely as some nonwheat varieties become mushy and disintegrate if cooked too long. Drain and rinse with cold water to stop the cooking. Drain thoroughly, and set aside.

3. Combine the tofu, soy milk, tahini, and salt in a blender or food processor, and purée until smooth. Add the corn and process briefly at high speed.

4. Place the cooked pasta in an oiled shallow 2-quart or 9-x-13-inch baking dish. Pour the puréed tofu over the pasta, mixing so that the pasta is evenly bathed in the sauce. Sprinkle liberally with paprika.

5. Bake for 30 minutes, or until the sauce is hot and bubbly. Serve hot.

PASTA WITH CHICKPEA-WALNUT SAUCE

YIELD: 4 SERVINGS

½ cup walnuts, toasted (page 19)

2 tablespoons sherry or dry red wine

½ cup chopped onion

2 tablespoons chopped garlic

2 cups cooked or canned chickpeas

1 ½ cups chickpea cooking liquid alone or combined with dry white wine, vegetable broth, or water if needed

Salt

1 pound broccoli, green beans, or snow peas

8 ounces whole grain pasta, such as linguini, spaghetti, spirals, shells, or wagon wheels

Crushed red pepper flakes

Although this dish has a number of steps, it is actually quite easy to make. The sauce is essentially a flavorful chickpea and walnut purée that takes just a few minutes to prepare with the aid of a blender or food processor. The vegetables are tossed in with the pasta to cook. Prepare a big salad and dinner is done.

1. Place the toasted walnuts in a blender or food processor and grind to a fine meal. Leave the nuts in the blender, setting aside.

2. Heat the sherry or wine in a medium-size saucepan over low heat. Add the onion and garlic and cook, stirring often, for about 3 minutes, or until softened.

3. Add the cooked onions and garlic, the chickpeas, and the cooking liquid to the walnuts in the blender or food processor. Purée until smooth.

4. Return the sauce ingredients to the saucepan and cook over medium heat, stirring frequently, for 5 to 7 minutes, or until warm and slightly thickened. Taste for salt and add if necessary.

5. To prepare the vegetable, divide the broccoli into small florets and peel and dice the stems; trim the ends from the green beans and break into 2-inch lengths; or trim the ends of the snow peas and leave whole.

6. Cook the pasta in a large pot of boiling water until al dente, or according to personal preferences. Add the vegetables during the last 2 minutes of cooking.

7. Drain the pasta and vegetables. Do not rinse. Transfer the mixture to a serving bowl and while still hot, coat generously with the sauce.

8. Serve hot with any remaining sauce on the side, along with red pepper flakes for individual seasoning.

LINGUINI WITH WHITE BEAN SAUCE

YIELD: 4 SERVINGS

3 stalks celery, sliced 1/4 inch thick

1 medium onion, chopped

1 cup diced red pepper

2 large cloves garlic, minced

2 tablespoons sherry

2 cups cooked or canned white beans, such as cannellini, Great Northern, or navy

1 1/2 cups bean cooking liquid, vegetable broth, or water

1/4 cup chopped fresh flat-leaf Italian parsley, divided

1/4 teaspoon crushed red pepper flakes

1/4 cup capers

Salt (omit if beans are salted)

Freshly ground pepper

10 ounces whole wheat linguini or other whole grain pasta

The sauce can be made with canned beans and their liquid if home-cooked beans are not available. To enhance the flavor, roast some garlic and squeeze out several cloves on top of the pasta before serving. Quick White Pita Pizzas (page 69) and a salad of fresh tomatoes dressed lightly with balsamic vinegar and olive oil can complete the meal.

1. To prepare the sauce, combine the celery, onion, red pepper, garlic, and sherry in a 3-quart pot. Cover and cook over medium heat for 5 minutes.

2. Add the beans, cooking liquid, 2 tablespoons of the parsley, and all of the red pepper flakes to the pot. Bring to a boil, reduce the heat to a simmer, and cook uncovered for 10 minutes.

3. Coarsely mash the beans with a potato masher to thicken the sauce. Add the capers. Season with salt, if needed, and with freshly ground pepper to create a highly seasoned sauce. Cook for about 5 minutes longer, or until the sauce is creamy.

4. Cook the pasta in a large pot of boiling water until al dente, or according to personal preferences. Drain the pasta well.

5. Stir the pasta into the hot sauce and mix to coat completely. Sprinkle with the remaining parsley and serve at once.

Multicultural Rice, Beans, and Greens

YIELD: 4 TO 6 SERVINGS

- Bean cooking liquid, sherry, or vegetable broth
- 3 large cloves garlic, sliced
- 12 ounces arugula, escarole, kale, or broccoli rabe, coarsely chopped (6 to 8 cups)
- 3 cups cooked brown rice
- 1/4 cup chopped fresh parsley
- 3 cups cooked or canned white beans
- Salt
- Freshly ground pepper
- Yogurt cream, optional (page 22)
- Grated Parmesan cheese, optional

The ethnic identity of this dish can be easily altered, as explained in the Variations at the end of the recipe. This is the Italian version.

1. In a heavy 15-inch skillet or pot, heat about 2 tablespoons of the bean cooking liquid, sherry, or broth over medium heat, just until hot.
2. Add the garlic to the pot and cook briefly.
3. Add the greens to the pot and cook, stirring frequently, for about 5 minutes, or until wilted and tender. Broccoli rabe will take a few minutes longer than the other greens to become tender.
4. Add the rice and parsley to the pot and cook, stirring, until warm.
5. Add the beans and a few more spoonfuls of the cooking liquid to the pot. Cook, stirring, until hot. Add additional liquid as needed to make the mixture creamy.
6. Season with salt and pepper to taste.
7. At serving time, top each portion with a generous dollop of yogurt cream, if desired, and pass grated Parmesan around the table.

Variations

- For Greek-Style Rice, Beans, and Greens, replace the parsley with chopped dill and in addition to the yogurt cream, crumble 2 tablespoons of feta cheese over each serving.
- For Southern-Style Rice, Beans, and Greens, use Swiss chard, turnip greens, beet greens, mustard greens, or collards as the greens of choice, and cooked black-eyed peas instead of white beans. Collard greens may take 5 to 10 minutes longer to cook than the other greens. Serve with your favorite hot sauce for individual seasoning.
- For Indian-Style Rice, Beans, and Greens, use spinach or mustard greens, replace half the parsley with chopped fresh cilantro, and use chickpeas and/or lentils instead of the white beans.

9. Side Dishes

The recipes in this chapter are designed to accompany main dishes and help round out a meal by adding more vegetables, grains, or beans—whatever would best complement your entrée. But don't feel that these dishes *must* be used in a supporting role. You can actually create a meal that is both balanced and satisfying by serving vegetable, bean, and grain side dishes together. Moreover, vegetable dishes can make a wonderful first course.

When choosing side dishes, you'll want to keep the following points in mind:

■ Where vegetables are concerned, the more the better. There is no limit to the number of vegetables you can serve in a meal or throughout a day.

■ When a meal could do with a protein boost, try a bean accompaniment.

■ Grains are an important part of the diet and should be served often as accompaniments to vegetable, tofu, tempeh, and bean dishes. The wide range of grains available makes this easy to accomplish.

If you haven't yet looked at Chapter 3, "Basic Training," you may want to refer to it now, as it provides simple step-by-step instructions for cooking dried beans and grains—the main ingredients used in many side dish recipes. Chapter 3 also details several different ways to cook vegetables, including steaming, stir-steaming, stewing, oven-roasting, grilling, and even pressure-cooking. Once you've learned these basic techniques and used some of them to prepare the recipes offered in this chapter, you may even find yourself making your old favorite side dishes in healthy new ways.

Making the Most of Vegetables

Many of us grew up in households that ruined vegetables by overcooking, or that—in an attempt to make vegetables more "interesting"—cooked them in fat or covered them with rich sauces. We now know that vegetables are best when cooked quickly and dressed as nutritiously as possible. No matter what vegetables you choose to serve, the following rules will help make them both appealing and healthful:

■ Select vegetables that are fresh and in season.

■ Cook vegetables only long enough to make them tender.

■ Keep added fat and calories down by steaming, stir-steaming, stewing, roasting, or grilling. (See Chapter 3 for details.)

■ Enhance the flavor of plain vegetables by adding a splash of wine vinegar, balsamic vinegar, or fresh lemon juice to the finished dish.

VEGETABLE SIDE DISHES

Spring Artichokes

YIELD: 4 SERVINGS

4 medium-size artichokes with stems

1/2 cup water

3 tablespoons lemon juice

3 strips lemon peel

1/2 teaspoon salt

1 small onion, cut into thin crescents

6 cloves garlic, sliced

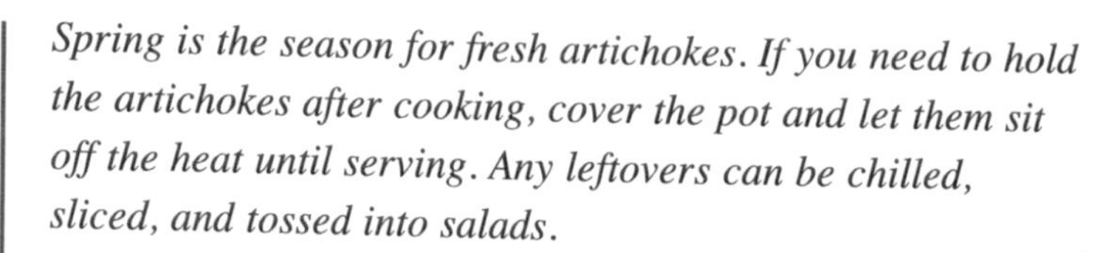

Spring is the season for fresh artichokes. If you need to hold the artichokes after cooking, cover the pot and let them sit off the heat until serving. Any leftovers can be chilled, sliced, and tossed into salads.

1. Prepare the artichokes by peeling the stems lightly, cutting off the top third of the bulb to remove the tips of the leaves, and removing any small tough leaves at the base. Cut each artichoke in half lengthwise and use a grapefruit spoon or small paring knife to scrape away the small hairy leaves (or choke) attached to the heart.

2. Combine the water, lemon juice, lemon peel, and salt in a broad pot that can hold the artichokes in a single layer. Dip the cut side of each artichoke in this lemon water. Then arrange the artichokes side by side in the pot with the cut sides up. Scatter the onion and garlic over the artichokes.

3. Bring the artichokes and liquid to a boil over high heat. Lower the heat to a simmer, cover, and cook for about 30 minutes, or until the artichokes can be easily pierced with a fork. Check periodically during cooking to see that the water is not boiling too rapidly and evaporating.

4. Serve each person 2 warm halves topped with some of the onions, garlic, and a little broth.

BROILED ASPARAGUS AND PEPPERS

YIELD: 4 SERVINGS

1 pound asparagus

2 red or yellow peppers

1 tablespoon balsamic vinegar

This is a simple way to enjoy fresh spring asparagus.

1. Preheat the broiler.

2. Snap off the tough ends of the asparagus. Cut the pepper into 1/2-inch-wide strips, discarding the seeds and trimming any thick ribs.

3. Arrange the vegetables in a single layer on a baking sheet. Broil 5 to 6 inches from the heat for 8 to 12 minutes, turning several times, until the vegetables are tender and lightly charred.

4. Transfer the vegetables to a serving dish and sprinkle with the balsamic vinegar. Serve warm or at room temperature.

BROCCOLI MASH

YIELD: 4 TO 6 SERVINGS

2 pounds broccoli, stems peeled and chopped, tops divided into tiny florets (about 4 cups)

1/2 cup water

1/2 teaspoon salt

4 cloves garlic, minced

2 teaspoons curry powder

1/2 cup yogurt cheese (page 22)

This broccoli is roughly mashed yet creamy, with a definite bite.

1. Combine the broccoli, water, and salt in a large skillet, and bring to a boil over high heat. Lower the heat to a simmer, cover, and cook for about 15 minutes, or until the broccoli is quite tender.

2. Add the garlic and curry powder to the skillet. Cook uncovered, mashing with a fork or potato masher until the broccoli is reduced to a rough purée. Add more water if needed to keep the mixture moist.

3. Remove the skillet from the heat and mash the yogurt cheese into the broccoli. If need be, return to very low heat and cook gently, while stirring, until the purée is hot.

Baked Acorn Squash

YIELD: 4 SERVINGS

2 medium-size acorn squash

Every winter, the market is filled with a variety of orange-fleshed squash, including acorn, hubbard, butternut, buttercup, and several other varieties. If desired, substitute your favorite squash for the acorn, cutting any larger squash into more manageable pieces to reduce cooking time.

1. Preheat the oven to 375°F.
2. Wash the squash, dry well, and cut each in half from the stem to the blossom end. Scoop out and discard the seeds.
3. Arrange the squash cut side down in a shallow baking pan. Add water to the pan to the depth of 1/2 inch to prevent scorching, and bake for 30 to 40 minutes, or until barely tender.
4. Invert the squash and return to the oven for 10 to 15 minutes, or until the flesh is tender. During this final stage of baking, a light sprinkling of cinnamon or nutmeg can be used for seasoning.

Baked Beets

YIELD: 4 SERVINGS

4 medium-size beets (4 to 5 ounces each)

Although beets are as easy to bake as potatoes, they are not commonly served this way. Enjoy them with a topping of Lemon Tahini Dressing (page 103) or Orange Parsley Dressing (page 101), or with a generous dollop of yogurt cheese (page 22).

1. Preheat the oven to 400°F.
2. Cut off any beet greens and set aside for another dish, cut off the stem right to the top of the beets, and remove the roots. Do not peel. Scrub clean and dry well.
3. Arrange the beets in a single layer in a baking dish, and cover tightly with a lid or with aluminum foil. Alternatively, enclose the beets entirely in foil.

4. Bake for an hour, or until the beets are tender and easily pierced with a sharp knife.

5. Remove the beets from the oven, and allow them to sit for about 10 minutes, or until they are cool enough to handle. Slide off and discard the skins.

6. Serve whole or cut into pieces, either plain or topped with the dressing of your choice.

ORANGE-LEMON BEETS

YIELD: 4 TO 6 SERVINGS

1 1/2 pounds red or golden beets

1/3 cup orange juice

1 teaspoon grated fresh ginger

1 small lemon

In this unusual dish, sweet beets are studded with tiny pieces of tart raw lemon. You will be amazed by the tenderness of the lemon peel. What also makes this recipe different is that beets are usually cooked whole without peeling, and then peeled and cut as desired. Here we cut up the beets first, dramatically reducing the cooking time.

1. Scrub and peel the beets, and cut into 1/8-by-1/2-inch matchsticks. To do this easily, begin by cutting each beet into 1/8-inch-thick slices. Stack several slices together and cut into 1/8-inch-wide strips. Cut strips into 1/2-inch lengths. You should have about 4 cups.

2. Place the beets in a small pot with the orange juice and ginger. Cover and cook over moderate heat for about 15 minutes, or until tender.

3. Cut the unpeeled lemon into very thin slices. Stack the slices and cut into small pieces. You should have about 1/2 cup.

4. Transfer the beets to a serving bowl and, while still hot, mix in the lemon pieces. Serve warm or at room temperature.

VARIATION

■ For Orange-Lemon Carrots, replace the beets with matchstick-size pieces of carrot.

Oven-Roasted Brussels Sprouts

YIELD: 4 SERVINGS

Olive oil

1 pint (10 ounces) Brussels sprouts, halved lengthwise through stem

1 teaspoon dried oregano or rosemary

Freshly ground pepper

Oven-roasting gives Brussels sprouts an irresistible flavor. (For more ideas on oven-roasting vegetables, see Chapter 3, page 26.)

1. Preheat the oven to 500°F.

2. Generously oil a baking sheet or shallow roasting pan, and arrange the Brussels sprouts in the pan in a single layer. Scatter the oregano or rosemary over the sprouts.

3. Bake for 20 to 25 minutes, or until the edges are delicately browned. Check occasionally during baking and use a spatula to loosen and move the vegetables around to promote even roasting and prevent sticking.

4. Transfer the Brussels sprouts to a serving bowl, season with freshly ground pepper, and serve.

Mustard Brussels Sprouts

YIELD: 4 SERVINGS

2 tablespoons sherry

1 tablespoon prepared mustard

1 pint (10 ounces) Brussels sprouts, cut into thin shreds

Perhaps because these Brussels sprouts are shredded, even people who claim not to like them enjoy this flavorful dish.

1. Place the sherry in a large skillet and cook over medium heat until aromatic.

2. Add the mustard and Brussels sprouts to the skillet and stir-cook for 5 to 8 minutes, or until tender. Serve at once.

Variation

- For Mustard Snow Peas, use snow peas instead of Brussels sprouts.

Stir-Steamed Sesame Cabbage

YIELD: 4 TO 6 SERVINGS

1 1/2 pounds cabbage

2 tablespoons sesame seeds

2 tablespoons Chinese rice cooking wine or rice vinegar

1 teaspoon Coleman's or Chinese mustard powder diluted in 2 teaspoons water

1 teaspoon toasted sesame oil, optional

Salt

If you use rice wine in this dish, it will keep the flavor mellow, while rice vinegar will make it more tangy. If for some reason you prefer not to add the toasted sesame oil, it can be served on the side as a condiment for individual seasoning. It takes very little of this oil to add intense flavor.

1. Slice the cabbage, including the core or "heart," into 1/2-inch-wide strips, and then into 1-inch segments. You should have about 8 cups. Set aside.

2. Place the sesame seeds in a large dry wok or heavy skillet and toast over medium heat until lightly colored and aromatic. Watch closely to avoid overbrowning.

3. Add the cabbage to the skillet and cook, stirring almost continuously, for about 3 minutes, or until the cabbage starts to wilt.

4. Add the wine or vinegar and the mustard mixture to the skillet. Mix well, cover, and cook over medium heat for about 5 minutes, or until the cabbage is tender but crunchy.

5. Remove the skillet from the heat and stir in the sesame oil if desired, and a pinch of salt if needed. Serve hot or at room temperature.

Creamy Cabbage with Sesame Seeds

YIELD: 4 SERVINGS

Olive oil

1/4 cup chopped onion

1 pound cabbage, thinly sliced (about 5 cups)

1 1/2 teaspoons soy sauce

2 tablespoons whole wheat flour

1 cup soy milk

1 teaspoon prepared mustard

1 tablespoon sesame seeds, toasted (page 19)

You can make a meal of this dish by pairing it with baked winter squash and cooked kasha.

1. Place enough oil in a large wok or skillet to just cover the bottom of the pan. Add the onion and sauté over medium heat for 3 to 5 minutes, or until it starts to color.

2. Add the cabbage to the skillet, cover, and cook over medium heat for 8 to 10 minutes, or until tender. Stir occasionally for even cooking.

3. Stir the soy sauce into the cabbage mixture. Sprinkle the flour evenly over the cabbage and mix well. Gradually stir in the soy milk and mustard.

4. Cook for a few additional minutes, stirring continuously, until the sauce thickens and comes to a gentle boil.

5. Transfer the cabbage to a serving bowl, sprinkle with the toasted sesame seeds, and serve immediately.

Asian Sesame Ginger Carrots

YIELD: 4 SERVINGS

1 tablespoon sesame seeds

2 tablespoons sherry

1 tablespoon minced orange zest

1 tablespoon minced fresh ginger

6 medium carrots, peeled and coarsely shredded (about 3 cups)

In this dish, crunchy cooked carrots are accented by sesame seeds, orange, and ginger.

1. Place the sesame seeds in a large dry skillet and toast over medium heat until lightly colored and aromatic. Watch closely to avoid overbrowning.

2. Remove the pan from the heat and let cool slightly; if the pan is too hot, the sherry will sputter when added. Then add the sherry, orange zest, ginger, and carrots to the skillet.

3. Cook over medium heat for about 8 minutes, stirring almost continuously, until the carrots are piping hot and just tender. Serve at once.

MEXICAN CHILI CARROTS

YIELD: 4 SERVINGS

1 tablespoon pumpkin seeds

2 tablespoons orange or apple juice

1 tablespoon minced orange zest

1 clove garlic, minced

2 teaspoons chili powder

1/2 teaspoon ground cumin

1/4 teaspoon salt

6 medium carrots, peeled and coarsely shredded (about 3 cups)

These carrots are crunchy with a gentle bite.

1. Place the pumpkin seeds in a large dry skillet and toast over medium heat for 1 to 2 minutes, or until lightly colored and beginning to pop. Watch closely to avoid burning.

2. Remove the pan from the heat and let cool slightly; if the pan is too hot, the juice will sputter when added. Then add the juice, orange zest, garlic, chili powder, cumin, salt, and carrots to the skillet.

3. Cook over medium heat for about 8 minutes, stirring almost continuously, until the carrots are piping hot and just tender. Serve at once.

PINK CAULIFLOWER OREGANATA

YIELD: 4 SERVINGS

1 small to medium cauliflower (1 1/2 to 2 pounds), broken into small florets (4 to 5 cups)

1 small onion, chopped

3 tablespoons cider vinegar, divided

2 tablespoons water

1 medium to large tomato, diced

1 teaspoon dried basil

1/2 teaspoon dried oregano

1/2 teaspoon salt

In this dish, cauliflower acquires a pale pink color from the tomato pieces and a perky flavor from the oregano.

1. Combine the cauliflower, onion, 2 tablespoons of the cider vinegar, and the water in a large heavy skillet. Cover and cook over medium heat, stirring occasionally, for about 15 minutes, or until the cauliflower is tender.

2. Add the tomato, basil, oregano, salt, and remaining tablespoon of cider vinegar to the skillet, and stir to combine. Continue to cook for a few additional minutes, just until hot, and serve.

BRAISED CAULIFLOWER WITH CURRANTS AND PINE NUTS

YIELD: 4 TO 6 SERVINGS

1 medium cauliflower (about 2 pounds), broken into small florets (about 5 cups)

1 medium red onion, chopped

4 cloves garlic, sliced

1 cup orange juice

$^1/_2$ cup canned crushed tomatoes

$^1/_4$ cup currants

3 tablespoons almond, cashew, or peanut butter

2 tablespoons pine nuts, toasted (page 19)

The cauliflower in this slightly sweet, delicate sauce gets its creaminess from your choice of nut butter. Serve with a bean entrée and cooked grain. Alternatively, for a main dish, use as a topping for grains or pasta, and complete the menu with a bean salad.

1. Combine the cauliflower, onion, garlic, orange juice, tomatoes, and currants in a large skillet, mixing well to coat the cauliflower.

2. Bring the cauliflower mixture just to a boil over high heat. Lower the heat to a simmer, cover, and cook for about 15 minutes, or until the cauliflower is tender. Stir occasionally to promote even cooking.

3. Remove the cover and cook for a few additional minutes, stirring to slightly thicken the sauce. If you are not ready to eat, cover and let stand off the heat until ready to serve. (Note that if the cauliflower becomes cool, you can reheat briefly before the next step.)

4. Just before serving, remove the skillet from the heat and stir in the nut butter, mixing until creamy. Toss in the pine nuts and serve.

Cauliflower with Tahini Gravy

YIELD: 4 SERVINGS

1/2 cup water

1 tablespoon soy sauce

1 medium cauliflower (about 2 pounds), broken into small florets (about 5 cups)

1 small onion, coarsely chopped

2 large cloves garlic, sliced

1/4 cup chopped fresh dill or parsley

2 tablespoons tahini (sesame seed paste)

1/3 cup vegetable broth or water

1 tablespoon lemon juice

Salt

In addition to imparting flavor, the tahini makes this gravy wonderfully creamy.

1. Combine the water and soy sauce in a shallow skillet large enough to hold the cauliflower. Add the cauliflower, onion, garlic, and dill or parsley.

2. Cover and cook over medium heat for 12 to 15 minutes, or until the cauliflorets are just tender.

3. Transfer the cauliflorets to a serving dish and set aside, leaving the liquid and seasonings in the pan.

4. Place the tahini in a small bowl, and use a fork to beat the vegetable broth or water into the tahini until smooth. Add to the liquid in the pan along with the lemon juice.

5. Place the pan over medium heat and simmer for 5 minutes, stirring continuously, until the gravy is hot and slightly thickened. Season with salt to taste.

6. Pour the gravy over the cauliflower, toss to coat, and serve immediately.

Variation

- For Green Beans with Tahini Gravy, replace the cauliflower with 1 pound of green beans, which have been left whole with ends trimmed off.

CORN PICADILLO

YIELD: 4 SERVINGS

1 tablespoon sherry

1/2 cup chopped onion

1/4 cup chopped green pepper

2 cups fresh corn kernels (cut from 2 big or 4 small ears) or frozen kernels

1 large tomato, diced

2 tablespoons chopped green or black olives

2 tablespoons currants or chopped dark raisins

1 tablespoon chopped fresh basil

This sprightly vegetable dish appeals to both the eye and the palate. Although it is most flavorful when made with fresh sweet summer corn cut right off the cob, it can also be made with frozen corn. Corn Picadillo provides a good accompaniment to grilled tofu or tempeh entrées along with a cooked whole grain.

1. Place the cooking sherry in a large shallow skillet, and heat. Add the onion and green pepper and cook over medium heat, stirring occasionally, for about 5 minutes, or until the onion softens.

2. Add all of the remaining ingredients to the skillet and continue to cook for about 8 minutes, or until the corn is tender and everything is heated through. Serve immediately.

SESAME GREEN BEANS

YIELD: 4 SERVINGS

1 pound green beans, trimmed but left whole

1 tablespoon lemon juice

1 tablespoon sesame seeds, toasted (page 19)

1 teaspoon toasted sesame oil

Salt

Freshly ground pepper

Sesame seeds enhance almost any vegetable. If you agree, try this recipe with steamed cauliflower and broccoli florets, as well.

1. Steam the green beans for 5 to 8 minutes, or until tender but still crunchy.

2. Transfer the warm beans to a serving bowl, and toss with the lemon juice, sesame seeds, and sesame oil. Add salt and pepper to taste and serve hot.

Blackened Green Beans

YIELD: 4 SERVINGS

1 pound green beans, trimmed but left whole

2 tablespoons soy sauce

4 cloves garlic, chopped

1 teaspoon chili powder

2 to 3 tablespoons water

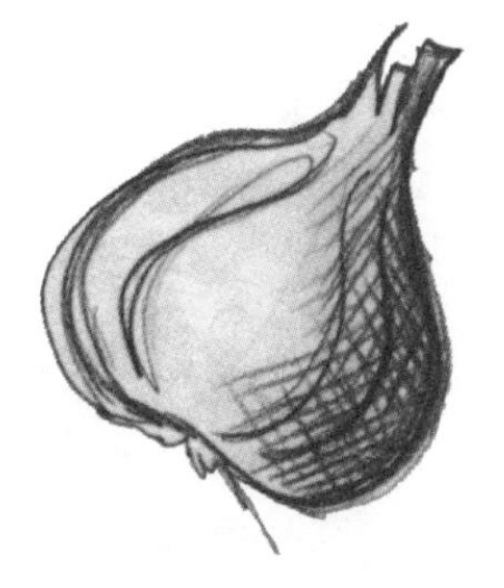

These crisply cooked beans have a subtle smoky taste and a hint of spiciness. If you like really hot food, use a potent chili powder or add a pinch of cayenne. Finally, if you're worried about cleanup, don't be. Just let the blackened pan soak for a while, and it will clean with ease.

1. Combine the green beans and soy sauce in a wok or large skillet. Cook over high heat, stirring continuously, for 5 to 10 minutes, or until the beans are singed and the soy sauce has evaporated. Add the garlic during the last minute or so of cooking.

2. Remove the pan from the heat, and immediately add the chili powder. Then add the water, 1 tablespoonful at a time, stirring to dissolve the blackened soy sauce in the pan. Do this carefully, as there will be some sputtering. Serve immediately.

Variations

- For Blackened Carrots, replace the green beans with a pound of carrots cut into 2-inch-long matchsticks (about 3 cups).

- For Blackened Asparagus, replace the green beans with a pound of stalks broken into 2-inch lengths (about 4 cups).

- For Blackened Broccoli, replace the green beans with 4 cups of broccoli stems, peeled and cut into 2-inch-long sticks.

Spicy Italian Greens

YIELD: 4 TO 6 SERVINGS

1 1/2 pounds leafy greens (beet greens, broccoli rabe, Swiss chard, chicory, escarole, frisée, or kale), chopped coarsely (about 12 cups)

1/2 cup canned crushed tomatoes or tomato purée

2 large cloves garlic, minced

2 tablespoons capers

1/2 teaspoon crushed red pepper flakes

This recipe is designed for the bitter greens listed at left, but can also be made using romaine lettuce combined with Italian flat-leaf parsley. A dollop of yogurt cheese on top of each serving provides a nice contrast.

1. Combine all of the ingredients in a heavy skillet or pot large enough to hold them. Cook, uncovered, over medium heat for about 5 minutes, or until the greens are wilted. Stir as needed for even cooking.

2. Cover the skillet or pot, and cook an additional 10 minutes, or until the greens are tender. Serve immediately.

Variation

- For a main dish, add 3 cups of cooked chickpeas, white beans, or lentils at the end of Step 2, and heat through. Serve as is or over a small-size pasta, such as bow ties, spirals, or shells. As an alternative, mix the cooked greens—with or without the beans—with cooked tortellini.

"When a man has pity on all living creatures then only is he noble."

–Buddha

Country Greens

YIELD: 4 SERVINGS

$1\frac{1}{2}$ pounds red or white Swiss chard

6 ounces cremini mushrooms

$\frac{1}{3}$ cup sliced shallots

2 tablespoons lemon juice

Salt

Freshly ground pepper

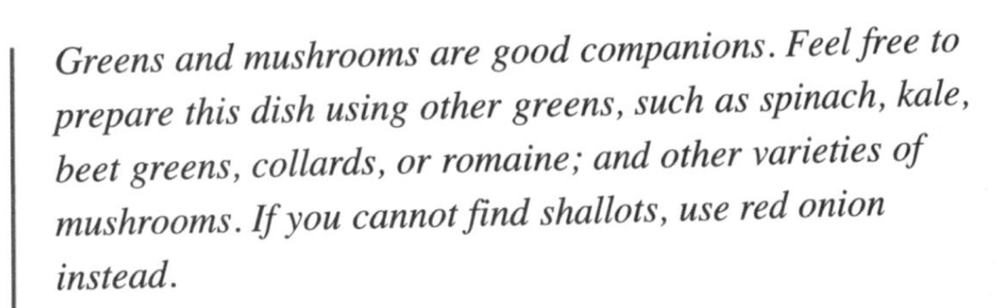

Greens and mushrooms are good companions. Feel free to prepare this dish using other greens, such as spinach, kale, beet greens, collards, or romaine; and other varieties of mushrooms. If you cannot find shallots, use red onion instead.

1. Remove the tough stems from the Swiss chard, and cut the leaves crosswise into $\frac{1}{2}$-inch-wide strips. You should have about 12 cups. Set aside.

2. Slice the mushroom caps and stems. You should have about 2 cups.

3. In a pot large enough to hold the greens, cook the mushrooms over medium heat, stirring occasionally to prevent sticking, for 5 to 8 minutes, or until they wilt and release their juices.

4. Add the shallots to the pot, and cook for 1 to 2 minutes.

5. Add the greens to the pot, and mix until they begin to wilt and cook down. (Tongs and chopsticks are both good tools for this job.)

6. Cover the pot and cook over low heat for 5 to 10 minutes, or until the greens are tender.

7. Remove the pot from the heat, stir in the lemon juice, and season with salt and pepper to taste. Serve hot.

Braised Leeks

YIELD: 4 SERVINGS

4 good-size leeks

1 teaspoon salt

2 tablespoons pine nuts

2 large cloves garlic, chopped

2 tablespoons balsamic vinegar

$\frac{1}{4}$ cup reserved leek cooking water

This dish makes a fine accompaniment to a meal, and also works well as part of an assorted appetizer plate.

1. Trim the dark green tops from the leeks and discard. Slice the leeks in half lengthwise. Wash well under cold running water to remove any dirt lodged between the layers. Cut into 3-inch sections.

2. Place a quart of water in a medium-size pot, and bring to a rolling boil over high heat. Add the salt and the leeks, and boil for 5 minutes.

3. Using a slotted spoon or tongs, remove the leeks from the pot, reserving $\frac{1}{4}$ cup of the cooking liquid. Place the leeks in a colander and run under cold water to refresh and stop further cooking. Drain well.

4. Place the pine nuts in a large skillet, and toast them over medium heat until they just begin to color. Add the drained leeks, garlic, and balsamic vinegar, shaking the skillet to coat the leeks with vinegar.

5. Increase the heat to high and cook for 1 to 2 minutes, stirring or shaking the pan continuously to lightly sear the leeks.

6. Reduce the heat to medium, add the reserved cooking water, and cook until the liquid is almost evaporated. Serve hot or at room temperature.

Variation

- For Braised Celery Stalks, replace the leeks with 8 celery stalks, cutting the celery into 3-inch sections and slicing any wide pieces in half lengthwise.

MUSHROOMS WITH CARROTS

YIELD: 4 SERVINGS

- 3 medium carrots, cut into 1/4-inch cubes
- 1/4 cup water
- 1 small onion, minced
- 12 ounces white mushrooms, sliced (about 4 cups)
- 2 tablespoons balsamic vinegar
- 1 teaspoon dried oregano
- 1/4 teaspoon salt

In this dish, the mild flavor of white mushrooms is vitalized by the sweetness of carrots and the sweet-tart taste of balsamic vinegar. To slice the mushrooms quickly and easily, use an egg slicer.

1. Combine the carrots and water in a large skillet, and bring to a boil over high heat. Then reduce the heat to a simmer, cover, and cook for about 5 minutes, or until barely tender.

2. Add the onion to the skillet and cook, uncovered, for about 5 minutes, or until the onion is wilted and the liquid has evaporated.

3. Add the mushrooms to the skillet and cook, stirring several times, for 8 to 10 minutes, or until the mushrooms are tender and have released their juices.

4. Add the vinegar, oregano, and salt to the skillet and boil gently for about 3 minutes. Serve hot.

GLAZED PLANTAINS

YIELD: 4 TO 6 SERVINGS

- 2 tablespoons fruit juice-sweetened orange marmalade
- 1/2 cup orange juice
- 3/8 teaspoon cayenne pepper
- 2 large ripe plantains (about 1 1/2 pounds), peeled and sliced 1/4-inch thick

Plantains—starchy fruits that look like bananas but taste more like potatoes—go well with South American dishes. This particular sweet-and-spicy version can be paired with Black Bean Soup (page 83), Quick Cuban-Style Black Beans (page 151), or Picadillo (page 134).

1. Place the marmalade in a large skillet, and melt over medium heat. Stir in the orange juice and cayenne pepper. Then add the plantains.

2. Reduce the heat to low and cook, turning a few times to coat, for 5 to 8 minutes, or until tender and covered with a thick glaze. Serve immediately.

Baked Onions

YIELD: 4 TO 6 SERVINGS

4 medium-size white or red onions

1/3 cup balsamic vinegar

We frequently serve this dish when entertaining. Although both white and red onions are suitable for baking, the red have more visual appeal.

1. Preheat the oven to 375°F.

2. Arrange the unpeeled, whole onions in a shallow baking pan just large enough to hold them comfortably and bake for about 1 hour, or until soft to the touch.

3. Transfer the onions to a serving plate. When cool enough to handle, cut each one in quarters almost down to the root so that the onions open like flowers, with the bottom still intact. Set aside.

4. Place the baking pan that held the onions on top of the stove and add the balsamic vinegar. Cook over medium heat while scraping the caramelized onion juice off the bottom of the pan, incorporating it into the vinegar. Cook until syrupy.

5. Spoon the vinegar reduction over the onions and serve.

"To consider yourself an environmentalist
and still eat meat is like saying
you're a philanthropist who doesn't give to charity."

–Howard Lyman
Former cattle rancher and founder of Voice for a Viable Future

BASIC BAKED POTATOES

4 medium-size baking potatoes (8 ounces each), such as Russet

This recipe can be easily increased or decreased to suit the size of your family. Naturally, if you use larger or smaller potatoes than those specified, you'll want to change the baking time accordingly. Serve simply with a sprinkling of salt and pepper, or slather on creamy yogurt cheese (page 22) for a more traditional topping.

1. Preheat the oven to 400°F.

2. Scrub the potatoes clean, and cut out any sprouts or eyes. Dry well with paper towels, and pierce each in several places with a fork to prevent bursting during baking.

3. Arrange the potatoes in a single layer on a baking sheet or directly on the rack of the oven, and bake for 45 minutes, or until the potatoes yield readily to gentle pressure with a mitted hand, or until a skewer will easily pierce the center. Serve immediately.

TIP

- To speed cooking time, spike each potato with a metal kebab skewer, and allow the skewer to stay in during baking. This will reduce the baking time by about a third.

MASHED POTATOES WITH GARLIC

YIELD: 4 SERVINGS

1 small leek, optional

1 1/2 pounds potatoes, unpeeled, cut into 1-inch chunks (about 4 1/2 cups)

8 cloves garlic, thinly sliced

1/2 cup water

1/2 cup soy milk

1/2 teaspoon salt

Freshly ground pepper

Paprika

This dish is low in fat, but not in flavor.

1. If using the leek, trim off and discard the dark tops, and cut the leek in half lengthwise. Then wash well to remove the dirt, and chop.

2. Combine the chopped leek with the potatoes, garlic, and water in a large pot. Bring to a boil over high heat.

3. Reduce the heat to low, cover the pot, and cook for 20 minutes, or until the potatoes are very tender. Once cooked, remove the peel or not, according to your preference.

4. Using a potato masher, mash the potatoes and other vegetables along with any liquid remaining in the pot. Then use a fork, whisk, or electric mixer to gradually beat in the soy milk until light and fluffy.

5. Season to taste with salt and pepper, and transfer to a serving bowl. Sprinkle the top generously with paprika before serving hot.

Seventh-day Adventists—who eat a mostly plant-based diet—live several years longer than most Americans and have a lower risk of heart disease and of lung, colon, stomach, bladder, and kidney cancers.

–Based on a study conducted by Loma Linda University

MASHED POTATOES WITH CELERIAC

YIELD: 4 SERVINGS

8 ounces celeriac

1 pound potatoes, peeled or unpeeled, cut into 1-inch chunks (about 3 cups)

1/4 cup white wine

1/4 cup water

2 tablespoons light miso, or 1/2 teaspoon salt

Freshly ground pepper

Celeriac, sometimes called celery knob or celery root, has a taste similar to that of celery but with a sweet undertone. Combined with potatoes, it makes a flavorful dish that is light in terms of both texture and carbs compared with regular mashed potatoes. If celeriac is not available, substitute peeled eggplant for a similarly light, low-carb dish and a novel flavor.

1. Trim the knobby portions of the celeriac and remove the peel using a potato peeler and small paring knife when necessary. Cut the celeriac into 1-inch chunks. You should have about 2 cups.

2. Combine the celeriac, potatoes, wine, and water in a large pot, and bring to a boil over high heat. Reduce the heat to low, cover, and cook for 20 minutes, or until the vegetables are very tender.

3. Drain the vegetables, reserving any liquid, and transfer the vegetables to a food processor. Add the miso or salt and process until smooth, light, and fluffy, adding the reserved liquid as needed.

4. Season generously with freshly ground pepper, and serve immediately.

POTATOES PEPPERONATA

YIELD: 4 SERVINGS

1 large red onion, chopped

2 cloves garlic, chopped

½ cup diced tomato

2 medium red peppers, cut into thin strips

2 medium potatoes (1 pound total), peeled or unpeeled, cut into ¾-inch cubes

½ teaspoon salt

Freshly ground pepper

Potatoes stewed with peppers and onions are both comforting and delicious. This Mediterranean classic complements Italian, Spanish, or Greek food, and goes well with traditional American fare, as well.

1. Combine the onion, garlic, and tomato in a large pot with a tight-fitting lid. Cover and cook over low heat for 10 minutes.

2. Add the red peppers, potatoes, and salt to the pot, replace the cover, and continue to cook, stirring occasionally, for 20 minutes, or until the potatoes are tender. The vegetables should expel enough of their own juices to cook the potatoes, but if the mixture seems dry, add a little water.

3. Season with a generous amount of freshly ground pepper before serving.

BAKED SWEET POTATOES OR YAMS

YIELD: 4 SERVINGS

4 medium-size sweet potatoes or yams (8 ounces each)

Like baked white potatoes, both baked sweet potatoes and yams are delicious when crowned with yogurt cheese (page 22). For a more substantial dish, though, try topping them with the flavorful cooked beans of your choice.

1. Preheat the oven to 375°F.

2. Scrub the potatoes clean, and cut out any sprouts or eyes. Dry well with paper towels, and pierce each in several places with a fork to prevent bursting during baking.

3. Arrange the potatoes in a single layer on a baking sheet or directly on the rack of the oven, and bake for 40 minutes, or until the potatoes yield readily to gentle pressure with a mitted hand, or until a skewer will easily pierce through the center. Serve immediately.

Louisiana Sweet Potatoes

YIELD: 4 SERVINGS

4 medium sweet potatoes, peeled and diced (7 to 8 cups)

1 tablespoon soy sauce

2 teaspoons paprika

2 teaspoons chili powder

1 teaspoon dried mustard powder

2 tablespoons water

This Cajun dish will add spice to any meal.

1. Place the sweet potato cubes in a large pot, and add water to cover. Bring to a boil over high heat. Then reduce the heat to a simmer and cook uncovered for 10 to 12 minutes, or until tender but still firm. Remove the potatoes, discarding the cooking liquid.

2. Combine the soy sauce, paprika, chili powder, and mustard powder in the pot in which the potatoes were cooked. Cook over medium heat, stirring continuously, for 1 minute.

3. Add the 2 tablespoons of water to the pot with the seasonings to dilute. Return the potatoes to the pot and mix until well coated with the spices. Then cook, stirring frequently, for 3 to 5 additional minutes, or until hot. Serve immediately.

Wine-Simmered Vegetables

YIELD: 4 SERVINGS

Dry red or white wine

4 cups carrots, green beans, zucchini, broccoli florets or stems, and/or cauliflorets, cut into bite-size pieces

A flavorful alternative to steaming, wine-simmering is an easy way to prepare vegetables that will be used as a side dish, served over grains, or dressed with a sauce. You can make this dish with a mixture of vegetables, or you can choose just one.

1. Pour enough of the wine into a large, heavy skillet to cover the bottom of the pan to a depth of $\frac{1}{4}$ inch, and place the skillet over medium heat.

2. When the skillet is hot and vapors just start to rise from the wine, add the vegetables. Cover and cook over low to medium heat for 10 minutes, or until the vegetables are done to taste. Serve hot.

Vegetables Baked in Red Wine

YIELD: 4 TO 6 SERVINGS

2 medium baking potatoes (8 ounces each), scrubbed

1 large sweet potato (12 ounces), peeled

1 medium cauliflower (2 to 2½ pounds), broken into florets (5 to 7 cups)

4 shallots, thinly sliced

4 cloves garlic, thinly sliced

1 cup dry red wine

1 teaspoon dried rosemary

1 teaspoon salt

Freshly ground pepper

Red wine adds wonderful flavor and color to this vegetable dish.

1. Preheat the oven to 400°F.

2. Cut the scrubbed baking potatoes into quarters lengthwise; then cut each quarter into 3 pieces. Cut up the peeled sweet potato in the same manner.

3. Arrange the cauliflower and potatoes in a 9-x-13-inch or shallow 2-quart casserole. The vegetables should fit in a snug single layer. Do not pile them up.

4. Scatter the sliced shallots and garlic over the vegetables. Then combine the wine, rosemary, and salt in a small bowl, and pour the mixture over the vegetables.

5. Cover the dish and bake for 20 minutes. Remove the cover, and season the vegetables with lots of fresh pepper. Stir so that all the surfaces are coated with the wine.

6. Return the dish to the oven and bake, uncovered, for about 45 minutes, or until the vegetables are tender. Stir occasionally to coat all the surfaces with the wine and promote even cooking. If the wine cooks out before the vegetables are done, add a little more wine or water to finish cooking and keep the pan from scorching. Serve hot.

BAKED YUCCA

YIELD: 4 TO 6 SERVINGS

4 medium-size yucca (7 to 8 ounces each)

Yucca—also called cassava and manioc—is a popular tuber of Latin American origin. While yucca is most commonly boiled, we prefer it baked and seasoned at the table, as you would prepare a baked potato. Choose a specimen with the bark-like brown skin intact, avoiding those with grayish fibers, discolored patches, or soft spots.

1. Preheat the oven to 400°F.

2. If the yucca appears to be coated with wax (most are), scrape under hot water with a paring knife or sharp vegetable peeler to remove the peel.

3. Arrange the yucca on a baking sheet and bake for 30 to 40 minutes, or until tender. Serve immediately.

SPICY GRILLED ZUCCHINI

YIELD: 4 SERVINGS

2 medium to large zucchini (about 10 to 16 ounces each)

¾ cup Spicy Marinade (page 216)

Grilling turns zucchini—a somewhat bland vegetable—into a delicacy. (For more details on grilling vegetables, see Chapter 3, page 28.)

1. Cut the zucchini lengthwise into ¼-inch-thick slices.

2. Pour the marinade into a shallow baking pan and place the zucchini in the marinade for 30 minute or longer. If the slices aren't completely submerged, turn them occasionally so that the marinade comes in contact with all of the zucchini.

3. Preheat a grill until the coals or elements are red hot. Oil the rack before you begin cooking.

4. Remove the zucchini slices from the marinade and place on the grill rack. Cook for 6 to 10 minutes on each side, or until grill marks appear on the surface. Serve hot off the grill or at room temperature.

ZUCCHINI A L'ORANGE

YIELD: 4 SERVINGS

1 1/2 pounds zucchini or yellow crookneck squash (2 to 4 squash), cut into 2-by-1/4-inch sticks

1/4 cup orange juice

2 tablespoons chopped fresh mint, or 2 teaspoons dried mint

1 teaspoon minced orange zest

1/4 teaspoon salt

2 oranges, peeled, separated into sections, each section cut in half

2 tablespoons pumpkin seeds, toasted (page 19)

1/2 teaspoon paprika

The sprightly flavors of orange and mint do an excellent job of making squash come alive in this summertime dish.

1. Combine the squash, orange juice, mint, orange zest, and salt in a large skillet, and stir over medium-high heat for 3 to 5 minutes, or just until the squash is tender.

2. Stir the orange pieces into the squash mixture, and cook briefly to warm through.

3. Transfer the squash mixture to a serving dish, top with the toasted pumpkin seeds, sprinkle with the paprika, and serve.

**"To be a vegetarian is to disagree—
to disagree with the course of things today.
Starvation, world hunger, cruelty, waste, wars—
we must make a statement against these things.
Vegetarianism is my statement.
And I think it's a strong one."**

–Isaac Bashevis Singer

BEAN SIDE DISHES

BLACK-EYED PEAS TRIPOLI

YIELD: 4 SERVINGS

1 small onion, chopped

2 cloves garlic, sliced

1/4 cup bean cooking liquid or water

3 cups cooked or canned black-eyed peas

2 stalks celery, chopped

1/2 cup chopped fresh cilantro

1/2 teaspoon salt (reduce if beans are salted)

Freshly ground pepper

1 to 2 tablespoons olive, flaxseed, or hemp oil, optional

Lemon wedges

For a Middle Eastern meal, serve this flavorful dish with cracked wheat, Tomato Couscous (page 199) or Warm Bulgur Salad (page 98), and a cooked vegetable or salad. This dish is also good with Cold Cucumber Yogurt Soup (page 86), Yogurt Cucumber Salad (page 90), or Quick White Pita Pizzas (page 69).

1. Combine the onion, garlic, and cooking liquid or water in a pot large enough to hold the beans. Cover and stew over medium heat for 5 to 8 minutes, or just until the onion is tender.

2. Add the beans, celery, cilantro, and salt to the pot, and cook uncovered, stirring frequently, for 2 to 3 minutes, or until the beans are heated through.

3. Remove the pot from the heat and season the bean mixture liberally with the pepper. Drizzle with the oil if desired, and serve accompanied by lemon wedges for individual seasoning.

VARIATION

- Replace the black-eyed peas with lentils (especially the firmer French lentils), small lima beans, or small white navy or pea beans.

Channa Dahl

YIELD: 4 SERVINGS

2 cups cooked or canned chickpeas, drained

1 cup chickpea cooking liquid, water, or vegetable broth

2 cloves garlic

1 tablespoon curry powder

½ teaspoon ground cumin

Salt

This Indian-style bean purée can be served as a side dish, spooned over baked potatoes or a cooked grain for an entrée, or served at room temperature as a dip with whole wheat chapati wedges and raw or lightly steamed vegetables. Be aware that the spiciness of the dish may vary with the curry powder blend used.

1. Combine all of the ingredients except for the salt in a blender or food processor, and purée until smooth.

2. Transfer the puréed mixture to a small saucepan, and cook for 2 to 3 minutes to warm through.

3. Salt the mixture to taste if necessary, and serve.

Variation

- To make Curried Hummus, reduce the chickpea cooking liquid to ½ cup, and chill the mixture well before serving.

Split Peas in Creamy Mustard Sauce

YIELD: 4 TO 6 SERVINGS

2 cups dried green split peas

6 cups water

2 bay leaves

2 tablespoons finely chopped fresh ginger

½ teaspoon turmeric

3 tablespoons prepared mustard

These rich, flavorful split peas are best accompanied by a grain—perhaps Nutted Rice with Raisins (page 201)—and a sprightly yogurt salad such as Carrot Raita (page 91). Whole wheat chapatis are excellent for scooping up the various dishes.

1. Combine the spit peas and water in a large pot, and bring to a boil over high heat.

2. Add the bay leaves, ginger, and turmeric to the pot. Reduce the heat to a simmer, cover, and cook over low heat for about 45 minutes, or until the peas are just tender, but not breaking apart. Stir occasionally during cooking and test frequently near the end so the peas do not overcook.

3. Remove and discard the bay leaves, and stir in the mustard. Then cook, stirring continuously, for 1 to 2 minutes, or until the mustard melts into the sauce and turns it rich and creamy.

4. Cover the pot, remove from the heat, and allow to sit for about 10 minutes so that the flavors develop before serving.

LEMONY LIMAS

YIELD: 4 SERVINGS

- 1 medium onion, chopped
- 2 cloves garlic, sliced
- 1/4 cup bean cooking liquid or water
- 1/4 cup lemon juice
- 1 teaspoon minced lemon zest
- 1/2 teaspoon salt (reduce if beans are salted)
- 1 stalk celery, chopped
- 1/4 cup chopped fresh parsley
- 3 cups cooked dried baby lima beans
- 1 tablespoon olive, flaxseed, or hemp oil, optional

Lots of fresh lemon melds nicely with the delicate flavor of lima beans. Lemony Limas store well in the refrigerator and make an excellent cold salad or filling for pita bread, so you may want to multiply the recipe for planned leftovers. Serve with a platter of grilled or oven-roasted vegetables and a simple grain.

1. Combine the onion, garlic, and cooking liquid or water in a pot large enough to hold the beans. Cover and stew over medium heat for 5 to 8 minutes, or just until the onion is tender.

2. Add all of the remaining ingredients except the oil to the pot, and cook uncovered for 2 to 3 minutes, or just until the lima beans are heated through.

3. Remove the pot from the heat and drizzle with the oil if desired. Serve warm or at room temperature. Leftovers can be chilled for a tasty salad.

VARIATION

- For Lemony Lentils, prepare the dish with the same amount of cooked lentils—preferably French lentils, as they maintain their shape well.

SPRING CHICKPEAS

YIELD: 4 SERVINGS

1 large onion, cut into thin crescents

2 carrots, thinly sliced

1 large clove garlic, chopped

1/4 cup chickpea cooking liquid or water

1/2 pound sugar snap or snow peas, cut into 1-inch segments (2 cups)

2 1/2 cups cooked or canned chickpeas

2 tablespoons chopped fresh parsley

1/4 teaspoon salt

Freshly ground pepper

This cheerful dish has the sprightly taste of fresh seasonal vegetables. For a spring meal, begin with Cold Cucumber Yogurt Soup (page 86) and pair the chickpeas with a flavorful grain dish and salad. As an alternative to the soup, accompany with Quick White Pita Pizzas made with a red pepper topping (page 69).

1. Combine the onion, carrots, garlic, and cooking liquid or water in a medium-size saucepan. Bring to a boil over high heat and cook uncovered for 5 to 8 minutes, or until the carrots are tender.

2. Add the peas to the saucepan and cook, stirring frequently, for 3 to 5 minutes, or until the peas are cooked but still crisp.

3. Add the chickpeas, parsley, and salt to taste, and cook just until the chickpeas are heated through.

4. Remove the saucepan from the heat and season liberally with freshly ground pepper before serving.

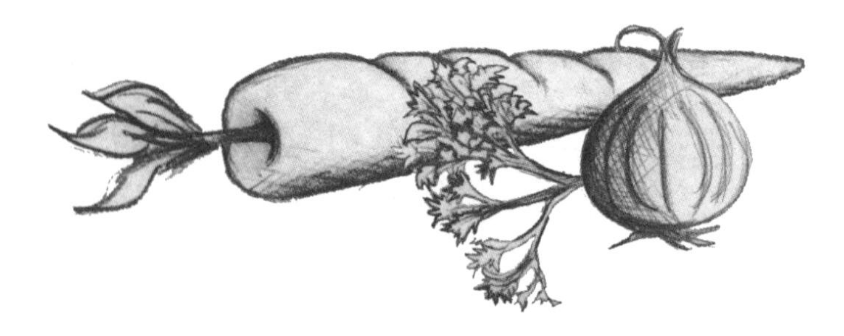

Soybeans Southern Style

YIELD: 4 SERVINGS

1 large sweet onion, such as Vidalia, Walla Walla, or Maui, chopped

1 tablespoon soy sauce

1 $^{1}/_{2}$ cups diced canned tomatoes, lightly drained

1 $^{1}/_{2}$ tablespoons molasses

1 $^{1}/_{2}$ tablespoons cider vinegar

3 cups cooked or canned soybeans, drained

Hot pepper sauce to taste

This is an especially good way to prepare the canned soybeans available in natural food stores. For an excellent Southern dinner, serve with Mashed Potatoes with Celeriac (page 187) or corn on the cob; Creamy Miso Mustard Cole Slaw (page 88) or Country Greens (page 181); and Golden Biscuits (page 46), corn bread, or even tortillas.

1. Combine the onion and soy sauce in a medium-size saucepan. Cover and cook over low heat for 5 minutes.

2. Add the tomatoes, molasses, and vinegar to the saucepan, and simmer uncovered for 5 minutes.

3. Add the soybeans to the pot, and season to taste with the hot sauce. Cover and simmer for about 10 minutes, or until the soybeans are quite hot and surrounded with sauce. Because soybeans hold their shape, longer cooking will not harm the dish, nor will reheating.

"The impact of countless hooves and mouths over the years has done more to alter the type of vegetation and land forms of the West than all the water projects, strip mines, power plants, freeways, and subdivision developments combined."

–Philip Fradkin
In *Audubon*, National Audubon Society, NY

GRAIN SIDE DISHES

BARLEY AND MUSHROOMS

YIELD: 4 TO 6 SERVINGS

12 ounces mushrooms, any type, sliced (4 cups)
1 cup chopped onion
2 tablespoons water
1 tablespoon soy sauce
1 1/2 cups hulled barley
4 cups boiling water
1/2 teaspoon salt
Freshly ground pepper

Hulled barley is the whole grain form, which is not the same as the more common—and more processed—pearl barley. In its hulled form, barley has a rich flavor and appealing chewiness. Barley takes a while to cook, but the time can be substantially reduced with a pressure cooker, as shown in the Variation at the end of the recipe.

1. Combine the mushrooms, onion, 2 tablespoons of water, and soy sauce in a large pot, and cook over medium heat, stirring occasionally, for 5 to 8 minutes, or until the mushroom juices run freely.

2. Stir the barley into the mushroom mixture and cook for 1 minute.

3. Add the boiling water to the pot, cover, and cook over low heat for 75 to 90 minutes, or until the barley is tender, stirring occasionally to prevent sticking. When done, the barley will be chewy but no longer hard.

4. Add the salt towards the end of cooking, and season generously with freshly ground pepper just before serving.

VARIATION

- To make Barley and Mushrooms in a pressure cooker, combine the mushrooms, onion, soy sauce, barley, and 3 cups of cold water in a pressure cooker. Then close the cooker, engage the pressure valve, and bring to pressure over medium heat. Lower the heat to just maintain pressure and cook for 50 minutes. Remove from the heat, let sit for 5 minutes, and reduce the pressure fully according to manufacturer's directions. Season to taste with salt and pepper, stir well to incorporate any remaining liquid, and serve.

Tomato Couscous

YIELD: 6 SERVINGS

1 1/2 cups water

1 1/2 cups tomato juice

2 cups whole wheat couscous or fine bulgur

Salt

This dish is quick, easy, and flavorful.

1. Combine the water and tomato juice in a medium-size pot, and bring to a boil over high heat.

2. Sprinkle the grain into the boiling liquid, stir once, and lower the heat to a simmer. Cover and cook for 5 minutes.

3. Remove the pot from the heat, and allow to sit covered for 10 minutes.

4. Fluff the grain with a fork, salt to taste, and serve.

Enjoying Grains

Chapter 3, "Basic Training," offers easy-to-follow instructions for preparing a variety of whole grains, and the recipes in this section illustrate how grains can be easily transformed into satisfying side dishes. As you experiment with your favorite grains, the following tips will help you broaden their appeal.

■ Add flavor to grains by varying the cooking medium, using vegetable broth, the liquid from drained canned tomatoes, any liquid left from cooking vegetables or beans, or even leftover tea in place of water.

■ Use herbs and spices to change the character of a grain. Cumin, curry powder, oregano, basil, rosemary, cinnamon, and such can be added in a ratio of 1/2 to 1 teaspoon per each cup of uncooked grains.

■ Toss on a garnish of sesame seeds, toasted sunflower or pumpkin seeds, pine nuts, walnuts, or slivered almonds, and add both crunch and flavor to your grains.

■ Make plain-cooked grains more substantial by adding a sauce or topping from Chapter 10. You will be surprised by how innovative and interesting these pairings can be.

■ Never toss out leftover cooked grains. Store them in the refrigerator for up to a week, and use them in salads, side dishes, and soups, or as a stuffing for vegetables.

Kasha with Stewed Onions

YIELD: 4 SERVINGS

2 cups boiling water

1 cup kasha (buckwheat groats)

1/2 teaspoon salt

2 large onions, chopped

2 tablespoons water

2 teaspoons soy sauce

Kasha and onions are a classic duo and an especially healthful one. You can embellish this dish with a topping of yogurt cheese (page 22) or Creamy Mushroom Gravy (page 215). Other variations include adding a cup of sliced mushrooms to cook along with the onions, or replacing half the kasha with bow-tie noodles for the famous dish kasha varnishkes.

1. Combine the boiling water, kasha, and salt in a medium-size saucepan. Cover and simmer over low heat for about 30 minutes, or until the liquid is completely absorbed and the grain is tender.

2. While the kasha is cooking, combine the onions, water, and soy sauce in a heavy skillet, and cook over medium heat until hot. Then cover, reduce the heat to low, and steep, stirring occasionally, for 10 to 15 minutes, or until the onions have a rich, velvety texture. If the onions become dry at any time during cooking, add more water, 1 tablespoon at a time, as needed.

3. Transfer the kasha to a serving dish, spoon the onions over the kasha, and serve hot.

Oat Pilaf

YIELD: 4 SERVINGS

1 egg

2 cups oats

1 cup water, vegetable broth, liquid from canned tomatoes, or a mixture of 1/4 cup tomato juice and 3/4 cup water

1 1/2 tablespoons soy sauce (reduce if liquid is salted)

4 scallions, sliced

3/4 cup frozen green peas

This quick, easy accompaniment has a moist texture reminiscent of stuffing.

1. Crack the egg into a medium-size saucepan and beat lightly until smooth. Stir in the oats, mixing until completely coated with the egg.

2. Place the saucepan over medium heat and cook, stirring almost continuously, until the surface of the oats is dry.

3. Add the liquid, soy sauce, scallions, and green peas to the saucepan, and bring to a boil. Reduce the heat to a simmer and cook gently, uncovered, for 5 to 8 minutes, or until the liquid is absorbed. Stir occasionally with a fork during cooking.

4. Cover and remove from heat until ready to serve.

Nutted Rice with Raisins

YIELD: 4 SERVINGS

1 cup brown rice

2 cups water

1/4 cup dark raisins

1/4 cup sliced almonds

2 tablespoons pumpkin seeds, toasted (page 19)

1/4 teaspoon ground cinnamon

If you have 3 cups of cooked brown rice in the fridge, simply warm it up and start preparing this fragrant dish with Step 2. In just a few minutes, you'll have a wonderful accompaniment for your entrée.

1. Combine the rice and water in a medium-size pot, and bring to a boil over high heat. Reduce the heat to a simmer, cover, and cook over low heat for about 45 minutes, or until the grain is tender and the liquid is completely absorbed.

2. Add all of the remaining ingredients to the rice, and toss gently with a fork or chopsticks. Replace the cover until ready to serve.

WILD RICE WITH MUSHROOMS

YIELD: 4 SERVINGS

1 small onion, chopped

3 ounces shiitake, cremini, chanterelle, oyster, or white mushrooms, coarsely chopped (about 1 cup)

2 tablespoons water

1 tablespoon soy sauce

$^{1}/_{2}$ cup wild rice

1 $^{1}/_{4}$ cups boiling water

Although used as a grain, wild rice is the seed of a native American grass. Perhaps because it is so expensive, wild rice is often combined with regular rice in recipes. But since it quadruples in volume with cooking, a little goes a long way, so consider using it alone. The Variation at the end of this recipe will guide you in speeding preparation.

1. Combine the onion, mushrooms, water, and soy sauce in a medium-size pot. Cover and cook over medium heat for 5 minutes, or until the onion is tender and the mushroom juices run freely.

2. Stir in the wild rice and boiling water, cover, and simmer gently for 50 minutes, or until the liquid is absorbed and the rice is tender. Serve hot.

VARIATION

- To make Wild Rice with Mushrooms in a pressure cooker, first cook the onion, mushrooms, water, and soy sauce as directed above, making sure the pressure valve is not engaged. Add the rice and 1 cup of cold water. Then close the cooker, engage the pressure valve, and bring to pressure over high heat. Lower the heat to just maintain pressure and cook for 25 minutes. Remove from the heat, let sit for 5 minutes, and reduce the pressure fully according to the manufacturer's directions. If the liquid is not completely absorbed, cover the pot to conserve heat and let the rice sit to absorb what remains.

MILLET POLENTA

YIELD: 4 SERVINGS

4 cups water

1 cup millet

1/2 teaspoon salt

2 cloves garlic, minced, optional

Salt

Freshly ground pepper

The standard ratio for cooking millet is 3 cups liquid per 1 cup grain. When cooked with additional water in the manner described here, millet develops the rich, creamy texture of cornmeal polenta. Serve topped with a saucy bean dish such as White Beans with Swiss Chard (page 142) or Creamy Italian-Style Garden Vegetables (page 114).

1. Bring the water to a boil in a medium-size saucepan. Stir in the millet, salt, and garlic, if using, and reduce the heat to a simmer. Cover and cook for 20 minutes.

2. Uncover the saucepan and, stirring frequently, continue to cook for 10 to 15 minutes, or until the polenta becomes thick and has a soft, creamy texture.

3. Season to taste with additional salt and freshly ground pepper before serving.

THREE-GRAIN POLENTA BREAD

YIELD: 4 SERVINGS

3/4 cup cornmeal

2 tablespoons soy flour

2 tablespoons flaxseed meal (page 17)

1/2 teaspoon baking soda

1/4 teaspoon salt

1 1/2 cups plain nonfat yogurt

1 tablespoon maple syrup

1 teaspoon canola oil

This dense, moist bread resembles baked polenta and provides an excellent bed for heavily sauced tempeh, tofu, beans, or vegetables—dishes such as Tofu Chili (page 126), White Beans with Swiss Chard (page 142), Quick Mixed Italian Vegetables in Tomato Juice (page 112), and Chili Rellenos (page 109).

1. Preheat the oven to 400°F.

2. Combine the dry ingredients in a medium-size mixing bowl. Add the yogurt and maple syrup and mix gently but thoroughly, until the dry ingredients are completely moistened.

3. Pour the oil into an 8-inch-square baking pan and place in the oven for 2 to 3 minutes, until hot.

4. Spread the batter in the hot pan and bake for 30 minutes, or until the edges are lightly browned. Cut into squares to serve.

MILLET POLENTA PATTIES

YIELD: 12 PATTIES

3 cups water

1 cup millet

$^1/_2$ teaspoon salt

$^1/_2$ cup shredded zucchini

$^1/_2$ cup shredded carrot

Salt

Freshly ground pepper

These broiled polenta patties are an excellent base for beans. Depending on the size of the meal, plan to serve 2 to 3 patties for each person. According to the capacity of your broiler, you may need to broil the patties in batches. If desired, you can form the patties as much as one day in advance and store them in the refrigerator until it is time to broil them.

1. Bring the water to a boil in a medium-size saucepan. Stir in the millet and salt. Then reduce the heat to a simmer, cover, and cook over low heat for 20 minutes.

2. Uncover the saucepan and continue to cook, stirring frequently, for about 10 minutes, or until the millet becomes quite thick and has a soft, creamy texture.

3. Remove the saucepan from the heat, and stir in the shredded vegetables. Season to taste with salt and freshly ground pepper.

4. Wipe a large baking sheet with olive or canola oil. Preheat the broiler.

5. Using $^1/_3$ cup of polenta at a time, shape the mixture into patties and arrange on the oiled baking sheet. Place 4 to 6 inches below the heat source in the preheated broiler, and cook for about 5 minutes on each side, or until very lightly browned. If you prepare the patties in batches, wrap the cooked patties in a clean cloth napkin or dish towel to keep them warm. If reheating is necessary, return to the pan briefly before serving.

SUNFLOWER RICE PATTIES

YIELD: 8 TO 12 PATTIES

3 cups cooked brown rice

2 eggs, lightly beaten

1/2 cup minced onion

1/4 cup minced green pepper

1/4 cup finely chopped fresh parsley

1/4 cup sunflower seeds

1/4 cup flaxseed meal (page 17)

1/2 teaspoon salt

While these tender patties make a great side dish, they are equally satisfying as a light entrée. Size them based on their intended role and people's appetites. Then garnish them with Roasted Sweet Red Pepper Purée (page 57) or Green Pepper and Avocado Mayonnaise (page 59), and serve with bean soup or chili.

1. Combine all of the ingredients in a large bowl, mixing well.

2. Wipe the bottom of a large, heavy skillet or griddle with oil, and place over medium-high heat. Unless you have a large griddle, you will need to cook the patties in batches.

3. Arrange the rice mixture in mounds on the hot skillet or griddle, using from 1/3 to 1/2 cup for each patty, as desired. Flatten each mound lightly with a spatula.

4. Cook for about 8 minutes per side, or until golden brown. Be sure to let the bottom brown before turning, as at this point the patties will hold together nicely. If you prepare the patties in batches, wrap the cooked patties in a clean cloth napkin or dish towel to keep them warm. If reheating is necessary, return to the pan briefly before serving.

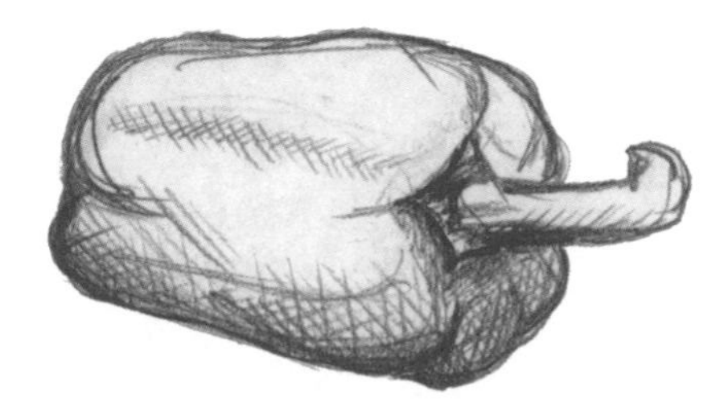

VEGETABLE CORN CAKES

YIELD: 8 CAKES

1 cup cornmeal

2½ teaspoons baking powder

1 cup soy milk

1 tablespoon light miso

1 teaspoon canola oil

6 ounces firm tofu, cut into ¼-inch cubes (1 cup)

½ cup fresh or frozen corn kernels

⅓ cup chopped red pepper

1 scallion, thinly sliced

These delicate corn pancakes provide a nourishing accompaniment that takes the place of bread. Plan on 2 corn cakes per person. Top with Pineapple Salsa (page 212), Salsa Cruda (page 212), or your favorite salsa, and serve with a bean entrée. Note that a nonstick pan is essential for this recipe.

1. Combine the cornmeal and baking powder in a large mixing bowl.

2. Add the soy milk, miso, and oil to the cornmeal. Mix gently but thoroughly so that the miso is distributed throughout, the cornmeal is completely moistened, and no lumps remain. Then fold in the tofu and vegetables.

3. Heat a nonstick frying pan or griddle over medium heat.

4. Drop the batter by ¼ cups onto the hot pan and cook for about 5 minutes on each side, or until brown. Turn each cake just once, and do it gently to keep the delicate cakes from breaking apart. If you prepare the cakes in batches, wrap the cooked corn cakes in a clean cloth napkin or dish towel to keep them warm. If reheating is necessary, return to the pan briefly before serving.

10. Sauces, Toppings, and Marinades

Sauces and toppings are what cooks all over the world rely on to make foods inviting. Almost any unadorned food—plain grains, simple steamed vegetables, basic beans, timid tofu or tempeh—can be brought to life by a shot of sauce or a tablespoon (or two) of topping. Similarly, marinades can be used to infuse everyday foods with extraordinary flavor.

Here are some ideas for choosing and using sauces, toppings, and marinades in your meals:

- Use vegetable- and fruit-based sauces to add to your daily produce intake.
- Choose sauces and topping containing beans, nuts, nut butter, or soy to add extra protein.
- For a homey dish, select a creamy sauce (or gravy) to moisten grains, pasta, tofu, and tempeh.
- For something lively, choose a pesto or flavorful tomato sauce to transform grains, pasta, tofu, tempeh, or vegetables.
- Use Better Than Ketchup on veggie burgers—or any other burgers, for that matter. You'll find that it surpasses any commercial offering.
- Use Spicy Marinade prior to cooking, or brush on Sweet Mustard Basting Sauce during cooking to enhance vegetables, tofu, and tempeh.
- Don't think of sauces simply as add-ons. They can also make spirited dips for vegetables.

The recipes in this chapter offer more than just good taste. Each mouthful actually boosts the nutrition of your meal. Because of their positive nature, we encourage you to indulge. Give grains plenty of gravy. Blanket those beans. Marinate those mushrooms. Smother your vegetables. And sop up all the sauce.

Portobello Mushroom Topping

YIELD: ABOUT 2 CUPS

4 cups sliced portobello mushrooms (about 12 ounces)

$^1/_2$ cup chopped shallots or red onion

2 large cloves garlic, minced

$^1/_4$ cup water

2 tablespoons soy sauce

$^1/_2$ cup chopped fresh parsley

$^1/_4$ cup balsamic vinegar

$^1/_4$ cup canned crushed tomatoes

The complex sweet-tangy flavor of balsamic vinegar melds with the earthiness of mushrooms, creating this dynamic topping for polenta, brown rice or other cooked grains, baked potatoes, pasta, or just a hearty slice of bread. If you want to economize, replace up to half the portobellos with another variety of exotic or even white mushrooms.

1. Combine the mushrooms, shallots or onion, garlic, water, and soy sauce in a large skillet. Cover and cook over medium-low heat for 10 to 15 minutes, or until the mushrooms are tender.

2. Add the parsley, vinegar, and tomatoes to the mushroom mixture. Leaving the pot uncovered, cook, stirring several times, for about 5 minutes, or until the mixture is heated through and the flavor of the vinegar infuses the mushrooms. Serve hot, or store for up to 5 days in the refrigerator. Rewarm over low heat.

Sea Vegetable Topping

YIELD: $^3/_4$ CUP

$^1/_2$ cup arame or hijiki seaweed

Warm water

1 tablespoon soy sauce

1 teaspoon toasted sesame oil

Arame and hijiki are both mild-tasting seaweeds and good choices for introducing nutritious sea vegetables to the table. Novices may prefer the less briny taste and tender texture of arame. Use this topping to garnish salads, vegetables, beans, and grains, or add to soups and sandwiches for flavor and nutrition.

1. Place the seaweed in a bowl, and add warm water to cover. Let soak for 5 to 10 minutes, or until the seaweed swells and softens. Drain, reserving $^1/_4$ cup of the soaking water.

2. Combine the seaweed, reserved soaking water, and soy sauce in a small saucepan, and simmer uncovered for 3 to 5 minutes, or until tender. The hijiki may require an additional few minutes.

3. Remove the saucepan from the heat, stir in the oil, and serve immediately, or store for up to 2 weeks in the refrigerator. Serve cold or at room temperature, or rewarm over low heat.

Chickpea Pesto

YIELD: 7/8 CUP

- 1/2 cup cooked or canned chickpeas, drained
- 2 tablespoons pine nuts, toasted (page 19)
- 2 cups lightly packed fresh basil leaves, or a mixture of fresh basil and parsley
- 2 cloves garlic, chopped
- 2 tablespoons chickpea cooking liquid or water
- 1 tablespoon olive oil
- Salt to taste

Chickpea Pesto can be used to dress 12 ounces of hot cooked pasta, just as you would use traditional pesto. Serve with grated Parmesan on the side. This pesto also makes an ideal topping for grilled eggplant slices, warm boiled potatoes, or Wine-Simmered Vegetables (page 189), as well as a filling for mushrooms (see Pesto-Stuffed Mushrooms on page 61).

1. Combine the chickpeas and pine nuts in a food processor, and process until well ground.

2. Add the herbs and garlic and purée to a thick paste.

3. Add the cooking liquid or water and process until evenly blended.

4. Add the oil and process until completely incorporated.

5. Adjust salt to taste and serve, or store for up to 5 days in the refrigerator.

Creamy Walnut Pesto

YIELD: 3/4 CUP

1/4 cup walnuts

2 cups lightly packed herbs or greens of choice, such as fresh basil, parsley, arugula, spinach, individually or in combination

2 cloves garlic, chopped

1/4 teaspoon salt

1/4 cup yogurt cheese (page 22)

1 tablespoon light miso

Serve this pesto on a baked potato, mix it with any hot steamed vegetable for a side dish, or stir it into mixed cooked vegetables and chickpeas or white beans for a main dish. For hors d'oeuvres, spoon some into raw mushroom caps or spread on tomato slices, raw zucchini rounds, or bread.

1. Place the walnuts in a food processor, and process until well ground.

2. Add the greens, garlic, and salt, and purée to a thick paste.

3. Add the yogurt cheese and miso, and process once more to a smooth thick sauce. Serve immediately, or store for up to 3 days in the refrigerator.

Tomato Almond Pesto

YIELD: 1 1/4 CUPS

1/2 cup almonds

1/2 cup lightly packed fresh basil leaves

1/2 cup lightly packed fresh parsley

1 cup drained chopped canned or fresh tomatoes

2 cloves garlic, chopped

1/2 teaspoon salt

1 tablespoon olive oil

Stir this pesto into brown rice or a mixture of steamed vegetables, such as carrots, cauliflower, zucchini, and green beans. For an interesting taste variation, replace the basil with cilantro.

1. Place the almonds in a food processor, and process until well ground.

2. Add the basil, parsley, tomatoes, garlic, and salt, and process until the garlic and herbs are finely minced and the ingredients are evenly blended.

3. Add the olive oil and process until incorporated. Serve immediately, or store for up to 5 days in the refrigerator.

Spicy Orange Nut Sauce

YIELD: ABOUT 1 1/2 CUPS

1 3/4 cups orange juice, divided

1/2 cup unsalted, unsweetened almond, cashew, or peanut butter

2 tablespoons lemon juice

1 tablespoon molasses

2 teaspoons soy sauce

1 teaspoon minced garlic

1 teaspoon minced fresh ginger

1/2 teaspoon crushed red pepper flakes

This mildly sweet and spicy sauce can be made with your choice of nut butters. Pour while still warm over steamed, grilled, or oven-roasted vegetables, tofu, tempeh, pasta, or grains. This is also good as a dipping sauce.

1. Combine about half the orange juice and all of the remaining ingredients in a small saucepan.

2. Place the saucepan over medium heat and cook, stirring continuously, until the nut butter softens and melts into the juice.

3. Stir the remaining juice into the sauce and continue to cook and stir until the sauce starts to simmer.

4. Simmer gently, continuing to stir, for 1 to 2 minutes, or until the sauce is thick and creamy. Serve immediately, or store for up to 5 days in the refrigerator. Rewarm over low heat.

Better Than Ketchup

YIELD: 3/4 CUP

1/2 cup tomato paste

1/2 cup apple juice

1/4 cup lemon juice or cider vinegar

2 teaspoons maple syrup

2 teaspoons minced fresh ginger

Pinch cayenne pepper

Here is the perfect condiment for burgers, Baked Tofu Sticks (page 117), eggs, or any other dish that you usually spice up with ketchup.

1. Combine all of the ingredients in a medium-size bowl, and beat with a fork to form a smooth sauce, just a bit thinner than commercial ketchup. Adjust the cayenne to taste.

2. Use at once, or store in the refrigerator for up to 2 weeks.

Salsa Cruda

YIELD: 1 $^{1}/_{2}$ CUPS

2 large ripe tomatoes

2 scallions, thinly sliced

1 clove garlic, minced

1 jalapeño pepper, minced (2 tablespoons)

2 tablespoons chopped fresh cilantro, or 2 tablespoons chopped fresh flat-leaf Italian parsley plus $^{1}/_{2}$ teaspoon ground cumin

2 tablespoons lime juice

You can reduce the heat of this very hot salsa by using only half a jalapeño pepper, or by replacing it entirely with a milder pepper. If cilantro is not available or not to your taste, use parsley and cumin in its place.

1. Chop the tomatoes and transfer to a serving bowl along with the juice released during chopping.

2. Add all of the remaining ingredients to the tomatoes and stir to mix well.

3. Cover and chill until serving time, storing in the refrigerator for up to 5 days.

Pineapple Salsa

YIELD: 2 CUPS

1 cup chopped fresh or canned pineapple

$^{1}/_{2}$ cup chopped red pepper

$^{1}/_{4}$ cup chopped onion of your choice

2 tablespoons minced chili pepper

2 tablespoons chopped fresh mint

1 teaspoon lemon juice

Enjoy this sweet and spicy salsa with grilled tofu or tempeh, Vegetable Corn Cakes (page 206), or Chickpea Roast (page 155). Choose the chili peppers you like and adjust the amount as desired, starting with less and tasting before adding more. If the finished salsa is not fiery enough, sprinkle in some cayenne pepper, crushed red pepper flakes, or hot pepper sauce.

1. Combine all of the ingredients in a small bowl, stirring to mix well.

2. Cover and chill until serving time, storing in the refrigerator for up to a week.

Quick Spicy Mexican Tomato Sauce

YIELD: 4 CUPS

- 1 1/2 tablespoons dry red wine or sherry
- 1 small onion, chopped
- 2 cloves garlic, chopped
- 2 tablespoons minced hot chili pepper, or 1/4 teaspoon cayenne
- 1 tablespoon chili powder
- 1 teaspoon ground cumin
- 4 cups tomato juice

When you need a Mexican-style tomato sauce, this one can be ready in just 15 minutes.

1. Combine the wine or sherry, onion, garlic, and hot chili pepper, if using, in a small saucepan. Cook over medium heat for 2 minutes, or until the onions are soft.

2. Stir the chili powder, cumin, and cayenne (if using) into the onion mixture, and cook briefly.

3. Add the tomato juice to the saucepan, and bring to a boil over high heat. Reduce the heat to a simmer and cook uncovered for about 10 minutes, or until the sauce is slightly thickened. Serve immediately, or store in the refrigerator for up to a week. Rewarm over medium heat.

15-Minute Italian Tomato Sauce

YIELD: 3 CUPS

- 1 medium green pepper, cut into thin 1-inch-long strips
- 2 cloves garlic, chopped
- 1 1/2 tablespoons dry red wine or sherry
- 3 cups tomato juice
- 2 tablespoons tomato paste
- 1 tablespoon chopped fresh basil, or 1 teaspoon dried basil
- 1 teaspoon dried oregano

This quickly made sauce is perfect for pasta and a variety of Italian-style dishes.

1. Combine the green pepper, garlic, and wine or sherry in a medium-size saucepan. Cook over medium heat, stirring several times, for about 5 minutes, or until the peppers have softened slightly.

2. Add all of the remaining ingredients to the green pepper mixture and bring to a boil over high heat. Lower the heat to a simmer and cook uncovered for about 10 minutes, or until the sauce is slightly thickened. Serve immediately, or store in the refrigerator for up to a week. Rewarm over medium heat.

PUTTANESCA SAUCE

YIELD: 2 CUPS

- 2 cups canned crushed tomatoes
- 1/4 cup chopped imported black or green olives
- 2 tablespoons capers
- 4 cloves garlic, sliced
- 1 tablespoon chopped fresh basil, or 1/2 teaspoon dried basil
- 1/2 teaspoon crushed red pepper flakes
- 1/2 teaspoon dried oregano
- 2 tablespoons light miso
- 2 tablespoons chopped fresh parsley
- 2 tablespoons pine nuts, toasted (page 19), optional

Puttanesca Sauce is excellent on cheese- or tofu-filled ravioli or tortellini, Eggplant Rollatini (page 128), or plain pasta. The sauce can also be spooned over grains, tempeh, or cooked vegetables such as potatoes, cauliflower, green beans, mushrooms, and squash. Two cups of sauce is enough for one pound of pasta.

1. Combine the tomatoes, olives, capers, garlic, basil, red pepper flakes, and oregano in a medium-size saucepan and bring to a boil over medium heat, stirring occasionally. Reduce the heat and simmer gently for 10 minutes. Remove from the heat.

2. In a small bowl, combine the miso with a little of the hot tomato sauce, stirring until the miso melts into the sauce. Add the miso to the saucepan along with the parsley.

3. Cover the saucepan and let sit for 5 minutes before using. If desired, sprinkle the toasted pine nuts on top of the sauced dish at serving time. Can be stored in the refrigerator for up to 5 days. Rewarm over low heat, stirring, until hot. Do not boil, as this will diminish the value of the miso.

VARIATION

- For a lighter sauce, replace the crushed tomatoes with lightly drained and chopped canned whole tomatoes or tomato pieces.

Creamy Mushroom Gravy

YIELD: ABOUT 3 CUPS

8 ounces thinly sliced mushrooms, any type ($2^1/_2$ cups)

2 tablespoons sherry or dry white wine

5 tablespoons whole wheat flour

2 cups soy milk

2 tablespoons light miso

Freshly ground pepper

Salt

Although this gravy is delicious made with plain white mushrooms, if you wish, you can get a more pronounced earthy taste by replacing up to half the mushrooms with chanterelles, creminis, shiitakes, or portobellos. If desired, enhance the gravy's visual appeal with a generous garnish of chopped fresh parsley.

1. Combine the mushrooms and sherry or wine in a medium-size saucepan, and cook over medium heat, stirring occasionally, for 5 to 8 minutes, or until the mushrooms are tender and release their juices.

2. Sprinkle the flour over the mushrooms and stir until evenly mixed. Gradually stir in the soy milk and cook over medium heat, stirring continuously, until the gravy thickens and begins to boil. Reduce the heat and simmer gently for 1 minute.

3. Remove the saucepan from the heat and stir in the miso until thoroughly melted. Season with a generous amount of freshly ground pepper and salt to taste, if desired. Serve immediately or store in the refrigerator for a day or 2. Rewarm over low heat and cook gently, while stirring, until warm. Do not boil.

Sweet Mustard Basting Sauce

YIELD: 6 TABLESPOONS

$^1/_4$ cup prepared mustard

2 tablespoons molasses

Use this basting sauce when grilling eggplant, onion, sweet potatoes, or winter squash slices. You should have enough sauce for dinner for four—for instance, two large sweet potatoes or one eggplant plus one large onion. Just baste the food on one side before placing it on the grill, and arrange it with the sauced side down. Then baste the top before turning.

1. Combine the ingredients, stirring well to mix. Use immediately, or store in the refrigerator for up to 2 weeks.

Spicy Marinade

YIELD: 3/4 CUP

- 1/2 cup white wine
- 1/4 cup soy sauce
- 2 cloves garlic, minced
- 1 hot pepper, minced, or 1/4 teaspoon crushed red pepper flakes
- 1 tablespoon toasted sesame oil

This recipe makes enough marinade for a pound of tofu or tempeh—enough to serve four people—or for half that amount, plus enough vegetables to serve two people. Fortunately, the recipe can be easily doubled as necessary. Besides marinating the food in this mixture for 1 to 2 hours, you can use it as a basting sauce during the grilling process.

1. Combine all the ingredients, stirring well to mix. Use immediately, or store in the refrigerator for up to a week.

Tahini-Mushroom Gravy

YIELD: 1 1/2 CUPS

- 1/2 cup dried porcini mushrooms
- 2/3 cup hot water
- 1/4 cup tahini (sesame seed paste)
- 1/2 cup cold water
- 1 tablespoon dark miso
- Juice from 1 lemon wedge

This rich, creamy gravy is excellent on cooked grains, tofu, tempeh, or chickpeas. Be aware that if the sauce curdles during cooking—which can happen if it gets too hot—you can simply remove it from the heat and stir vigorously with a fork to recombine.

1. Place the dried mushrooms in a bowl, cover with the hot water, and let stand about 10 minutes to soften. Then drain the mushrooms through a strainer, reserving the liquid. Tear the mushrooms into pieces.

2. Place the tahini in a small saucepan, and gradually beat the reserved mushroom liquid into the tahini with a fork. Beat in the cold water until smooth, and add the mushrooms.

3. Place the saucepan over low heat and cook, stirring continuously, until the sauce just starts to boil.

4. In a small bowl, combine the miso with a little of the hot sauce just until the miso is melted. Stir the mixture into the sauce along with the lemon juice, and heat briefly without boiling. Serve immediately, or store in the refrigerator for a day or 2. Rewarm over very low heat and cook, stirring gently, until warm. Do not boil.

SWEET ONION GRAVY

YIELD: ABOUT 2 CUPS

- 2 cups coarsely chopped red onion or sweet white onion
- 2 tablespoons sherry
- 1/4 cup whole wheat flour
- 2 cups soy milk
- 2 tablespoons light miso
- Freshly ground pepper
- Salt

The gentle stewing of onions gives this gravy a rich velvety texture and a sweet mellow taste.

1. Combine the onions and sherry in a small saucepan. Cover and cook over low heat for 8 to 10 minutes, or until the onions are quite tender.

2. Sprinkle the flour over the onions, and stir until evenly mixed. Gradually stir in the soy milk and cook over medium heat, stirring continuously, until the gravy thickens and begins to boil. Reduce the heat and simmer gently for 1 minute.

3. Remove the saucepan from the heat and stir in the miso until thoroughly melted. Season with a generous amount of freshly ground pepper and salt to taste, if desired. Serve immediately or store in the refrigerator for a day or 2. Rewarm over low heat and cook gently, while stirring, until warm. Do not boil.

AGLIATA

YIELD: 3/4 CUP

- 1 to 2 slices whole grain bread
- 1/2 cup soy milk
- 1/4 cup walnuts
- 1 large clove garlic, coarsely chopped
- 1 1/2 tablespoons lemon juice
- 1 tablespoon olive oil
- 1/8 teaspoon salt

Rich garlic sauces are popular in many cultures. The French have mayonnaise-based aioli, and the Turks have tarator. Agliata is the name for the Italian sauce that inspired this recipe. Serve on Tofu-Stuffed Artichokes (page 66) or Tofu-Stuffed Sweet Red Peppers (page 130), or use on rice or steamed vegetables.

1. Trim the crusts from the bread, and tear the remainder into small pieces to make 1/2 cup lightly packed crumbs.

2. Combine the bread crumbs and soy milk in a blender, and allow to sit without processing for just a few minutes, or until the bread has absorbed the liquid and become soft.

3. Add the walnuts, garlic, lemon juice, olive oil, and salt to the blender, and process to form a smooth sauce with the consistency of thick heavy cream. Use immediately, or store in the refrigerator for a day or 2.

Greek Garlic Sauce

YIELD: 1 CUP

- 2 small new or red potatoes (6 ounces total), quartered
- $^1/_2$ teaspoon salt, divided
- 2 cloves garlic, crushed
- $^1/_4$ cup finely chopped fresh parsley, or $^1/_4$ chopped fresh parsley and dill
- 2 tablespoons lemon juice
- 2 tablespoons olive oil

This sauce resembles a garlicky mayonnaise, without the egg and with very little oil. It can be spread on raw tomato slices, cucumber slices, or toast rounds; spooned over grilled eggplant slices, beans, or steamed vegetables; or slathered on toast and floated in a bowl of soup. For a raw vegetable dip, add some yogurt cheese (page 22).

1. Place the potatoes in a small saucepan and add just enough water to cover. Bring to a boil and add $^1/_4$ teaspoon of salt. Reduce the heat to a simmer, cover, and cook gently for about 15 minutes, or until the potato is quite tender. Drain, reserving the liquid.

2. Allow the potatoes to cool slightly. Remove and discard the peel. Set aside.

3. In a small bowl, mash the crushed garlic with the remaining $^1/_4$ teaspoon of salt using a mortar or the back of a spoon. Add the drained potato and use a potato masher or fork to mash it until no lumps remain.

4. Using a fork or wire whisk, beat in the parsley, lemon juice, and $^1/_3$ to $^1/_2$ cup of the reserved cooking liquid as needed to produce a sauce a little thicker than mayonnaise. Then beat in the oil. Serve at once, or store in the refrigerator for a day or 2.

11. DESSERTS

A wedge of sweet watermelon, a bowl of ripe berries, a juicy peach, a crisp apple. These are nature's most simple and delectable dessert offerings. Of course, fruit can be made even more enticing as a dessert through presentation, the addition of natural flavorings such as orange and lemon juice, and wholesome adornments such as nuts. It is also possible to prepare impressive and tantalizing baked goods that do not result in an overdose of fat, sugar, and refined grains. Here are some tips:

■ Base your fruit selection on what is fresh and in season.

■ Cut fruit into wedges and arrange on a plate surrounded by pecan halves and dates.

■ Cut pineapple pieces into triangles and attach toothpicks holding red grapes.

■ Place wedges of lime around cantaloupe and honeydew slices. As you'll discover, lime juice brings out the flavor in even lackluster fruit.

■ Combine peeled kiwi rounds with sweet red cherries.

■ Instead of topping your wholesome desserts with high-fat or imitation toppings, use our all-natural, protein-rich Whipped Yogurt Cream or Whipped Tofu Topping.

■ Reinvent favorite baked desserts by adding oats, nuts, and other healthful ingredients; replacing refined flours with whole-grain products; and substituting maple syrup or honey for granulated sugar. It may take some experimenting to get it right, but your efforts will be lavishly rewarded.

In this chapter you will find some additional ideas for embellishing fruit, as well as some baked goods that you can prepare and serve with confidence. As you'll learn, it's not just possible but also easy to treat your family and friends to desserts that provide the taste and comfort that we all expect from these sweets, and real nourishment as well.

Maple-Orange Nectarines

YIELD: 4 SERVINGS

4 firm but ripe nectarines

1/2 cup orange juice

2 tablespoons maple syrup

2 tablespoons slivered almonds

Sweet poached nectarines in a maple-orange syrup make an excellent dessert whether served warm, at room temperature, or chilled. For added appeal, garnish with Whipped Yogurt Cream (page 224) or Whipped Tofu Topping (page 224). You can also enjoy this sweet treat on top of pancakes or unfrosted cakes, or you can mix it with plain yogurt.

1. Cut the nectarines into slices. You can do this by cutting the fruit from stem to blossom end, gently twisting to pry the halves apart, removing the pit, and cutting into wedges; or by using a small paring knife to cut the whole fruit into wedges from stem to blossom end, and gently prying the pieces off the pit.

2. Combine the orange juice and maple syrup in a medium-size skillet, and bring to a boil over medium heat. Add the nectarines and cook, stirring occasionally, for 5 minutes.

3. Transfer the nectarines to a bowl, using a slotted spoon so that the liquid remains in the skillet. Simmer the liquid for 3 to 5 minutes, or until slightly thickened. Pour over the nectarines and let sit at room temperature for at least 15 minutes.

4. Serve the nectarines while still warm, at room temperature, or chilled, spooning the slices into individual dishes and topping each bowlful with some of the slivered almonds.

The Best Antioxidant Fruits

In a scientific ranking by the U.S. Department of Agriculture of the antioxidant capability of twelve fruits, strawberries ranked highest, followed in descending order by plums, oranges, red grapes, kiwi, pink grapefruit, white grapes, bananas, apples, tomatoes, pears, and honeydew melon. The antioxidant activity of strawberries was twice the capacity measured in oranges and red grapes, seven times that of bananas and apples, eleven times that of pears, and sixteen times that of melon.

Asian Melon

YIELD: 6 SERVINGS

1 orange

$^3/_4$ cup water

$^1/_4$ cup honey

1-inch piece fresh ginger, peeled and thinly sliced

4 cups sliced or cubed honeydew, cantaloupe, or other muskmelon

Fresh mint leaves, optional

Gently spiced ginger syrup imparts an Asian flavor to this simple melon dessert.

1. Use a vegetable peeler to remove 2 long strips of peel from the orange. Combine the peel in a small saucepan with the water, honey, and ginger, and bring to a boil over high heat. Reduce the heat to a simmer, cover, and cook for 15 minutes, or until the syrup has thickened slightly and is reduced to about $^1/_2$ cup.

2. Pour the syrup into a bowl large enough to accommodate the fruit, and allow to cool to room temperature. When cool, remove the orange peel and ginger.

3. Squeeze the orange and add $^1/_4$ cup of juice to the syrup. Add the melon to the syrup, turning to coat, and chill until serving time.

4. Spoon the chilled melon into serving dishes and garnish with fresh mint leaves, if desired. Serve immediately.

Favorite Fruit Salad

YIELD: 4 SERVINGS

2 apples, diced

2 bananas, sliced

1 $^1/_2$ cups other seasonal fruit, such as pears, grapes, mangos, kiwi, melon, and berries

Juice of 3 oranges

8 to 12 dried dates, cut into small pieces

$^1/_3$ cup walnut pieces

Almost any combination of fruit can be included in fruit salad, but to make it extra special, we like to add walnuts and dates.

1. Combine the apples, bananas, and other fruit in a bowl. Stir in the orange juice and toss to coat to preserve the color and provide a syrup.

2. Stir the dates into the salad, mixing to distribute well. If prepared ahead, chill until needed. Top with the walnuts and serve immediately.

MARINATED FIGS

YIELD: 4 TO 6 SERVINGS

12 dried golden figs

2 tablespoons dark raisins

1 1/4 cups apple juice

2 tablespoons lemon juice

Figs are one of the sweetest fruits available. Marinated in juice, they produce a dessert of elegant simplicity. Although this dish takes only a few minutes to prepare, it should be done ahead of time since at least 8 hours of marinating are needed.

1. Combine the figs, raisins, and apple juice in a small saucepan, and bring to a boil. Lower the heat to a simmer and cook for just 1 minute. Remove from the heat.

2. Stir the lemon juice into the fig mixture, and transfer the mixture to a bowl. Cover and marinate in the refrigerator for at least 8 hours before serving.

BANANA SOFT SERVE

YIELD: 4 SERVINGS

4 bananas

All you need are frozen bananas and a food processor to produce one of the creamiest desserts around. People are amazed when they learn that there is no cream or sweetener in this luscious treat.

1. Peel the bananas, and wrap them together in airtight, freezer-proof packaging. Freeze for at least 24 hours, or up to 3 months.

2. Just before serving, unwrap the bananas and break them into chunks. Place in a food processor fitted with a steel blade and process until the banana breaks up, passes through the icy stage, and becomes creamy and whipped with air. The consistency will be that of soft-serve ice cream. Serve at once.

STRAWBERRY FROZEN YOGURT

YIELD: 1 PINT

- 2 cups fresh strawberries
- 3 tablespoons fruit juice-sweetened berry preserves
- 1 cup yogurt cheese (page 22)
- 1 to 2 tablespoons maple syrup
- ½ teaspoon vanilla extract

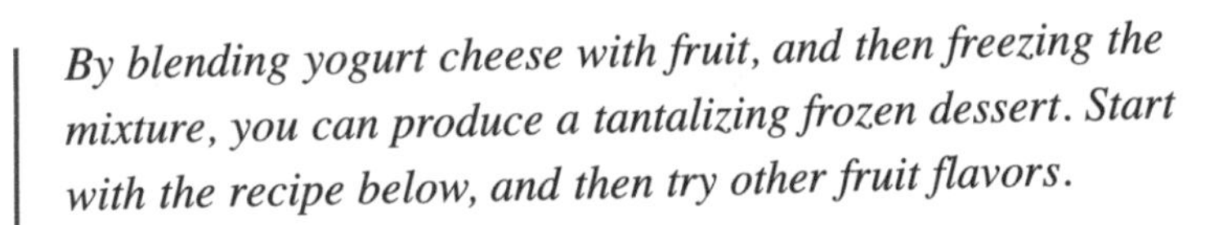

By blending yogurt cheese with fruit, and then freezing the mixture, you can produce a tantalizing frozen dessert. Start with the recipe below, and then try other fruit flavors.

1. Combine the berries and preserves in a food processor or blender, and process into a purée. Transfer the mixture to a medium-size mixing bowl.

2. Using a fork or whisk, beat the yogurt cheese, maple syrup, and vanilla extract into the berry mixture until evenly combined. The amount of maple syrup needed will depend on the sweetness of the berries and individual taste; begin with 1 tablespoon, taste, and adjust if needed.

3. Transfer the mixture to a shallow metal pan or freezer container, and freeze for 2 to 3 hours, or until firm.

4. Return the mixture to the processor or blender, breaking it into chunks. Process at high speed until smooth, stopping and scraping the sides as needed until the frozen yogurt begins to soften. Continue until the mixture is the consistency of soft-serve ice cream.

5. Either eat the frozen yogurt at this point, or return it to a freezer container and freeze solid. If refrozen, remove it from the freezer about 10 minutes before serving to soften slightly.

Nutritious Toppings for Fruit and Baked Goods

Just about any dessert, whether fresh fruit, pie, or cake, can be made even more appealing with a whipped topping. But regular whipped cream adds a high dose of fat, while most commercial lower-fat alternatives are laden with chemicals. Fortunately, the next two recipes provide delicious options. You can serve these with confidence, adjusting the sweetness according to your own preferences and the dessert being topped. While a sweeter taste may be desired on plain cakes, baked apples, or tart fruit, a more subdued topping will better complement sweeter desserts. One cup of topping will serve four generously, but with these recipes—which are a good source of protein and calcium, but sparing in the way of calories and fat—you can afford to be lavish.

Whipped Yogurt Cream

With half the calories, five times the protein, and six times the calcium of regular whipped cream, but very little fat, this is what we call a "no worry" topping.

YIELD: 1 CUP

1 cup yogurt cheese (page 22)
1 tablespoon honey or maple syrup
1 teaspoon vanilla extract

1. Place all of the ingredients in a small bowl, and use a fork or whisk to beat together until creamy. Use at once or refrigerate for up to 4 days. If the topping thickens in the refrigerator, beat it with a fork to lighten the consistency.

Variation

- For Whipped Orange Yogurt Cream, use honey as the sweetener and replace the vanilla extract with 2 tablespoons of orange juice and 1/2 teaspoon of grated orange zest.

Whipped Tofu Topping

Tofu as a dessert topping may seem unusual, but it is very tasty and bears no resemblance to tofu in block form.

YIELD: 1 CUP

8 ounces soft tofu (1 cup mashed)
3 tablespoons apple juice
1 1/2 tablespoons maple syrup
1/2 teaspoon almond or vanilla extract

1. Place all of the ingredients in a blender or food processor, and process until creamy. Use at once or refrigerate for up to 4 days.

Chewy Oat Cookies

YIELD: 30 COOKIES

1 1/2 cups whole wheat flour
1/2 cup oats
1/2 cup chopped walnuts
1/4 cup chopped dark raisins
3 tablespoons flaxseed meal (page 17), wheat germ, or a mixture of the two
3/4 teaspoon baking soda
1/2 teaspoon baking powder
1 teaspoon minced orange zest
2/3 cup unsweetened applesauce
1/2 cup honey
2 tablespoons maple syrup

This low-fat cookie has great texture and flavor without being cloyingly sweet like most commercial low-fat baked goods.

1. Preheat the oven to 325°F.

2. Combine the flour, oats, walnuts, raisins, flaxseed meal and/or wheat germ, baking soda, baking powder, and orange zest in a large bowl. Add the applesauce, honey, and maple syrup, and stir until the dry ingredients are thoroughly moistened.

3. Drop the dough by tablespoons onto oiled baking sheets, spacing the cookies about an inch apart to allow for spreading. Flatten gently with the prongs of a fork.

4. Bake for 20 minutes, or until the cookies are golden. Transfer to a wire rack to cool, and serve immediately or store for up to 2 weeks in an airtight container.

"How can you eat anything with eyes?"

–Will Kellogg

GOLD CHIP COOKIES

YIELD: 28 COOKIES

1 1/2 cups oats

1 cup whole wheat flour

1/4 teaspoon salt

1/4 teaspoon baking soda

1/2 cup chopped almonds or hazelnuts

3/4 cup chocolate or carob chips

1/2 cup maple syrup

1/3 cup unsweetened applesauce

2 tablespoons canola oil

1 teaspoon vanilla extract

Here is an enhanced version of a traditional favorite.

1. Preheat the oven to 375°F.

2. Place the oats in a blender or food processor, and grind to a coarse flour.

3. Combine the oat flour, whole wheat flour, salt, and baking soda in a large bowl, and mix well. Add the nuts and chips, and mix again.

4. Combine the maple syrup, applesauce, oil, and vanilla extract in a small bowl, whisking to mix well. Stir the wet ingredients into the dry, mixing until thoroughly moistened.

5. Drop the dough by tablespoons onto oiled baking sheets, spacing the cookies about an inch apart to allow for spreading. Flatten gently with your hands or the prongs of a fork.

6. Bake for 15 to 20 minutes, or until the cookies are lightly browned on the bottom. Transfer to a wire rack to cool, and serve immediately or store for up to 2 weeks in an airtight container.

OAT NUT CLUSTERS

YIELD: 20 COOKIES

6 tablespoons tahini (sesame seed paste)

1/4 cup honey

1 cup oats

1/4 cup sliced Brazil nuts or almonds

1/2 teaspoon ground cinnamon

These cookies are appealingly crunchy with a subtle sweetness.

1. Preheat the oven to 350°F.

2. Place the tahini and honey in a large mixing bowl, and beat with a fork until smooth.

3. Work the oats, nuts, and cinnamon into the tahini mixture to form a stiff dough, using your hands if necessary.

4. Scoop up teaspoonfuls of dough and shape them into compact balls. Arrange them on oiled baking sheets, spacing the cookies about an inch apart. Flatten gently with the palm of your hand.

5. Bake for 12 to 15 minutes, or until the cookies are golden. Allow to cool for a minute or 2 before transferring to a wire rack to cool completely. Serve immediately or store for up to 2 weeks in an airtight container.

Ginger Cookies

YIELD: 24 COOKIES

1 teaspoon hot water
1/2 teaspoon baking soda
1/2 cup molasses
1 tablespoon canola oil
1 1/2 teaspoons ground ginger
1/2 teaspoon ground cinnamon
1 3/4 cups whole wheat flour

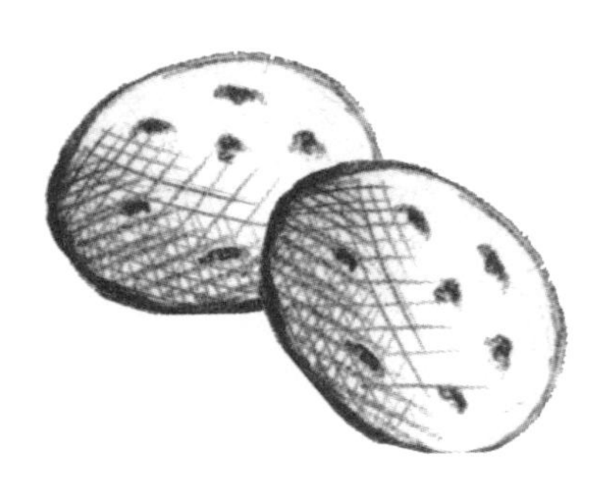

These delicate cookies are crunchy and spicy.

1. Preheat the oven to 325°F.

2. Place the hot water and baking soda in a large mixing bowl, and stir to dissolve. Add the molasses, oil, ginger, and cinnamon, and mix well.

3. Add enough flour to the molasses mixture to make a dough firm enough to roll. Use your hands if necessary to work it in.

4. Place the dough on a floured surface, and roll it out until it is quite thin—about 1/8 inch in thickness. Cut the dough into the desired shapes with a cookie cutter and arrange on an oiled baking sheet.

5. Bake for about 10 minutes or until just lightly colored, taking care not to overbake. Transfer to a wire rack to cool, and serve immediately or store for up to 2 weeks in an airtight container.

BROWNIES

YIELD: 16 SQUARES

- 3/4 cup whole wheat pastry flour
- 1/2 cup chopped walnuts or pecans
- 1 teaspoon baking powder
- 1/4 teaspoon salt
- 1/2 cup mashed tofu (4 ounces), any type
- 1/3 cup maple syrup
- 1/4 cup unsweetened cocoa or carob powder
- 2 tablespoons canola oil
- 2 tablespoons honey
- 1 teaspoon vanilla extract

These brownies are lean and mean, and deceivingly low in fat despite their rich taste.

1. Preheat the oven to 350°F.
2. Combine the flour, nuts, baking powder, and salt in a large bowl, stirring to mix.
3. Combine the tofu, maple syrup, cocoa or carob powder, oil, honey, and vanilla extract in a blender or food processor, and process until completely smooth.
4. Add the tofu mixture to the flour mixture and stir until completely blended. If the mixture is too thick to blend together, add a tablespoon or so of water.
5. Spread the batter in an oiled 8-inch-square baking pan and bake for 20 to 25 minutes, or until firm. Do not overbake. Allow to cool in the pan for at least 15 minutes before cutting into squares and serving. Store any leftovers for up to 2 days in an airtight container, or up to 5 days in the refrigerator.

Orange Oatmeal Coffee Cake

YIELD: 8 TO 12 SERVINGS

1 1/2 cups orange juice

1 cup oats

2 eggs

1/2 cup honey

1/4 cup canola oil

1 1/2 cups whole wheat pastry flour

1/2 cup nonfat dry milk powder

1 tablespoon chopped orange zest

1 teaspoon baking powder

1 teaspoon baking soda

1/2 teaspoon ground cinnamon

1/4 teaspoon salt

Coconut Topping

1/2 cup chopped walnuts

1/2 cup shredded unsweetened coconut

3 tablespoons maple syrup

This Goldbeck family favorite is soft and moist.

1. Preheat the oven to 375°F.

2. Place the orange juice in a small saucepan, and bring to a boil. Place the oats in a medium-size bowl, and pour the hot juice over the oats. Allow to sit while assembling the remaining ingredients.

3. Place the eggs, honey, and oil in a large mixing bowl, and beat together with a fork until light and foamy. Set aside.

4. Combine the flour, milk powder, orange zest, baking powder, baking soda, cinnamon, and salt in a medium-size bowl, stirring to mix well. Alternately add the flour mixture and the softened oats to the egg mixture, beating gently with a fork or wooden spoon until smooth.

5. Pour the batter into an oiled 10-inch round baking pan and bake for 20 minutes.

6. While the cake is baking, combine the topping ingredients in a small bowl. Sprinkle the mixture over the cake and bake for 10 additional minutes, or until a toothpick inserted in the center of the cake comes out clean. Allow to cool completely in the pan before cutting into wedges and serving. Leftovers will keep for a day or 2 if wrapped to prevent the cake from drying out.

APPLESAUCE DATE CAKE

YIELD: 16 SQUARES

1 cup unsweetened applesauce

3/4 cup honey

1/2 cup plain low-fat or nonfat yogurt

1 teaspoon vanilla extract

1 teaspoon minced orange zest

1/2 teaspoon ground cinnamon

1/4 teaspoon salt

2 cups whole wheat flour

1/4 cup soy flour

1 teaspoon baking powder

1 teaspoon baking soda

1/2 cup cut-up dates

This dense cake with a moist, pudding-like texture is delicious as is, and excellent topped with Whipped Yogurt Cream (page 224).

1. Preheat the oven to 350°F.

2. Combine the applesauce, honey, and yogurt in a large bowl. Using a fork or whisk, beat in the vanilla extract, orange zest, cinnamon, and salt.

3. Combine the flours, baking powder, baking soda, and dates in a medium-size bowl. Gradually add the dry ingredients to the wet ingredients, mixing gently but thoroughly until the dry ingredients are completely moistened.

4. Spread the batter in an oiled, floured 8-inch-square baking pan, and bake for 35 minutes, or until the center is firm and a toothpick inserted in the center of the cake comes out clean. Cool completely in the pan before serving. Leftovers will keep for a day or 2 if wrapped to prevent the cake from drying out.

Apple Crumble

YIELD: 4 SERVINGS

3 medium apples, peeled and cut into bite-size pieces
2 tablespoons dark raisins
2 tablespoons sliced almonds
1/2 teaspoon ground cinnamon
3/4 cup oats
1/4 cup whole wheat flour
Pinch salt
2 tablespoons canola oil
1/2 cup apple juice
3 tablespoons honey or maple syrup

This deep-dish crumb-topped dessert should be served warm, either plain or topped with sweetened yogurt or Whipped Tofu Topping (page 224).

1. Preheat the oven to 350°F.
2. Combine the apples, raisins, almonds, and cinnamon in an oiled, shallow 1-quart baking dish. Set aside.
3. Combine the oats, flour, and salt in a small bowl. Add the oil, and mix until crumbly. Sprinkle the oat mixture over the apple mixture.
4. Combine the apple juice and honey or maple syrup, heating gently if necessary to blend. Pour the mixture over the crumb topping.
5. Bake for 30 to 40 minutes, or until the apples are fork-tender. Serve warm.

"Until we have the courage to recognize cruelty for what it is . . . whether its victim is human or animal . . . we cannot expect things to be much better in this world."

–Rachel Carson

Very Berry Shortcakes

YIELD: 6 SERVINGS

Shortcake

2/3 cup whole wheat flour

1/3 cup cornmeal

2 tablespoons wheat germ

1 teaspoon baking powder

1/4 teaspoon baking soda

2 tablespoons canola oil

1/3 cup plain nonfat yogurt

1 tablespoon maple syrup or honey

Fruit

2 1/2 cups sliced strawberries, divided

1/4 cup orange juice

1 tablespoon maple syrup or honey

1 1/2 cups blueberries

Whipped Topping

1 cup Whipped Yogurt Cream (page 224) or Whipped Tofu Topping (page 224)

Each component of these fruit-topped cakes—the shortcake, the fruit, and the whipped topping—can be made ahead of time if you wish, and assembled just prior to serving. When shopping for the berries, figure on using 1 pound or 1 dry pint of strawberries, and about 8 ounces of blueberries.

1. Preheat the oven to 425°F.

2. To prepare the shortcake, combine the flour, cornmeal, wheat germ, baking powder, and baking soda in a large mixing bowl. Stir in the oil and mix with a fork, whisk, or pastry blender until completely incorporated. Then add the yogurt and maple syrup or honey, and mix until the ingredients are well combined and can be formed into a ball of dough. Towards the end, it is best to knead gently with your hands.

3. Oil a baking sheet or the removable bottom of a 9-inch tart pan. Place the dough on the pan and pat into an 8- to 9-inch circle, 1/4 inch high. Using the prongs of a fork, score the circle of dough into 6 pie-shaped wedges without separating the wedges. Bake for 15 minutes, or until golden.

4. To make the filling, combine 2 cups of the strawberries with the orange juice and sweetener in a blender or food processor, and process quickly to a coarse purée. Transfer the mixture to a bowl and stir in the blueberries and the remaining strawberries. If prepared in advance, cover and chill until serving time.

5. To assemble the shortcakes, separate the round cake into 6 wedges. Split each wedge by piercing through the center with a fork, and arrange 2 halves soft side up on each serving plate. Top generously with the fruit and with 2 rounded tablespoons of the whipped topping, and serve.

FRESH FRUIT TART WITH CHEESE FILLING

YIELD: 8 TO 10 SERVINGS

Cheese Filling

1 1/2 cups yogurt cheese (page 22)

2 tablespoons honey

1 teaspoon vanilla extract

Crust

1/2 cup whole wheat flour

1/3 cup cornmeal

1 tablespoon flaxseed meal (page 17)

1/2 teaspoon baking powder

1/4 teaspoon baking soda

2 tablespoons canola oil

1/4 cup yogurt

1 tablespoon honey

Fruit Glaze

3 cups fresh peeled and sliced peaches or nectarines, or strawberry halves, blueberries, or raspberries, individually or in combination, divided

2 tablespoons honey

2 tablespoons lemon juice

1 tablespoon cornstarch or arrowroot

This elegant tart tastes as impressive as it looks. It is best to make the cheese filling first and refrigerate it while you prepare the crust and fruit glaze. Since the tart needs to be well chilled before serving, it should be made from several hours to as much as a day in advance.

1. To make the cheese filling, place the yogurt cheese, honey, and vanilla extract in a small bowl, and beat with a fork until well combined. Cover and chill until ready to use.

2. To prepare the crust, preheat the oven to 425°F. Combine the flour, cornmeal, flaxseed meal, baking powder, and baking soda in a medium-size bowl. Stir in the oil and mix with a fork, whisk, or pastry blender until completely incorporated and crumbly. Then add the yogurt and honey, and mix until the ingredients are well combined, kneading gently in the bowl with your hands to form a ball of dough.

3. Oil a 9-inch tart pan or a pie pan with a removable bottom, and press the dough over the bottom and up the sides of the pan to make a thin shell. Prick the surface liberally with a fork and bake for 10 minutes, or until golden. Allow to cool.

4. To make the fruit glaze, place 1 cup of the fruit in a small saucepan, and mash with a fork or potato masher. Stir in the honey, lemon juice, and starch, and cook over low heat, stirring continuously, until the mixture is thick and translucent and no longer has a milky appearance. Remove from the heat and allow to cool for a few minutes.

5. To assemble the tart, fill the cooled crust with the cheese filling. Arrange the remaining 2 cups of fruit over the filling, and use a spoon to gently spread the glaze over the fruit. Chill for several hours before serving.

Fruit and Tofu Tart

YIELD: 8 SERVINGS

Crust

1 1/4 cups crumbs made from whole grain cookies and/or whole grain ready-to-eat cereal

1/4 cup wheat germ

2 to 4 tablespoons orange juice

Filling

1 pound firm tofu

1/4 cup honey

2 to 4 tablespoons orange juice

1 teaspoon vanilla extract

1/2 teaspoon almond extract

Topping

1/3 cup orange juice, divided

1/4 cup fruit juice-sweetened orange marmalade

1 teaspoon honey

1 1/2 teaspoons arrowroot or cornstarch

1 tablespoon lemon juice, divided

2 cups peeled orange segments, thin kiwi wedges, sliced bananas, and/or strawberries

If you have never tried tofu pie, or have tasted one but were disappointed, this creamy tart with its fresh fruit topping is sure to win you over.

---

1. To make the crust, preheat the oven to 350°F. Combine the crumbs with the wheat germ, and add just enough juice to keep the mixture together when pressed between your fingers. The amount of juice will vary, depending on how soft or crisp the crumbs are.

2. Press the mixture over the bottom and sides of a 9-inch pie pan and bake for 8 minutes, or until just beginning to color. Allow to cool for at least 5 minutes before filling.

3. To make the filling, pat the tofu dry and crumble it into a blender or food processor. Add all of the remaining filling ingredients, using just 2 tablespoons of the juice initially. Purée until completely smooth and creamy, adding additional juice if necessary. The firmness of the tofu will influence how much juice is needed.

4. Spread the filling evenly in the cooled crust and bake for 20 to 25 minutes, or until set and barely colored. Allow to cool to room temperature.

5. To prepare the topping, combine all but 1 tablespoon of the orange juice and all of the marmalade and honey in a small saucepan, and cook over low heat until melted. Then mix the remaining tablespoon of orange juice into the arrowroot or cornstarch until dissolved, and add it to the hot marmalade mixture. Cook, stirring constantly, until thick and translucent.

6. Remove the saucepan from the heat, and stir in the lemon juice. Then fold the fruit into the mixture, and allow to cool to room temperature.

7. Spread the cooled fruit topping over the pie, and chill for several hours before serving.

METRIC CONVERSION TABLES

Common Liquid Conversions

Measurement	=	Milliliters
¼ teaspoon	=	1.25 milliliters
½ teaspoon	=	2.50 milliliters
¾ teaspoon	=	3.75 milliliters
1 teaspoon	=	5.00 milliliters
1¼ teaspoons	=	6.25 milliliters
1½ teaspoons	=	7.50 milliliters
1¾ teaspoons	=	8.75 milliliters
2 teaspoons	=	10.0 milliliters
1 tablespoon	=	15.0 milliliters
2 tablespoons	=	30.0 milliliters

Measurement	=	Liters
¼ cup	=	0.06 liters
½ cup	=	0.12 liters
¾ cup	=	0.18 liters
1 cup	=	0.24 liters
1¼ cups	=	0.30 liters
1½ cups	=	0.36 liters
2 cups	=	0.48 liters
2½ cups	=	0.60 liters
3 cups	=	0.72 liters
3½ cups	=	0.84 liters
4 cups	=	0.96 liters
4½ cups	=	1.08 liters
5 cups	=	1.20 liters
5½ cups	=	1.32 liters

Converting Fahrenheit to Celsius

Fahrenheit	=	Celsius
200–205	=	95
220–225	=	105
245–250	=	120
275	=	135
300–305	=	150
325–330	=	165
345–350	=	175
370–375	=	190
400–405	=	205
425–430	=	220
445–450	=	230
470–475	=	245
500	=	260

Conversion Formulas

LIQUID		
When You Know	Multiply By	To Determine
teaspoons	5.0	milliliters
tablespoons	15.0	milliliters
fluid ounces	30.0	milliliters
cups	0.24	liters
pints	0.47	liters
quarts	0.95	liters

WEIGHT		
When You Know	Multiply By	To Determine
ounces	28.0	grams
pounds	0.45	kilograms

INDEX

OTHER BOOKS BY NIKKI & DAVID GOLDBECK

AMERICAN WHOLEFOODS CUISINE

OVER 1,300 MEATLESS, WHOLESOME RECIPES FROM SHORT ORDER TO GOURMET

A classic of contemporary vegetarian cooking, plus 300 pages of valuable kitchen information. Considered "the new Joy of Cooking" by authorities from Food & Wine to Vegetarian Times. Over 250,000 in print. (580 pages/Paper)

HEALTHY HIGHWAYS

THE TRAVELERS' GUIDE TO HEALTHY EATING

State maps and local directions guide you to 1,900 healthy eateries and natural food stores throughout the U.S. Plus travel tips, dining advice and other useful resources. Free online supplement keeps the book up to date. (420 pages/Paper)

CHOOSE TO REUSE

AN ENCYCLOPEDIA OF SERVICES, PRODUCTS, PROGRAMS & CHARITABLE ORGANIZATIONS THAT FOSTER REUSE.

This revolutionary guide is the first to show the ingenious ways that individuals, businesses and charitable organizations can profit from reuse—the second environmental "R." More than 200 topics and 2,000 resources from Air Filters to Zippers. A Book-of-the-Month Club selection. (480 pages/Paper)

THE GOOD BREAKFAST BOOK

Contains 450 vegetarian recipes to jumpstart the day. Quick weekday getaways to elegant brunches. Great for families. Includes recipes suitable for vegans, as well as people with wheat, dairy and egg sensitivities. (206 pages/Paper)

EAT WELL THE YOCHEE WAY

Enjoy rich creamy dishes without the fat and calories. High-protein, calcium-rich YoChee (yogurt cheese) is the ideal substitute for cream cheese, sour cream or mayonnaise. Improve your diet without forgoing your favorite dishes. Simple directions and 275 recipes. (310 pages/ paper) Also, YoChee makers (available online).

THE ABC'S OF FRUITS AND VEGETABLES

DELICIOUS ALPHABET POEMS PLUS FOOD, FACTS AND FUN FOR EVERYONE

A collaboration of Steve Charney and David Goldbeck. Actually two books in one. In Part One, the ABCs are taught via twenty-six funny and clever fruit and vegetable poems. Part Two continues to delight older children with a mix of fruit and vegetable jokes, tongue twisters, fun facts, kid-friendly recipes, shopping tips, and more. (112 pages/Illustrated/Color throughout/Paper)

Ceres Press • PO Box 87 • Dept EOS • Woodstock, NY 12498
Phone/FAX 888-804-8848 • visit www.HealthyHighways.com for online specials

OTHER SQUAREONE TITLES OF INTEREST

EAT SMART, EAT RAW

Creative Vegetarian Recipes for a Healthier Life

Kate Wood

As the popularity of raw vegetarian cuisine continues to soar, so does the mounting scientific evidence that uncooked food is amazingly good for you. From healing diseases to detoxifying your body, from lowering cholesterol to eliminating excess weight, the many important health benefits derived from such a diet are too important to ignore. However, now there is another compelling reason to go raw—taste! In her new book *Eat Smart, Eat Raw,* cook and health writer Kate Wood not only explains how to get started, but also provides delicious kitchen-tested recipes guaranteed to surprise and delight even the fussiest of eaters.

$15.95 US / $21.95 CAN • 184 Pages • 7.5 x 9-inch quality paperback • ISBN 0-7570-0261-7

GOING WILD IN THE KITCHEN

The Fresh & Sassy Tastes of Vegetarian Cooking

Leslie Cerier

Go wild in the kitchen! Be creative! Venture beyond the usual beans, grains, and vegetables to include an exciting variety of organic vegetarian fare in your meals. Step outside the box and prepare dishes with beautiful edible flowers; flavorful wild mushrooms, herbs, and berries; tangy sheep and goat cheeses; tasty sea vegetables; and exotic ancient grains like teff, quinoa, and Chinese "forbidden" black rice. Author and expert chef Leslie Cerier is crazy about the great taste and goodness of organically grown foods. In this exciting cookbook, she shares scores of her favorite recipes that spotlight these fresh, wholesome ingredients.

$16.95 US / $25.50 CAN • 240 Pages • 7.5 x 9-inch quality paperback • ISBN 0-7570-0091-6

GREENS AND GRAINS ON THE DEEP BLUE SEA COOKBOOK

Fabulous Vegetarian Cuisine from The Taste of Health Cruises

Sandy Pukel and Mark Hanna

You are invited to come aboard one of America's premier health cruises. Too busy to get away? Well, even if you can't swim in the ship's pool, you can still enjoy its gourmet cuisine, because natural foods expert Sandy Pukel and master chef Mark Hanna have now put together *Greens and Grains on the Deep Blue Sea Cookbook*—a titanic collection of healthful and delicious vegetarian recipes that are among the most popular dishes served aboard the Taste of Health voyages offered through Costa Cruises.

$18.95 US / $23.95 CAN • 256 Pages • 7.5 x 9-inch quality paperback • ISBN 0-7570-0287-0

For more information about our books, visit our website at www.squareonepublishers.com

FOR A COPY OF OUR CATALOG, CALL TOLL FREE: 877-900-BOOK, ext. 100